POLITICAL WOMEN

Volume 8
Sage Yearbooks in WOMEN'S POLICY STUDIES

POLITICAL WOMEN

Current Roles in State and Local Government

Edited by

JANET A. FLAMMANG

SAGE PUBLICATIONS
Beverly Hills   London   New Delhi

To Joseph and Gloria Flammang

For information address:

SAGE Publications, Inc.
275 South Beverly Drive
Beverly Hills, California 90212

SAGE Publications India Pvt. Ltd.
C-236 Defence Colony
New Delhi 110 024, India

SAGE Publications Ltd
28 Banner Street
London EC1Y 8QE, England

Printed in the United States of America.

Library of Congress Cataloging in Publication Data

Main entry under title:

Political women.

(Sage yearbooks in women's policy studies ; v. 8)
Bibliography: p.
1. Women in politics—United States—Addresses, essays, lectures. I. Flammang, Janet A. II. Series.
HQ1236.5.U6P65   1984   320′.088042   84-6922
ISBN 0-8039-2139-X
ISBN 0-8039-2140-3 (pbk.)

FIRST PRINTING

CONTENTS

PREFACE

Political Women: Current Roles in State and Local Government is the eighth volume in the Sage Yearbooks in Women's Policy Studies. This collection of original works constitutes the first book on women and politics with an exclusively state and local focus. It can be seen as a complement to Volume 7 in this series: *Women in Washington: Advocates for Public Policy,* edited by Irene Tinker, which covers the Washington political arena. It is a tribute to the women's movement that its policy accomplishments are significant and numerous enough to warrant consideration at all levels of American politics.

I am grateful to Susan Carroll of Rutgers University for her help in the planning stages of the book. I extend my thanks also to the contributors for their seriousness of purpose, sensitivity to deadlines, and openness to suggestions. It was a pleasure to work with such a cooperative group of scholars.

Timely completion of this project would not have been possible without the generosity of a Presidential Research Grant and a course reduction from the University of Santa Clara; the proficient research assistance of Nancy Plimpton and Garrette Clark; the extraordinary typing skills and cheerfulness of Debra Kolsrud; and the patience and moral support of loved ones. My deep appreciation to all concerned.

INTRODUCTION:
A REFLECTION ON THEMES OF A
"WOMEN'S POLITICS"

By the early 1980s, there was good reason for both strategists of the women's movement and scholars of American politics to shift their attention from national politics to state and local politics. To the leaders of the women's movement, the policy achievements of the 1960s and 1970s emanated from the nation's capital: these included legislation prohibiting sex discrimination in employment and credit and congressional approval of the Equal Rights Amendment. However, when the ERA went down to defeat in state legislatures, the National Organization for Women (NOW) shifted its ratification strategy to target nonsympathetic state legislators and support sympathetic ones. The Reagan administration's New Federalism meant the fate of many women's programs was handed increasingly to state and local officials. And, in the face of major cutbacks in federal programs like Medicaid, Aid to Families with Dependent Children (AFDC), and food stamps—the majority of whose recipients were and are women—state and local governments increasingly bore the burden for maintaining services. The women's movement sounded the alarm over the feminization of poverty at all levels of government.

For scholars of American politics, attention to state and local politics revealed that a quiet revolution in women's electoral, organizational, and policy accomplishments had been taking place throughout the 1970s. On the electoral front, while women still held fewer than 15 percent of all offices, during the 1970s there was a dramatic increase in the percentages of female officials at all levels. The congressional percentage, however, hovered around three to four percent. Between 1971 and 1983, there was a steady increase in the proportion of female state legislators from 4.7 percent to 13.3 percent; and of female mayors from 1 percent to 8.7 percent (National

Women's Political Caucus [NWPC], 1983: 10). Between 1975 and 1980 the proportion of female county officials doubled (from three percent to six percent) and that of municipal officials tripled (from four percent to thirteen percent) (Center for the American Woman and Politics [CAWP], 1981). On the organizational and policy fronts, women's efforts in settings as diverse as consciousness-raising groups, rape crisis centers, health collectives, welfare rights organizations, neighborhood associations, and local chapters of the League of Women Voters, National Organization for Women, and National Women's Political Caucus, produced impressive policy achievements and challenged political scientists to expand what was considered to be "political."

The focus of this volume is on three areas of this quiet revolution at the state and local levels: women's *policy* accomplishments, the increasing number of female *officials*, and women's political *activism*. The articles that follow deal with state and local policies such as ERA ratification, abortion funding, AFDC eligibility requirements and payment levels, child custody and support, child care tax incentives, battered women's shelters, and housing for single parents. Articles about female officials explore their recruitment, electoral obstacles, relations with political parties and interest groups, organizational strategies in caucuses, role as cue-givers to male colleagues, and distinctive attitudes and behavior. And women's political activism is discussed in articles about the motivation of party activists; how grassroots women's groups are performing partylike functions; and how individual activists and women's collaborative activities are leading to a redefinition of the political.

Most prior research has been conducted in the area of women's state and local officeholding.[1] Studies of women's policy accomplishments and political activism at the state and local levels are recent and few in number.[2] For the most part, this literature describes women's politics as resembling that of men. Women organize, lobby, raise funds, run for office, pressure officeholders, and educate their communities. In fact, authors of those few textbooks mentioning women as a political force in state and local politics are typically skeptical about women's increased participation resulting in significant changes in these arenas (for example, Dye, 1981: 80).

There are certain methodological problems that arise in any attempts to determine the nature and extent of differences between men's and women's politics. Studies of women's activism are recent and few in number; few studies are drawn from comparable male and female samples; and self-report data on gender differences are difficult to verify in actual practice. While these are good reasons for caution in drawing generalizations about gender differences in politics, one can nonetheless advance tentative interpretations regarding such differences.

In the articles in this volume, one finds evidence for both similarities and differences in men's and women's politics. However, woven throughout these articles are certain claims about differences that are provocative and merit attention since, taken together, they could make a plausible case for a distinctive women's politics. I will briefly discuss four of these claims in order to alert the reader to them: (1) Women are transforming traditional political concepts and paradigms; (2) female officials have a distinctive politics; (3) parties are still problematic for women, and (4) there is a significance in women's token status in government and majority status as voters. Such claims to differences have been made elsewhere with regard to women's national-level politics, but this volume represents the first attempt to consider the evidence for these claims in state and local arenas. While one can only speculate in the absence of further research, it is possible that, to the extent that there are differences between men's and women's politics, they are more likely to surface in subnational settings. In these settings, relative to Washington politics, female officials are found in greater numbers and women's lack of monetary resources can more easily be compensated for by the strength of their mobilized numbers.

TRANSFORMATION OF TRADITIONAL POLITICAL CONCEPTS AND PARADIGMS

Several of the articles in this volume suggest that women's political efforts have resulted in the expansion and reshaping of state and local political agendas. For example, Anne Wurr, in her "Community Responses to Violence Against Women: The Case of a Battered Women's Shelter," provides an example of agenda expansion in her account of the creation of a local battered women's shelter. And, in her "State and Local Policies on Motherhood," Emily Stoper describes the nature of the controversies surrounding abortion, child care, and child support and custody, and indicates how women have expanded public debate on these issues.

In addition to reshaping the political agenda, women are presenting challenges to classical liberal formulations of the political. For the most part, they seem to eschew inhabiting a Hobbesian or Lockian political world of isolated, competitive individuals. While this framework may seem natural to men of affairs, it does not appear to jibe with most women's experiences. Many women in these studies proffer a politics of connectedness that is seen as resonating with their experiences in society's gender division of labor (compare Gilligan, 1982). While it is not exactly clear how this politics of connectedness might transform the lexicon of political scientists, at least two possibilities are raised in the following essays.

The first pertains to the intrinsic/extrinsic model Diane L. Fowlkes employs in her article, "Conceptions of the 'Political': White Activists in Atlanta." In her earlier analysis of these women, Fowlkes found that politically ambitious women tended to have an intrinsic view of politics (that is, one included oneself as an active agent in politics), while nonambitious women held an extrinsic view (that is, politics was seen as outside of, or happening to, oneself). This is in keeping with the findings of other studies that have employed similar political science dichotomies such as that between "participants in" and "subjects of" political regimes (for example, Almond and Verba, 1965). However, struck by the frequency with which women saw themselves as simultaneously extrinsic to formal officeholding and intrinsic to advocacy for political change, Fowlkes pursued the research presented in this volume. Here she argues that these women provide an expanded sense of the political lodged in their social connections with friends and family, and more active in its advocacy stance than the terms "extrinsic to" and "subject to" convey. The upshot of Fowlkes's analysis is that women see themselves as connected to politics in ways that most political scientists have not appreciated.

A second provocative claim about a politics of connectedness is that put forth by Martha A. Ackelsberg in her "Women's Collaborative Activities and City Life: Politics and Policy." She argues that most research about urban life implicitly adopts a model of disconnected and isolated individuals whose world is split into workplace and community. But, she claims, this model reflects men's experiences, not women's, for whom work and community are experienced as connected in the course of their day-to-day negotiations with landlords, markets, social service agencies, and the like. Ackelsberg maintains that women are not isolated and self-interested captives of their households, but rather part of communities and social networks. She goes on to say that women's, and men's, relationships, not their interests, are the cornerstones of a democratic policy (compare Diamond and Hartsock, 1981). One implication of Ackelsberg's analysis is that women's experiences in the gender division of labor could provide an alternative model of political community and democracy, a model predicated on a politics of connectedness.

As for women in public office, the authors in this volume seem to suggest that female officials' politics of connectedness is reflected in three ways: their sense of obligation to current and prospective female officials, their "delegate" model of representation, and their criteria for evaluating their influence as officials. In her "Women in Local Government: An Overview," Denise Antolini classifies most local female officials as "Sisters" (i.e., recognizing obligations to women who proceeded and will succeed them) rather than "Queen Bees" (i.e., feeling they have made it on their own with little obligation to other women). The implication is that women most likely feel connections not always experienced by their male counterparts or noticed by traditional political science scholarships. However, Marianne Githens maintains in her "Women and State Politics: An Assessment," that female state legislators do not perceive their *primary* obligation as serving as a role model to inspire would be female officials or as representing women's issues per se. Rather, she says, they choose the role of delegate reflecting the interests of all their constituents. Githens argues that the passivity and reactiveness usually conveyed by the present political science definition of delegates (in contrast to the active, autonomous trustees who use independent judgment) does not accurately reflect women's understanding of their delegate functions. She says that traditional legislative role typologies should be reformulated to see delegates as more active. Women's advocacy and community service are the criteria they use to evaluate their influence and success as officials. These are less passive roles than currently connoted by the term "delegate." Githens urges us to pay attention to how elected women provide a new gloss on a standard paradigm.

FEMALE OFFICIALS HAVE
A DISTINCTIVE POLITICS

Most of the studies in this volume refer to the well-documented gender differences in patterns of recruitment to political office: Women typically have volunteer and homemaker backgrounds while men typically have business and professional experiences. These differences are thought to have a bearing on what women do once in office. For example, Antolini discusses evidence from local studies suggesting that women spend more time than men on constituency service; but if they have been employed, women spend the same amount of time on constituents as men. In light of this finding, Antolini raises some questions for consideration: To what extent are other perceived differences between male and female officials (for example, women are less beholden to economic special interests) more a function of employment status than of gender per se? And will women's attitudes and behaviors come to resemble those of men as their economic and political careers come to look more like men's?

Like observers elsewhere, some authors in this volume are not anxious to jettison whatever it is that women's distinctive backgrounds might enable them to bring to public office. For example, Fowlkes is sympathetic to a Georgia state legislator who tells her she is prepared to be patient in her protracted struggle for women's issues in a hostile statehouse. The legislator told Fowlkes that she gained the ability to be patient from her experiences raising children. Patience is thus portrayed as a political asset for a member of an outgroup.

Women's outgroup consciousness is reported by female officials at all levels when asked if they still feel excluded from informal centers of male power in their respective government bodies (Johnson and Carroll, 1978). Female officials have devised various strategies in response to this exclusion. Carol Mueller, in her "Women's Organizational Strategies in State Legislatures," details how women's perceptions of their male colleagues determine which kind of organizational strategy they will choose to pursue. Most states were found to have both formal and informal women's social networks, coalitions, and caucuses. Mueller reports that women's efforts are often so low-key and bipartisan that their male colleagues are surprised to learn post facto that women even had their own legislative agenda, let alone a successful one.

When is comes to the question of attitudinal differences between male and female officials, the most comprehensive survey of state and local male and female officials concludes that women are more liberal and more feminist than their male counterparts (Johnson and Carroll, 1978). The fact that such sentiments are not always visible among female candidates for office has given rise to a "closet feminist" hypothesis advanced by Carroll (1979) and discussed by authors in this volume. This hypothesis says that female candidates may not recognize or accept the degree to which their own concerns coincide with those of the feminist movement because they find themselves in environments hostile to such a recognition.

The closet feminist hypothesis might be in for some modification if Edmond Costantini and Julie Davis Bell's findings about California party activists (convention delegates) are indicative of a trend elsewhere. In their "Women in Political Parties: Gender Differences in Motives Among Party Activists," they report that female party activists held more extreme views that did male party activists: Republican women were found to be more conservative and Democratic women more liberal than their respective male partisans. While most women in their sample were less likely than men to say they became interested in party politics to pursue elective office, in recent years there has been a significant increase in the amount of feminists in the Democratic party in California who are interested in public office. If this trend emerges in other states, it may be that there will be fewer closet and more self-described feminist candidates for public office.

PARTIES ARE STILL PROBLEMATIC FOR WOMEN

Several authors discuss earlier research findings showing that while political parties have been anxious to secure women's volunteer and secretarial services, they have been hesitant to slate them as candidates. Or, when slated, they are sacrificial lambs with little chance of winning. And, once elected, they face a hostile reception from party leaders in their chambers. The articles in this volume detail some of the ways in which parties remain problematic for women.

In their study "Women as Legislative Candidates in Six States," Janet Clark, R. Darcy, Susan Welch, and Margery Ambrosius report that there is still some support for the sacrificial lamb hypothesis. In the six states they studied, a higher proportion of female candidates (relative to men) were slated in two low-win types of races: against incumbents (who typically win over ninety percent of the time), and as candidates in the state's minority party. By contrast, they found that the obstacle of voter hostility to female candidates, while present before 1976, seems to have virtually disappeared since that time.

Women in the Georgia state legislature told Fowlkes that they felt that the Democratic party leadership was not receptive to women's new ideas. This prompted one woman to run on the Republican ticket and a Democratic woman to work quietly with women of both parties in the legislature to form a women's caucus to coordinate women's issues. In the same vein, female state legislators from around the country told Mueller that the stronger the state's partisan loyalties, the harder it was to form a women's caucus. And in her study of women in the judiciary, "Women on the State Bench: Correlates of Access,"

Beverly B. Cook finds that strong partisan competition in an area reduces the likelihood of finding women on the bench. She argues that the more compeitive the election, the less anxious is the party to take risks with what it considers to be a potential liability: female gender.

In defense of parties, Costantini and Bell point out that female party activists in California have not always been interested in running for public office. Only recently has such an interest been expressed primarily by women who are younger, members of feminist organizations, and ERA supporters. However, the authors also note that there is still a gender division of labor within parties, with women performing most of the internal housekeeping tasks and men taking on most of the party's external relations. They voice the concern that if women reach parity with men in public officeholding, one unintended consequence may be the further debilitation of political parties as effective organizations, since they rely so heavily on women's support functions.

Political parties have been debilitated at the state and local levels as a result of turn-of-the-century Progressive electoral reforms. Today three-quarters of all cities hold nonpartisan elections (Dye, 1981: 272). In my article, "Filling the Party Vacuum: Women at the Grassroots Level in Local Politics," I argue that grassroots women are performing five partylike functions in nonpartisan Santa Clara County politics: ward heelers, informal and ad hoc networkers, political educators, political recruiters and endorsers, and campaign fundraisers and workers.

THE SIGNIFICANCE OF WOMEN'S TOKEN STATUS IN GOVERNMENT AND MAJORITY STATUS AS VOTERS

A final way in which women's politics can be said to differ from that of men results, somewhat paradoxically, from their token status in government bodies and their majority status at the ballot box. In her review esssay on women in local government, Antolini elaborates on Rosabeth Kanter's (1977b) theory about how token women in organizations become, in the eyes of the numerically dominant men, symbols of women as a group. As such, women are closely scrutinized by their male peers and feel they have to work harder than men to prove themselves to men. In her article, Cook argues that a female judge "does not enjoy the presumptions of competency and objectivity that shield the establishment-style judge. Her behaviors are subject to a more intensive and critical oversight; she must be prepared to rationalize decisions that would have been accepted without special notice if emanating from a less visible judge.'' She concludes that in the climate of judicial "objectivity," responsiveness to women's interests may be more difficult for a female than a male judge. And Githens contends that female state legislators' small numbers limit their bargaining ability and that their colleagues' scrutiny of them as a group constrains their leadership potential.

However, in the short run at least, the possibility is also raised that women's small numbers may have some positive consequences as well. David B. Hill, in his article, "Women State Senators as Cue-Givers: ERA Roll-Call Voting, 1972-1979," argues that male state senators turned to the few women in their chambers for cues on how to vote on ERA ratification, which women favored about eighty percent of the time. Men deferred to the expertise of their female colleagues, particularly those with seniority. However, as the ERA became more controversial and opposition mounted, male legislators began relying on outside cues as well.

Another consequence of women's minority status in government is a consciousness that they are in a unique position to increase the numbers of appointed women around them. Cook says that when a woman is in a position to appoint judges, whether as a governor or a member of a nominating board, the chances of female candidates improve since women are more likely to be found in her social networks. Once women lost their token status, they may not feel as keen a sense of obligation to shepherd the careers of other women.

Ultimately, however, most authors agree that women have the most to gain by increasing their numbers in government bodies—greater coalition and bargaining powers and relief from excessive scrutiny. Githens also points out that women can be more themselves in greater numbers (compare Flammang, forthcoming). She argues that while at one time female officials had to act more like men to be accepted, there is evidence today that women feel less pressure to exhibit masculine personality traits.

There is a little question that women benefit from their numbers at the ballot box, especially insofar as male officials preceive a female voting bloc in their constituencies. The presence of a "women's vote" is most clearly visible in a local constituency. In her article on a battered women's shelter, Wurr maintains that female activists were successful in pressuring candidates in local district attorney and sheriff races. And in my case study, both female and male politicians attributed their electoral victories to mobilized women in their constituencies.

Finally, Ellen Boneparth, in her overview essay, "Resources and Constraints on Women in the Policy-Making Process: State and Local Arenas," sees the gender gap as a major resource for women, with implications for the future of state and local politics. She argues that while this gap may have originated in concerns outside the purview of state and local governments—such as militarism, nuclear weapons, interventionist foreign policies—it is the domestic-issue component of the gender gap that is most keenly felt at state and local levels: welfare mothers with reduced food budgets, laid-off female government employees who are the sole support of their families, and reduced government funds for commissions on the status of women and battered women's shelters.

Perhaps, as Githens cautions, male state legislators have been able to relegate to their female colleagues peripheral concerns such as women's rights and social welfare issues. But as the domestic-issue component of the gender gap looms larger in states and localities; as cutback victims continue to register to vote in increasing numbers; and as women continue with their quiet procession into decision-making posts in state and local governments, male perceptions of the "peripheral" are bound to change. A "women's politics," as the articles in this volume seem to indicate, is becoming an ever-increasing presence on the American political landscape.

ORGANIZATION OF THE BOOK

The articles are presented in four sections. In the first, Antolini and Githens provide their overviews on women in local and state politics. The second section deals with women as political activists: Fowlkes's white Atlanta activists, my grassroots women in Santa Clara County, and Costantini and Bell's California party activists. In the third section, authors discuss female officials: Clark, Darcy, Welch, and Ambrosius look at female candidates in six states' legislative races; Mueller studies the organizational strategies of women in eighteen state legislatures; Hill considers the influence of female senators in thirty-one state legislatures; and Cook traces the correlates of women's access to local and state judiciaries nationwide. The final section considers state and local public policies: Wurr provides a case study of a battered women's shelter; Ackelsberg discusses the political and policy women's shelter; Ackelsberg discusses the political and policy implications of urban women's collaborative activities; Stoper outlines four motherhood policies; and Boneparth looks at overall resources and constraints on women's policymaking in state and local arenas.

NOTES

1. An indispensable source of information about elected state and local women is the Center for the American Woman and Politics (CAWP), part of the Eagleton Institute of Politics at Rutgers University. In 1972 CAWP sponsored a conference for fifty female state legislators and commissioned Kirkpatrick's book about them, *Political Women* (1974). CAWP conducted national surveys of women in municipal, county, state, and congressional offices in 1975 (Johnson and Stanwick, 1976) and in 1977 (Johnson and Carroll, 1978). CAWP's director published an account of female candidates at all levels in 1976 races (Mandel, 1981). And the 1982 CAWP conference of female state legislators was the occasion for Mueller's observations about women's caucuses in state legislatures (this volume).

Aside from Diamond's classic *Sex Roles in the State House* (1977) and some of Gruberg's anecdotal accounts in *Women in American Politics* (1968), most writing on female state and local officials is scattered throughout journals and anthologies. Examples of local studies are Karnig and Walter (1976), King and McAuliffe (1976), Lee (1976), MacManus (1981), Merritt (1977), Mezey (1978a, 1978b, 1978c), Van Hightower (1977), and Welch and Karnig (1979). State studies include Blair and Henry (1981), Dubeck (1976), Githens and Prestage (1979), Jones and Nelson (1981), Welch (1978), Werner (1968), and Werner and Bachtold (1974). Githens and Prestage's *Portrait of Marginality* (1977) contains several articles with a state and local focus (e.g., those of Currey, Githens, King, Stoper, and Prestage). And Stewart's anthology *Women in Local Politics* (1980c) is the first with a local focus, featuring case studies of women in parties (Margolis), courts (Cook), city councils (Mezey and Merritt) and commissions on the status of women (Stewart).

2. Policy studies are found in such anthologies as Diamond's *Families, Politics, and Public Policy* (1983) and Boneparth's *Women, Power and Policy* (1982). Stewart (1980b) examines the local policy achievements of commissions on the status of women. Several articles in the *Signs* special issue "Women and the American City" (1980) have a policy focus. For studies of women's state and local activism, see the same *Signs* issue, and articles in anthologies like *Quest*'s *Building Feminist Theory* (1981), Bernice Cummings and Victoria Schuck's *Women Organizing* (1979), and Gloria T. Hull, Patricia Bell Scott, and Barbara Smith's *But Some of Us Are Brave* (1982). Jo Freeman's *The Politics of Women's Liberation* (1975) looks at women's activism and policy achievements at both the local and national levels. For studies of women as state and local party activists, see Costantini and Craik (1972); Fowlkes, Perkins, and Rinehart (1979); Jennings and Farah (1981); Jennings and Thomas (1968); Porter and Matasar (1974); and Wells and Smeal (1974).

I

OVERVIEW AND ASSESSMENT

This section contains two articles reviewing the literature on the recruitment, attitudes, and behavior of female officials in local and state governments.

Denise Antolini, in "Women in Local Government: An Overview," discusses the impact of local female officials on public policy and politics. She begins with a look at women's impact on the governing process and the practice of representation. Next, she considers the evidence for the influence of elected women on public policy. Finally, she examines the effect of female officials' attitudes and behavior on the access of other women to positions of power.

Marianne Githens reviews existing research on women's recruitment and performance in state politics. Her essay, "Women and State Politics: An Assessment," is divided into three parts: recruitment of women to the political elite, performance of women as political elites, and new directions for further research.

1

WOMEN IN LOCAL GOVERNMENT: AN OVERVIEW

Denise Antolini

More than two thousand years ago, Aristophanes suggested that women in power would have a radical influence on politics. In his comedy *Ecclesiazusae*, wives of Greek assemblymembers accomplish a coup d'etat and institute a rigidly egalitarian system of communal property, eating, and sex (Aristophanes, 1967). Aristophanes' assumptions about the impact of women in politics remain popular today. Yet, despite the recent increase in the number of female officeholders, particularly at the local level, the real effect of women in power remains a question largely unexplored.

This overview examines these assumptions about women's political behavior by analyzing the influence of female officeholders at the city and county level of government. The large number of women at this level of office permits some speculation about the impact of women in politics generally. The local level of office also represents the most rapidly changing context for women's political experiences. Twenty times more women serve at the city and county level of government than at the state and federal levels combined (CAWP, 1981: 1). Between 1975 and 1980 alone, the number of elected women at the municipal and township level more than tripled, increasing from 4650 in 1975 to 14,136 in 1980 or thirteen percent of the total positions (CAWP, 1981: 1; according to the same data, the number of women holding *county* office increased by only three percent to 1444 during the same period).

Though less glamorous than the state or national scene, local politics significantly affects the lives of women and men at the community level. The women's movement has long recognized the great potential for policy change at the local level; areas targeted for reform include "women's issues" (for example, day care and rape crisis centers), as well as issues that affect women's lives more subtly (education and zoning policy, for instance). The doubling of the number of local commissions on the status of women between 1975 and 1980 indicates the growing emphasis on local government as a vehicle for change in the economic, political, and social condition of women (Stewart, 1980a: 199).

This analysis of the impact of local female officals on public policy and politics examines three related areas: local women's impact on governing processes and the practice of representation; the influence of elected women on public policy; and the effect of the attitudes and behavior of female officeholders on the access of other women to power. Four studies in particular shed light on this inquiry: Susan Mezey's study of fifty female (and a corresponding sample of 50 male) Connecticut councilmembers from 1976 to 1977; the survey of municipal legislators in Chicago in 1977 by Sharyne Merritt; the comprehensive national study of the attitudes of female officeholders by the Center for the American Woman and Politics (CAWP) in 1977; and Trudy Bers's 1974 to 1975 examination of 235 women and men on boards of education in Cook County, Illinois.

PUBLIC SERVICE VERSUS POLITICS

The recent impressive increase in the number of women in local office nationwide prompts the questions, "So What?," or, "Are female representatives any different than their male colleagues?" Female officeholders do have a gender-distinctive theory and practice of representation according to several surveys of the attitudes of local women in office.

The most noted differences researchers found between women and men on local councils centered on the divergent attitudes of the sexes toward their constituencies. Women, much more than men, resembled the stereotype of the local officeholder as "public servant" rather than as "politician." The public service orientation has deep roots in the history of local politics. Dye (1969: 198) traces this notion of public service to the municipal reform movements of the Progressive era, which resulted in a preference for nonpartisan, antiseptic, consensual, and moral community rule in the public interest. Women's bid for public office after suffrage as reformers—labeled "petticoat politics"—conformed with this popular attitude toward local government. Many women ran on all-female slates (often defeating their husbands running for re-election), served a short, but impressive term, then quit. A typical example of this phenomenon of the early 1920s to mid-50s—chronicled in Gruberg's (1968) extensive anecdotal history of the era—is the story of the "City Mothers" of Stephenson, Michigan. The village elected a slate of women to all of its offices in 1929. After a few years in office, the City Mothers resigned. They had entered politics, they stated, "to further community projects, not merely to be office holders" (p. 203). This service orientation of women in office continues to be evident in the current cohort of female politicians.

This history strongly suggests that women view their role as that of a "delegate" rather than a "trustee" of the electorate (Wahlke et al., 1962: 272-280; Gross, 1978: 359). A delegate tends to regard her or his mandate as "instructions from his constituency," while a trustee views her or himself as "a free agent acting on the moralistic directives of his own conscience" (Gross, 1978: 361). An examination of the theoretical orientation of women and men in office is important because an official's adoption of either role—or components of each—affects the legislative process as well as its policy outcomes.

Bers's (1978) study of board of education members in Cook County, Illinois, confirms that elected women tend to view themselves as public servants, while men consider themselves politicians. Forty-six percent of the women surveyed (compared to only nineteen percent of the men) stated that one of the major responsibilities of a board of education member was to "represent [the] public" (p. 385). And, nearly fifty percent of the men believed that "exercise of administrative oversight" was a primary function of their office, while fewer than one-third of the women felt similarly. The strong public service motivations of female members who surfaced in a third area—their "perceived contributions to the board." Eight percent more women than men answered "community representation;" ten percent more noted "public relations" (p. 387). The emphasis women place on their responsibilities to the public complements the delegate model; in contrast, men in local office apparently feel greater freedom—or duty— to act independently of public sentiment.

These findings support the hypothesis that women tend to possess a gender-distinctive approach toward their political careers and the legislative process. However, the importance of structural (e.g., occupational) rather than gender-specific factors is suggested by Neuse's (1978) examination of the attitudes of women working in state government agencies. In his survey of 725 professional state employees, Neuse found "women were more likely than men . . . to value public input and participation in administrative processes, rejecting the belief that administrative policy makers could fare well without citizen or clientele participation" (p. 438). This significant difference diminished, however, when the occupational situation of the women studied was considered; most of the women worked in agencies that primarily administered "benefit transfer" or service programs (i.e., health, education, and welfare agencies). Thus, why women exhibit a preference for constituent participation and public service is not clear; either women are excluded from the male-dominated areas of public administration and are restricted to service careers, or their occupational choice is a manifestation of this belief in democratic participation.

A re-examination of Bers's (1978) and Mezey's (1978a, b, c) data demonstrates a similar relationship between women's "structural situation," or official role in the political body, and their devotion to public service. Nearly twenty percent of the female school board members (compared to only eight percent of the males) in Bers's study sat on "Publicity or Community Relations" committees. In contrast, nearly one-third of the men were members of "Negotiations" committees (compared to twenty percent of the women). The divergent delegate and trustee beliefs discussed above can be seen as logical extensions of the different official roles chosen by or relegated to women and men on school boards.

Mezey also suggests that the varying enchantment of women and men with public service is occupationally linked. Bargaining skills are developed in the traditionally male-dominated occupations such as law and business from which most men enter politics; few women have yet to enter these professions, and women tend to come from volunteer and community involvement backgrounds that emphasize cooperation rather than conflict. Although Bers did not break her sample down by occupation, note that twenty-four percent of the men studied and none of the women valued highly their contributions to the board arising from their business knowledge or background (Bers, 1978: 387). One effect of this occupational difference is that the legitimacy of female officeholder's political expertise may be undermined. As discussed further below, forty percent of the women in Mezey's sample reported that "women never get to inner circles of power"; twelve percent of the men agreed (Mezey, 1980: 184). Given the perception of many women that they are excluded from the nucleus of the political power, and men's low awareness of this barrier, it becomes less surprising that women turn toward the public and more closely resemble delegates than trustees.

The theory that elected women and men have different political relationships with the public is supported by behavioral as well as attitudinal evidence. Women's emphasis on serving constituencies manifests itself in the sheer amount of time they devote to official duties. The time women devote to office seems generally to be affected by two forces: the demands of their constituents and women's own dedication to the work.

With respect to the quantity of commitment, those studies that explored the question reveal that women devote more time to their duties than do men. Merritt (1980), in her study of 102 local councilmembers in suburban Chicago, noted this positive relationship: "On the average, women spend seventeen hours per week, while men spend an average of fourteen hours per week" on matters related to the functions of their office (p. 119). The comprehensive, national CAWP survey implied a similar finding. Female councilmembers nationwide spent an average of ten hours a week on office duties (the same average as for men for *all* levels of office nationwide—the only reported comparable figure; CAWP, 1978: 24, 25, 29).

Gender, then, seems to be one predictive variable of the quantity of time devoted to local office. However, this glosses over the significant employment status differences between female and male officeholders. Employment outside the home should have an influence on time commitment at the local level because of the relative ease with which homemakers can devote more time to local office (relative to higher office), particularly because of their proximity. Though the job demands vary greatly among cities—depending on the council's size and power—the average time commitment required for holding city council positions is low. The majority of women and men in local office serve in districts with populations under 25,000, and pay at this level is nominal; ninety-five percent of the women on local councils in 1977 reported salaries under $5000 (CAWP, 1978: 24). The profile of the typical officeholder is that of a community businessperson for whom holding office is a part-time job (Dye, 1969: 235-36). However, while eighty-six percent of the men in CAWP's local sample held other jobs, forty-four percent of the women were not employed outside the office (CAWP, 1978: 17, 10). Thus, a substantially greater proportion of women than men have more free time (i.e., a more flexible schedule) to devote to official duties.

Employment does seem to be a key variable in predicting women and men's commitment to office. When Merritt (1980) compared working women and men, she found "no difference in the number of hours devoted to office activity. Each group averaged fourteen hours a week." However, women who did not work outside the home averaged nineteen hours a week on official business—twenty-six percent more than that spent by employed women (Merritt, 1980: 120). The CAWP (1978) study also found that outside employment decreased the time commitment of women by thirty percent. CAWP concluded: "The greater commitment of time by women is accounted for almost entirely by women with no outside employment" (CAWP, 1978:29).

Does the quantity of time commitment to office by women reflect greater devotion to constituent needs? Again, employment status seems to be a determinant. Merritt found that employed women saw an average of twenty-six constituents a month, while women without outside employment received thirty-two. (The averages for all women and all men in the sample were identical—thirty constituents; Merritt, 1980: 120). This finding lends further support to the hypothesis that some of the major behavioral distinctions between women and men at the local level of office are not directly attributable to gender, but to differences in employment status (which reflect deeper socioeconomic gender differences).

Female officials not only resemble the delegate model with respect to the *quantity* of time commitment, but also there is a distinctive *quality* to their performance as representatives. Two available measurements of performance are: degree of preparation and emphasis on action as opposed to process. Here, again, it appears that both external and internal pressures reinforce gender-distinctive behavior of women in local office.

Studies indicate that women in local office work hard to be more knowledgeable and better prepared than their male colleagues. One-third of the councilwomen in Merritt's (1980) study (compared to only fourteen percent of the men) cited "preparation" as the main reason for their level of influence (p. 123). For school board members, Bers (1978) found that eighteen percent of the women and only six percent of the men believed "being informed" was one of their major responsibilities as a representative. And, twice as many women as men perceived their "knowledge or information" as a contribution to the board (pp. 385, 387). Sixty-one percent of the local councilwomen nationwide surveyed by CAWP in 1977 rated themselves superior to their colleagues in "general knowledge" and "intelligence" (CAWP, 1978: 27). The preponderance of evidence indicates that women place a higher value on knowledge and preparation as an essential part of their obligation to the public. Notably, Merritt (1980) found the strength and direction of this relationship remained unchanged when employment status was held constant (p. 123). What explains this consistent pattern of women's emphasis on work?

First, as "token" members on virtually all local councils, women may be motivated by their underdog status to try harder simply to achieve influence. The term "token" refers to group members who, because of their small number and physical appearance (e.g., sex or race), are treated by others ("dominants") as symbols of their "group" rather than as individuals. In her insightful study of token women in male-dominated groups, Kanter (1977b) suggests that minority status dramatically increases pressure to perform; for example, women in her study "had to work twice as hard [as men] to prove their competence" (p. 973).

Moreover, as relative newcomers to electoral politics—seventy-one percent of the local councilwomen nationwide in 1977 were serving in their first public office (CAWP, 1978: 22)—these women may react as many people would who undertake an unfamiliar task under public scrutiny, that is, work harder than incumbents to gain power and legitimacy. In addition, councilwomen may work harder to overcome the presumption that women are politically incompetent. This obstacle was noted by thirteen percent of the councilwomen nation-wide as a major difficulty experienced in office (CAWP, 1978: 40). Perceptions of women's incompetence come partially from male col-leagues; seventeen percent of male officeholders nationwide (com-pared to four percent of the women) thought "deficiency of qualifica-tions" a difficulty for their female colleagues (CAWP, 1978: 43). Similarly, Mezey (1980) found in her study of Connecticut council-members that significantly more women than men (eighty-two percent and forty-two percent respectively) believed that "women on local councils have to work extra hard to prove themselves to their male col-leagues" (p. 183). This presumption of incompetence intensifies the pressure on women to work harder than men.

Finally, the tendency for women to expend greater energy on their political duties may result from a principled belief in reform and political action. For example, women in Merritt's (1980) survey were more satisfied by concrete end products, such as service delivery or public construction, than by processes, such as negotiations or work with colleagues (p. 127). CAWP (1978) found similarly that for office-holders at all levels, more women than men cited developing policy (fifty-five percent compared to forty-six percent) and sponsoring legislation (thirty-four percent compared to twenty-nine percent) as a major emphasis of their work (CAWP, 1978: 29).

Merritt suggests three explanations for women's emphasis on political action over process: women lack social experiences that develop bargaining and negotiating skills; they may see political action as the means to the end of public service; and, women may consciously avoid or be barred from process because of the historical discrimination which has systematically excluded them from "the informal arenas in which negotiations take place" (Merritt, 1980: 122). Perhaps more important, though, may be the ideological motivation of women who seek local office. Merritt reported that the women she studied were more reformist than the men (p. 89). Lee's study of Westchester community leaders also revealed that more women than men thought that urgent community problems seemed perpetually put off (sixty-six percent compared to forty-nine percent; Lee, 1973: 81).

An additional gender difference in officials' relationship with their constituents is their degree of responsiveness to constituent concerns. In Bers's (1978) study, twice as many women as men believed that "commitment or caring" was their major contribution to their boards of education—fifteen percent compared to seven percent (p. 387). For local women in the CAWP survey, this deeper commitment manifested itself both through greater "responsiveness to constituents" and through emphasis on "helping on [constituents'] individual problems" (CAWP, 1978: 27, 29). Merritt's findings also suggested that constituents trusted women much more than men councilmembers and demanded more from them (Merritt, 1980: 120-121). That constituents expect more from female officeholders may result both from the stereotypical perception that women are selfless and from the fact that nonemployed representatives are assumed to be more available. One councilwoman commented:

> People call me because they know I'm here [at home] during the day—even people from outside my ward. They don't call the other aldermen because they're at work and no one wants to disturb them. But since I'm usually at home during the day everyone calls me with their problems [Merritt, 1980: 121; brackets in original].

As one would expect, given the importance of the employment variable in determining the general availability of officeholders, employment status does significantly affect this "demand" relationship (Merritt, 1980: 121).

In addition, the high degree of trust that constituents place in local female officeholders may reflect both the greater responsiveness of women to the needs of individuals and the popular notion of the moral superiority of women. Another councilwoman explained that

> people think women are more honest. I don't see why they should, but that's the general assumption. No matter who you are, if you're a woman people just assume you won't lie [Merritt, 1980: 120].

The idea that female politicians are less corrupt than their male colleagues remains popular, though it is probably waning. Women's political purity is due in part to their lack of experience in government and their weak economic ties to traditional circles of power. As the Tolchins (1976) noted, "[women have] been spared the years of entangling alliances that ensnare most veteran male politicians," and women's virtue results from their "ostracism and their lack of political IOUs" (Tolchin and Tolchin, 1976: 244). The trust relationship between female officials and their constituents seems attributable to the unsullied record of this group of women (and women in other realms) rather than to women's incorruptibility.

In short, the profile of female councilmembers described by attitudinal surveys stands in stark contrast to the traditional characterization of local male politicians. Prewitt found that councilmen approach their job as a duty to direct the community—"a middle-class version of noblesse oblige" (Prewitt, 1970: 10). By contrast, women have a strong delegate orientation, which may withstand even the convergence of the employment status of the sexes.

POLICY IMPACT

The second obvious question to ask about the growing participation of women in American politics is, "Have women made a distinctive impact on policy?" Without implying that women must make a gender-distinctive contribution to justify their political participation, this overview aggregates data on some important indicators of the influence of female officeholders on local policy.

Perhaps the question most often asked about female officials is, "Do women represent women?" Surveys show that most women in local government are sympathetic to feminism and are strong supporters of women's issues. These results suggest that they do operate within a gender-distinctive attitudinal framework that directs their policy decisions. Women's issues are defined here as those topics of public interest that directly and immediately affect women more than men, including reproductive rights, child care, and family policy; tax, insurance, and credit equity; and employment discrimination, affirmative action, and the Equal Rights Amendment. Feminism can be measured by assessing feminist attitudes and behavior. As Carroll (1979) explains:

An individual is an attitudinal feminist if she favors the elimination of societally prescribed sex roles and the removal of any legal constraints that prohibit women from pursuing their potential for individual development just as fully as men. An individual is a behavioral feminist if she engages in behavioral acts that reflect such beliefs—e.g., joining organizations that espouse those beliefs, publicly advocating measures consistent with these beliefs, developing legislation of projects as an extension of these beliefs [p. 5].

In determining the strength of the feminist attitudes of female politicians, it is important to view the existing data cautiously. Since few studies have approached the question directly, the data represent incomplete, yet meaningful, fragments of an answer.

From her study of councilmembers in Connecticut, Mezey (1978b) concluded that the women possessed weak feminist orientations— twenty percent said that their male colleagues viewed them as feminists (p. 490). Mezey failed to report, however, whether women's self-ratings were higher. Bers's exploration of this area also proved inconclusive. Only six percent of the female board of education members she surveyed cited "the woman's point of view" as a particular contribution of theirs to the board. Bers concluded that if in fact "such an identifiable perspective exists . . . it is not salient to these women" (Bers, 1978: 388). Again, however, the phrasing of the question probably negatively biased the response. Would more women identify themselves with the more concrete notion of women's interests rather than a single, cohesive point of view that is a demanding and abstract description of the feminist orientation?

Merritt's (1980) study of Cook County councilors supports the hypothesis that correct assessments of the attitudes of female officeholders depend not only on which questions are asked, but also on how women's responses compare to those of men. Merritt asked three specific questions that measured support for equality in the areas of domestic roles (Should the wife and husband equally share housework?); economic equality (Should the man necessarily be the breadwinner?); and political opportunity (Should women be considered as seriously as men for executive and high political positions?). On the latter two questions, women's responses were significantly more feminist than those of men—the correlation between the feminist response and gender was $+.26$ (p < .005) and $+.36$ (p < .001) respectively (Merritt, 1980: 124). On the private sphere question, women and men were equally supportive of changing domestic roles. Carroll (1979: 17) has suggested the most satisfactory explanation for the attitudinal divergence between the sexes seen in these studies. In her study of female candidates, she noted that "while most candidates support feminist concerns, many may not recognize and accept the degree to which their attitudes and concerns coincide with those of the feminist movement."

The studies examined here reveal a significantly higher degree of support by local female officeholders than by their male colleagues for feminist positions on salient political issues. The tendency of the female officeholders to be more feminist than their male colleagues is best determined by looking at specific issues. Mezey (1978b) found interesting differences in attitudinal support among the 100 local Connecticut legislators she studied. Though the women and men were very close on the issues of safe abortion and rape crisis centers, opinions differed noticeably on the issues of day care, affirmative action in politics, legalization of prostitution, and sexism in education—eighteen percent, ten percent, seventeen percent and ten percent, respectively (Mezey, 1978b: 489).

The 1977 CAWP survey provides the most comprehensive assessment of the strength of female officeholders' feminist attitudes. On the questions CAWP used as indications of support for women's issues, clear differences of opinion were apparent between the sexes. In the unmatched sample of women in local office, support *for* the ERA, homemaker social security, and child care, and *against* an abortion amendment to the Constitution ran at sixty-two percent, fifty-nine percent, thirty-nine percent, and sixty-seven percent, respectively. A matched sample of elected women and men with district populations under 10,000 showed women's support to be very close to the above levels, while men were *less supportive* by a margin of twenty-one percent, fifteen percent, seven percent, and twelve percent, respectively ("strong" and "moderate" responses combined) (CAWP, 1978: 33, 37). The survey reveals the strong feminist orientation of local women, particularly on the issues of ERA ratification and homemaker social security. But, are the differences attributable directly to gender? Cross-tabulations of data by CAWP indicated that several other variables such as ideology, party affiliation, level of education, and age may be explanatory variables. For example, though CAWP found support for women's issues strong among "conservative" women, agreement with the feminist position was significantly higher among "liberal" women (CAWP, 1978: 33, 37).

Another approach to explaining the feminism of local women in office is to view these attitudes as only one facet of a broader "humanist" ideology. Though the greater humanism of women is often cited in the literature (CAWP, 1978: 35; Johnson and Stoper,

1977), little analysis has focused on the strength of this apparent relationship. Evidence in the studies examined here is also sparse, but suggestive.

Merritt found the women in suburban Chicago politics "more likely to express an interest in social topics" as opposed to "physical or regulatory" issues (Merritt, 1980: 126). The relationship disappeared, however, when Merritt controlled for employment status. She concluded that, "the greater appeal of social issues to women is less a function of traditional sex-role socialization than it is of home-centered experience" (Merritt, 1980: 126). The CAWP survey found pronounced liberal tendencies among women on five specific issues: busing, criminal penalties, defense spending, mandatory retirement, and federal revenue for cities. The opinion of women in local office was more liberal than that of their male colleagues by four percent on busing, nine percent on criminal penalties, four percent on defense spending, eight percent on mandatory retirement, and seven percent on federal revenue for cities, "strong" and "moderate" responses combined (CAWP, 1978: 45, 37). CAWP concluded that women have a more humanistic approach to public policy issues (CAWP, 1978: 35A).

Though local female politicians seem to exhibit gender-distinctive political attitudes, it is crucial to inquire about the institutional forces that operate for and against women's ability to implement these political goals before reaching any conclusions about women's impact on policy.

Women occupy about thirteen percent of local legislative offices nationwide, have participated formally in politics only since the 1920s, continue to have lower economic status than men, and still experience varying degrees of invidious discrimination. Can one expect women's approach to politics to be similar to that of men who have played with power for centuries? The behavior patterns exhibited by women in local politics may be "unnaturally" suppressed by three interrelated institutional pressures—realpolitik, tokenism, and institutional sexism.

Female officeholders do not operate in a vacuum, and they cannot focus on their particular interests to the exclusion of the demands of a wide variety of pressing issues any more than can men. The influence of realpolitik on women's policy preferences is suggested by Mezey's (1978b) finding that when women's issues competed with other community problems, women and men officeholders ranked the importance of issues similarly; for example, on five out of seven policy proposals, women and men's ranking differed minimally (pp. 489-491).

She reported that although "the large majority of women has approved of day care facilities and rape crisis centers, especially the latter, they were not willing to assign these issues to the highest ranks" (p. 490). This means, Mezey says, that "women's support for women's policy tends to 'dissipate' when other issues are introduced on the political agenda." However, to say support dissipates misstates the findings and inaccurately portrays these women as uncommitted to women's issues. A realignment of priorities does not necessarily mean a change in the degree of support for policy issues. The reluctance of female politicians to place women's issues above all others may indicate only their recognition of the realities of politics; it also negates the stereotype of the female politician as a single-purpose legislator. Merritt suggested this same conclusion in her study: "It may be that problems facing the communities are so well articulated (or so limited) that there is general agreement on which are most pressing" (p. 125).

The minority status of women on most councils may also increase the pressure on women not to stray far from the mainstream. Kanter's (1977b) study of the effects of skewed sex ratios on token women members of competitive groups suggests several reasons why the small number of women in local politics may itself constrain their preferences. Kanter found that the women she studied (members of high-level sales groups in a Fortune 500 company) experienced significantly more performance pressure than men in the same situation. Women responded to the additional pressure in two ways, by "overachieving" or by limiting their visibility and avoiding "conflict, risks, and controversial situations" (Kanter, 1977b: 974).

Some evidence suggests that women on councils where they are the visible minority are, indeed, constrained by their token status. Mezey (1978b) noted: "[Women's] roles as politicians are determined—at least in part—by their political environment, and it may be the institutional setting which attenuates or negates the feminist attitudes of women politicians. Since the women, usually, if not always, operate as minorities in this setting, it is plausible that their views would be the first to be compromised" (pp. 490-491). Mezey (1980) asserts later that there is no statistical relationship between sex ratio (or the absolute number or percentage of women) on a council and role perceptions: "None of the measures of tokenism or marginality in a sex-skewed ratio affected [women or men's] perceptions of women's roles" (p. 191). But the impact of the minority status of local women on their ability to effect *policy* has yet to be examined.

Kanter's (1977b) study suggests the "political marginality" of women—a recurrent theme in the literature on women's political par-

ticipation. The classic work, *A Portrait of Marginality*, by Githens
and Prestage (1977) fully discusses this phenomenon.

The final obvious explanation for the difference between womens'
feminist philosophy and their limited power to effect real change is institutional sexism, the systematic exclusion of women from political
prestige and power. Mezey's study reveals several independent indicators of the patriarchy encountered by local councilwomen. For instance, forty percent of the women, but only twelve percent of the
men, agreed that "women never get to the inner circles of power."
Twenty-eight percent of the women, but only twelve percent of the
men felt that "women [are] likely to be frozen out of informal
political contacts." Yet ninety-two percent of the women and eighty-
four percent of the men agreed that it was precisely these informal activities that were critical to the work of a politician (Mezey, 1980:
184-185). The CAWP survey found a similar pattern of women's
heightened consciousness of institutional discrimination. Nearly half
of all the women surveyed named "chauvinism, stereotyping" as a
difficulty encountered in office (CAWP, 1978: 43). In addition to the
barriers mentioned above, institutional sexism denies women the
legitimacy they need to operate effectively in local government.

ACCESS TO POWER
FOR OTHER WOMEN

Another important way in which women might influence politics is
to facilitate the entrance of other women (and other under-franchised
political groups such as minorities) into politics. The future of other
women in politics depends upon the willingness of women currently in
office to recognize the connection between themselves and other
women who also aspire to office, who want access to their government, and who want policy changes. The tendency of women in office
today to remember their roots is not always evident. Some of the
most famous women in politics—national leaders such as Margaret
Thatcher and Indira Ghandi—who are paraded as examples of the
political equality of the sexes are fine specimens of what Stains et al.
(1974) refer to as "Queen Bees." This typology refers to professional
women who believe that their success was entirely their own doing; that
they encountered little or no discrimination on the way up; and that "if
only other women would try, they could do it too." Women with the
opposite attitude about the abilities and motivations of women will be
referred to here as "Sisters." These women perceive a commonality of

interests with other women; believe that discrimination has limited women's opportunities and abilities; and feel that they share responsibility for lowering the ladder to other women and for aiding their entrance into politics.

Do women in local office fit either of these stereotypes? Merritt found the councilwomen she surveyed resembled the Sister model. On the Queen Bee statement that "most women have only themselves to blame for not doing better in life," the correlation was $+.27$ ($p < .001$) between sex (female) and disagreement with the statement (Merritt, 1980: 124-125). The women faulted the political environment rather than themselves for barriers to success, and indicated a "general sensitivity to the women's movement rather than merely reflection of their own personal stake in public domain equality" (p. 125).

Mezey's extensive inquiry into the attitudes of female officeholders toward women's political roles led to a similar conclusion. She found that "women politicians are more concerned about the minority group of female public figures than men are; they are more sympathetic to their problems and more sensitive to discriminatory patterns of behavior within the institution," but that women and men were "essentially alike in their approval of the formal elements of the women's movement and in viewing traditional femininity with approbation" (pp. 496, 494). This latter finding appears to contradict the hypothesis that projects a higher degree of sympathy on the part of councilwomen for other women; but, the response may again be biased by the nature of the question—that is, individuals tend to see their own situation as the most salient. Moreover, women and men in office may feel similarly about issues, but possess different levels of motivation and ability to act upon their attitudes as discussed above. Data from the nationwide CAWP survey indicate that, in fact, local women strongly favor improving the status of women and are much more supportive than their male colleagues of the women's movement. A strong majority of local women (districts with populations less than 10,000) felt that more should be done to assure women's rights by the federal and state governments and by private industry (sixty-one percent, sixty-three percent, and seventy-four percent, respectively); men's favorable responses were much lower (thirty-seven percent, thirty-six percent, and fifty-five percent, respectively) (CAWP, 1978: 32, 37).

On the attitudinal level, then, women in local politics appear to be much closer to the Sister than the Queen Bee model. This heightened awareness may result from the greater degree of discrimination women encounter in the male-dominated world of politics. Mezey noted that "when women exist as a minority of a dominant population, especially in a setting where women are not 'generally' accepted, they may develop an increased awareness of the differences between the sexes" (Mezey, 1978b: 494). Although women in her sample exhibited a greater gender-based concern for women's political status than the general social or economic situation of women, implicit in this perception is a broader range of concerns, for political status is difficult to separate from women's social and economic condition.

As "descriptive" representatives (Pitkin, 1967) of a recognizable component of local constituencies, female representatives are standard-bearers for the entire movement seeking greater involvement of women in the spheres of power. Subsequently, the performance of female politicians is scrutinized by both women and men. The former often look to women as role models of successful women. Ninety-eight percent of the women Mezey surveyed agreed that "women in politics serve as examples to women in society" (Mezey, 1980: 189). And men often evaluate all women in politics on the basis of a few prominent examples who are in their minds obvious exceptions to the female populace.

An innovative study of the effect of the attitudes of the electorate toward women in office by MacManus (1981) demonstrates that female politicians are correct in perceiving that their performance (and existence) has wider political and social ramifications than that of a man in the same position. A poll of voter attitudes in Houston toward women in politics indicated that dramatic changes in voter attitudes were attributable to the strong performance of then city controller (now mayor) Kathy Whitmire. "One-third of the persons polled attributed personal changes in attitudes toward women in city politics directly to the performance [of Whitmire] . . . of this third, the overwhelming majority (94%) claimed their attitudes toward women's participation in local office had become more positive" (p. 99). Thus, a woman's performance in local office (assuming the office is a significant one and the performance is good) can break down the barriers for other women aspirants. This gender-based contribution to politics embodies the essense of the notion of democratic participation and suggests particularly that unrepresentative political bodies can encourage disenfranchisement.

How willing are local female officeholders to facilitate the realization of women's interests or to be the vanguard for the movement? Evidence indicates that women in local office do accept such responsibility. Fifty-six percent of the women in Mezey's survey (compared to twelve percent of the men) agreed that "women politicians have special responsibility to represent the interest of women in society"; sixty-eight percent (compared to forty-eight percent of the men) felt that women members of local councils should take leading positions on women's issues; and eighty-two percent felt that other women looked to them to take such positions (Mezey, 1980: 189).

Women's activists and feminist groups often tend to operate on this assumption that women in office are automatically "standing for" their interests (Pitkin, 1967: 60-91). "Women politicians are typically the target of efforts to lobby for favorable policy positions and women's groups devote much energy to increasing the assumption that women accord a higher priority to women's policy issues than men do" (Mezey, 1980: 486). Given that a primary task of many women's groups is to gain access to the policy-making process (usually with very limited resources), it is not suprising that they look toward female legislators for aid and leadership.

Gaining access to power is, however, only the prelude to using it. For feminists, the coalition of activists and officeholders on women's issues that help translate concerns into issues is often crucial to legislative success. Research on alliances formed by women's interest groups and female legislators at the local level is lacking, although some have suggested this link at other levels of office (e.g., Gelb and Palley, 1977).

SUMMARY

Though research remains sketchy, the attitudes and behavior of women in local office suggest gender-distinctive impacts in the areas of representative theory, women's issues and social policy, and the access of other women to power. Unlike the debutante City Mothers of Stephenson, Michigan, women in local office today are no longer anomalies; they must be concerned with their impact on the political system, the policy agenda, and other women.

A recent study of the recruitment of women to city councils concluded that structural (aggregate demographic, socioeconomic, and formal political) characteristics of cities do not explain the continuing low rate of female officeholding at the local level (Welch and Karnig, 1979: 491). This suggests that the most basic questions about the real constraints on women in local politics today remain unresolved. Combined with the barriers of realpolitik and partriarchy, Kanter's theory of tokenism greatly elucidates these problems, but prompts the question, "How many women must serve on councils and in politics for their 'normal' behavior to reveal itself?" Kanter estimates that even a minority presence of twenty percent is not always large enough to overcome the problems encountered by tokens. Considering that the percentage of women in local politics is only about thirteen percent, Kanter's conclusion makes the study of the impact of women in politics at present necessarily tenuous.

The hypothesis that women's entrance into power would radicalize politics was satirically proposed in Greek comedy more than two thousand years before women were allowed to hold office in the United States. Recent empirical research on the attitudes and behavior of women at the local level of government suggests that Aristophanes' prediction was partially accurate. Although women in city and county offices have not radically changed modern local politics, research on their attitudes and behavior indicates a growing liberal and feminist influence on this traditional bastion of male power.

2

WOMEN AND STATE POLITICS: AN ASSESSMENT

Marianne Githens

Since the late 1960s, when the first scholarly efforts to explore women's political behavior began to appear in print, considerable emphasis has been placed on women's participation in elite politics. This was to be expected. In the first place, when the environment of the sixties with its calls for "opening up the system" and participatory democracy spurred interest in looking at who the political decision makers were, just a cursory glance showed how few women there were among the ranks of public officeholders. This absence of women in public leadership positions raised a number of questions. Did women eschew positions of political power because they were too passive and submissive by nature? Were they socialized to be subordinate? Was their primary role of wife and mother too demanding to permit other kinds of activity? Or were there some special circumstances that militated against women's representation in public office?

Second, at the same time that the paucity of women in the political elite was becoming so glaringly apparent, the nascent Women's Liberation movement started to call attention to the insensitivity of public policy to women and to press for changes that would make it more congruent with women's concerns and requirements. The growing legitimacy of this demand for policy change, at least among women, along with many male politicians' obliviousness to women's needs, suggested an urgency for getting more women into public office. But how could this goal be achieved if the causes of women's underrepresentation were not understood? Both feminist scholars and activists needed answers. Pompous explanations based on conventional wisdom or rooted in crude sex stereotyping would no longer do.[1]

Although national policy was, and is, highly critical to the well-being of women and their representation at the federal level woefully inadequate, the study of women in the national political elite did not seem to be a particularly promising field. For one thing, there are simply not enough women in either elected or appointed federal positions to permit any meaningful empirical study. This is not to say that those case studies of congresswomen and higher-echelon federal appointees that have appeared have not presented much interesting and useful data. They have. Scholarly research, such as that of Gehlen (1977a), Kincaid (1978), Rosenberg (1972), Lepper (1974), Werner (1966), Bullock and Heys (1972), Tolchin and Tolchin (1976), and Chamberlin (1974), has provided many important insights about the ways in which these women are recruited and perform. However, because of the small number of women involved, the findings have not allowed widely applicable conclusions to be drawn.

Nor is the problem of statistical reliability stemming from such a small database the only difficulty involved in studying women at the federal level. Politics is largely a matter of working one's way up, and the research suggests that women need more experience than men in order to run for Congress (Diamond, 1977). As a consequence, women could not be expected to hold national positions if they had not already held subfederal posts. The dearth of women in the national political elite could, therefore, be easily explained by the fact that there is only a small pool of women eligible to move into such positions. Under these circumstances, it seemed to make a great deal more sense to look at women's political recruitment and performance at the state and local levels.

As with studying national elites, examining women in local politics also has certain limitations. Since local communities often differ substantially from each other, conclusions about women's participation in one local political arena may not be applicable to women elsewhere. Of course, if a representative sample of local communities is used, general conclusions can be drawn; but such projects require the kind of funding rarely available to those whose primary focus is women's political participation. Furthermore, since local politics is not the sole entry point for a political career, it is not imperative to investigate female participation at this level. Studying women in elite politics at the state level might be prefered because this course avoided the pitfalls encountered in research on women in both national and local elites. Or at least so some researchers thought.

State politics seemed the ideal level on which to concentrate. At the state level, the problem of an insufficient database is circumvented, for even in the 1960s there were enough women holding state office, especially in state legislatures, to gather statistically meaningful data. Also, if a sample of states that took into account variables such as political and party structures, political culture, the degree of urbanization, minority group presence, and income distribution were selected, generalized conclusions might be drawn. Because the costs of such comparative state studies in contrast to those involved in surveying a broad range of local communities are not as overwhelming, it appeared to make sense to focus research efforts on women's political behavior at that level.

In this chapter, the research on the recruitment and performance of women in state politics will be reviewed. The findings and questions raised by this research will be discussed, and the problems and prospects they pose for continued work on this topic presented. This will provide a context for the contemporary research directions found in subsequent chapters of this book.

THE RECRUITMENT OF WOMEN TO
THE POLITICAL ELITE

Political Woman (Kirkpatrick, 1974) did not appear until approximately eight years after the initial efforts to do serious, systematic research on women and elite politics; yet three of the four hypothetical constraints advanced by Kirkpatrick in her ground-breaking study of female state legislators have dominated all scholarly discussion of this subject.[2] To be sure, these constraints have been refined, modified, clarified, and extended to include structural barriers and have led to the application of other theoretical approaches, such as marginality (Githens and Prestage, 1977). Nevertheless, the core of Kirkpatrick's constraints remains the basic focus for all research on women in the political elite. Thus today, as in the 1960s, when the body of literature on women's political participation first began to appear, the effects of cultural constraints—especially those arising from socialization—role constraints; "male conspiracy," and situational and structural factors stemming from these constraints are central to both the empirical investigations and the explanations of female public officeholder's patterns of recruitment and performance.

Studies of political socialization done in the late 1950s and the 1960s had a significant impact on the research dealing with the recruitment of women. These socialization studies all conclude that there were important gender differences in political interest. Boys were consistently found to have a greater interest in politics than girls, to possess more political information, and to follow the national news more closely (Hyman, 1959; Greenstein, 1965; Easton and Dennis, 1969). In contrast, girls were found to be more attracted to personal figures than boys, to have a higher level of trust and reliance on the inherent goodness of the political system, and less likely to be task oriented or to see benefit in conflict and disagreement (Hess and Torney, 1967; Greenstein, 1965).

Although the accuracy of these findings was subsequently questioned and contradictory evidence presented (Merelman, 1971; Orum et al., 1977; Jennings and Niemi, 1974; Keller, 1978; Baer, 1978), the fundamental assumption of those initially engaged in the study of women and politics was that women were less positively oriented to politics than men and that women's lack of involvement in political activity, particularly at the elite level, resulted from socialization to sex role and sex-role-appropriate behavior.[3] For all intents and purposes, this orientation was seen as precluding politics as a career option for women.

Of course some women, few though they were, did enter the political arena—seeking and sometimes getting elected to office. Since this politically active woman was in such sharp contrast to the passive female depicted in the socialization studies, it was assumed that she was unlike ordinary women. An examination of ways in which these women differed from women in the general population and how closely they resembled males in the political elite seemed in order. Thus, initial studies of women in state politics investigated the demographic and personality characteristics of these women in order to isolate their distinctive qualities.

All the data collected pointed to certain similarities shared by women recruited to the political elite. These women were most likely to be married, to have children, to be in their 40s when first elected to public office, to be middle class and to be drawn from a somewhat different range of occupations, including employment in the home, than male politicians (Werner, 1966, 1968; Werner and Bachtold, 1974; Gruberg, 1968; Costantini and Craik, 1972; Githens, 1977; Soule and McGrath, 1977; Bullock and Heys, 1972; King, 1977; Githens and Prestage, 1978, 1979; Kirkpatrick, 1974, 1976; Jennings and Farah, 1981; Johnson and Stanwick, 1976; Johnson and Carroll, 1978; Mandel, 1981; Main and Schapiro, 1979).

In terms of gender differences, there were some interesting findings. Perhaps the most striking was that women were likely to be considerably older than their male peers at the time of their initial election to public office. This age difference is even more significant in light of the fact that, at least in the case of state legislators, men become interested in politics at a later age than women (Main and Schapiro 1979). As far as a range of occupations was concerned, though, homemaking and other traditional female vocations were not as dominant as many researchers had anticipated, for while women were not drawn in the same numbers as men from the more prestigious brokerage occupations, such as law and business, a fairly significant proportion of them did come from a variety of professional careers (Githens, 1977; Main and Schapiro, 1979; Dubeck, 1976; Welch, 1978).

In addition to these general characteristics, some studies found that elite women were more likely than women at the citizen level to possess a configuration of masculine personality characteristics. Specifically, female state legislators were found to be more liberal in their attitudes, more unconventional, and more adventuresome than women at the citizen level (Werner, 1968; Werner and Bachtold, 1974; Soule and McGrath, 1977). In particular, Werner and Bachtold (1974) found female state legislators more likley to be dominant, that is to say stubborn, assertive, and competitive, more adventuresome, more unconventional, and radical in the sense of being experimental and more liberal and free thinking than women in the general population; and in comparison with their male peers, they were more likely to be assertive, imaginative, and liberal.

Although both Kirkpatrick (1974) and Mandel (1981) alluded to the feminine qualities of women in state politics, most of the research assumed them to be socialized to somewhat masculine norms of behavior. Data on female state legislators gathered in 1978 show them, however, to possess a much broader range of personality characteristics (Githens and Prestage, 1981). Indeed, these research findings suggest that female state legislators are just as likely to have a strong as a weak orientation to authority, to be adventuresome as conventional, and only slightly more likely to be conflictual than consensual in style. When these findings are taken into account, the widely accepted description of women state legislators as especially adventuresome, independent minded in terms of authority, and unconventional seems unwarranted.

What can account for these contradictory findinds? Well, it may be that, given the initial premise that women in the political elite had to be different, that is to say more attuned to masculine norms, these characteristics were exaggerated in the early studies. It is, of course, also possible that when there were so few women in the state legislatures, as was the case in the late 1960s and early 1970s, when many of the studies were done, women had to be somewhat masculine in their characteristics in order to get elected and to function in an overwhelmingly male environment. Perhaps with the dramatic increase in the number of women sitting in state legislatures, women may no longer feel the need to be especially independent, aggressive, or different. Now that they are in a less exclusively male setting, perhaps they sense an improved chance for effective participation in the legislative process, and, as a result, they may have adopted a less militant demeanor that allows them to fit in better and to enhance their power. It is also conceivable that the changes in general attitudes about women permit a more diverse cross-section of women to get elected to public office and encourage women with less distinctively male or aggressive personality characteristics to seek and win public office. But, whatever the explanation for the contradictory findings may be, the notion of the female legislator as someone necessarily socialized to male behavioral norms is now suspect.

Since even today comparatively few women sit in state legislatures and socialization to male personality characteristics does not satisfactorily explain this phenomenon, what factors do affect their recruitment? The two most consistently cited are a generalized socialization to sex role or sex role appropriate behavior and situational constraints. Research dealing with socialization as an explanatory variable contends that normative behavior internalized by women limits their aspirations for public office. For example, in their study of Michigan delegates to national party conventions, Jennings and Farah (1981) found that although there were few differences between men and women in terms of social backgrounds, political status, political careers and perceptions of the political process, there were real gender differences in ambition and aspiration. This finding conforms with Sapiro and Farah's (1980) contention that there is a differential development of political ambition among women, with female ambition being dependent on such factors as home, family, employment role, and feminism. Elsewhere, Sapiro (1983) has expanded on this theme and argued that the gender role of what she calls "privatization" influences women's political ambition and mode of citizen participation. Similarly, Fowlkes et al. (1979) found gender differences in both ambition and activity among party members that led them to conclude that men are more ambitious than women. Welch who, unlike Fowlkes et al. argues that active discrimination affects the recruitment of women to public office, also agrees that socialization to sex role reduces the number of female candidates for public office.

Thus, all these studies substantiate the notion of cultural constraint advanced by Kirkpatrick (1974).

As will be discussed a little later on, gender differences in ambition and aspiration may, however, have less to do with socialization to feminine passivity or sex-role-appropriate behavior than with women's rational assessment of how their energies can best be utilized to affect political decisions. Perhaps women perceive the traditional political process as being less malleable and responsive to issues of concern to them than men do, and that this has prompted women to define their participatory role in politics somewhat differently. By limiting consideration of women's ambition and aspirations to the arena of traditional elite political activity, the extent of their political ambition and aspiration may be obscured.

Much discussion of women's limited participation in the traditional political elite has also focused on situational factors, particularly the strains and conflicts resulting from the multiple roles of mother, wife, and politician. The emphasis female public officeholders give to their roles of mother and wife, as well as to the barriers imposed by societal definitions of appropriate female roles and the obligations associated with them, have led many to hypothesize that role strain and conflict significantly affect women's recruitment. For example, Lee (1977) has argued that in order for women to participate in political activity, they must have adequate financial resources to pay others to perform services associated with traditional female roles such as child care and housekeeping. As she puts it, "If they can afford a house cleaner and baby sitter to get away from the house, they can pursue other interests" (p. 25). Lynn and Flora (1977) go further and claim that there is societal punishment for women who deviate from traditional female roles, particularly the role of mother, and that this punishment affects patterns of female political participation. Currey (1977), Mandel (1981), Kirkpatrick (1974, 1976), and Sapiro (1983) have also maintained that role strain or conflict has an impact on women in the political elite. Even recent data on politically active women gathered by the National Women's Education Fund (1981) present a picture of politically involved women as individuals who acutely feel role strain or conflict. In other words, these studies suggest that socialization to the notion of the primacy of women's roles as mother and wife means that their involvement in other nontraditional female activity is contingent upon their first meeting traditional female role obligations. As a result, politically active women continuously face the strain or actual conflict of being above all else a wife and mother and simultaneously a full-time, dedicated, professional politician. In turn, the difficulty of meeting these dual demands dissuades women from participating in elite politics.

The application of the theory of marginality to women in politics grew out of this notion about the role strain that female politicians experience from attempting to fulfill the roles of wife/mother and politician. The nature of this conflict and strain has been described in *A Portrait of Marginality* (Githens and Prestage, 1977: 8) in the following way:

> Women who have moved into the political elite feel intensely the pressure of the two conflicting groups. Much time, effort and energy goes into seeking some reconciliation of the roles of women and politician. Political women want to be respected by their male colleagues; yet they also feel the need to serve dinner on time, clean the house and so forth.

Recent research, however, raises questions about how gender-specific the role strain and conflict of parenting and a political career really are. Although the support of spouse and children appears to be much more critical for women in politics than for men, Stoper (1977) contends that conflicting roles may effect a cost on male politicians as well; and Blair and Henry's (1981) study of the effects of family on legislative turnover seems to support her in this assertion. Furthermore, recent analyses of data that test the hypothesis of marginality indicate that the strain female state legislators experience may be much more dependent on their aspirations to be accepted as politicians by their male peers and on their perceptions that their male colleagues continue to see them as a distinctive and unequal subgroup than on the conflict arising from the discordant demands of wife/mother and a career in politics (Githens and Prestage, 1980, 1981, 1982).

Other situational and structural variables have been investigated as well. MacManus (1976), Kirkpatrick (1974, 1976), Githens (1977), Githens and Prestage (1977, 1980), Mezey (1976), and Welch (1978) have all pointed to gender differences in skill areas. The most noteworthy of these skills differences is the small number of women, as compared to men, who are drawn from the brokerage professions, such as law and business. As Main and Schapiro (1979: 7) have pointed out,

> Despite the high percentage of women engaged in nontraditional occupations, there is still a significant disparity between the numbers of

men and women who occupy the legal and other brokerage professions from which a disproportionate share of political recruits come.

The small number of women lawyers and the effects of this on the recruitment of women to the political elite in general, and state legislatures in particular have been especially noted (Githens, 1977; Kirkpatrick, 1974). Indeed, Kirkpatrick (1974: 83) has gone as far as to say:

> A woman who is a lawyer can win nomination and be elected to the legislature without the years of party or community service that characterizes most of women's careers. Presumably a legal education can be substituted for apprenticeship in community affairs.

A little further on she reports one of her respondents as saying "if you are a woman and a lawyer . . . you have an instant credibility" (p. 83).

In some research, however, gender differences in terms of occupation do not seem to explain fully the meager recruitment of women. For example, Welch (1979: 379) concludes that

> while women do not yet posses the same educational and occupational levels as men, their overall achievements in these areas would lead one to expect a greater percentage of female legislators than actually exists. Thus, if this were a "sex blind" but occupation and education sensitive process, about one quarter of the legislators would be female. Thus, structural characteristics are an important set of factors keeping women out of this kind of public office.

In contrast to Kirkpatrick's assertion, Githens and Prestage's (1980, 1982) research shows female lawyers to be the most disadvantaged of all female state legislators in terms of office held in their legislative chamber and in their party organization. Indeed, even after controlling for the length of time in the legislature, the data show that women with only a high school diploma hold more offices within their legislatures than do more highly educated women, and that female lawyers are the least likely of all female occupational groups to perceive themselves as being successful or as having influence.

Education and socioeconomic status have also been cited as barriers to recruitment. Here, the research suggests that the combination of higher levels of educational achievement and affluence erodes male/female differences in political recruitment. For example, Jones and Nelson (1981) found that highly educated women from affluent families were the most stable source for political recruitment to the lower chambers of state legislatures. Similarly, Powell et al. (1981)

found that education, childhood family status, and the political interest of parents minimized male/female discrepancies in elite participation. However, if Welch is correct in her assertion that education does not fully account for the disproportionately small percentages of women recruited to public office, then even though more highly educated, affluent women more often participate in elite politics than do other women, education and affluence do not solely account for the poor showing of women. Rule (1981: 76) concurs in this assessment and observes: "Generally the small proportions of women legislators is related less to eligibility factors—such as availability of women professionals—than to selection/nomination contextual elements."

Some of the literature dealing with structural variables has made much of the fact that women spend a greater amoung of time in political party activity than men. From this it has been assumed that since males are much more often tapped by their political organizations than women, it is the party organizations that constitute a significant constraint on women's recruitment to public office. However, research findings suggest that the barriers for women may be somewhat more complex than were originally supposed. In the first place, while women's party activity is more extensive than men's, women tend to be more involved in routine party matters than in decision making. In contrast, men are clustered in the decision-making levels of the party. Although one may argue that this, in itself, is an indication of a structural barrier, the findings do not demonstrate that women are necessarily relegated to certain areas of party activity. Indeed, some of the studies have suggested that the socialization of women to sex role encourages them to participate in party affairs in a different way than men (Lee, 1977; Sapiro and Farah, 1980). In terms of political parties and election outcomes, Fowkles et al. (1979) do not find that parties impose constraints on women. This leads them to conclude that "the underrepresentation of women in elective office is more a result of a paucity of women candidates than discrimination against them at the polls" (p. 7). Similarly, Darcy and Schramm (1977) found sex to have no effect on election outcomes, except for incumbent Democratic women who do significantly better than their male counterparts.

Perhaps the best and certainly the most comprehensive study of structural barriers to women's participation in state politics is Diamond's book, *Sex Roles in the State House* (1977). She found that women are more likely to be successful in those states where this office is viewed as less desirable by men, is more poorly paid, and is considered less professional. Interestingly enough, in a study of female mayors in Brazil, Blay (1979) comes to a similar conclusion; her findings show women most likely to be elected in the poorest, least industrialized, and least urbanized states. Jones and Nelson (1981: 11) found that although "highly industrialized states with a highly educated population of women provide the ideal milieu for the recruitment of women to the lower chambers of state legislatures," neither lower party competition nor a legislature of high quality is positively associated with the political recruitment of women. This prompts them to speculate that the recruitment of women may in fact depend on other factors, such as state expansion in population, heterogeneity and an increase in the percentage of U.S. representatives, with this combination of factors "leaving avenues for women to enter the lower house of the states" (p. 14).

Some doubts about Jones and Nelson's rather optimistic conclusions are implicitly raised, however by Rule's (1981: 76-77) research on the relationship of female state legislators to women's recruitment to Congress. Arguing that there is a Catch 22 operating for women she writes:

> where many women are elected to state legislatures—in states with Republican party dominance of the legislatures and low population states—few women are elected to Congress. Where few women are elected to state legislatures—states with Democratic party dominance of the legislature and high population states—also few women are elected to Congress. This "Catch 22" . . . explains why there is a negligible relationship between the proportions of women in particular state legislatures and women's representation in the same states' congressional delegations.

She argues further that certain contextual factors other than eligibility are significant; these include adverse economic conditions, the lack of an egalitarian heritage, and unfavorable expenditures for public welfare.

In the final analysis, all the research on the political recruitment of women at the state level suggests the existence of some degree of cultural constraint that stems from the socialization to sex role and sex-role-appropriate behavior. This socialization restricts women in their choice of a career in politics, or encourages them to pursue a somewhat different pattern of political involvement; possibly both. At the same time, the role constraints of wife and mother would appear to be rather more complex and less gender-specific than was originally supposed; certainly they are not as crucial as were once thought. Indeed, role constraint defined as the strain or conflict of wife/mother versus politician may be less important than the limitations of culturally defined life/career options that most men and women are taught and come to internalize. Structural and situation variables also play some part in the political recruitment process for women, although once again in a more complicated way than was initially expected. Affluence and education are important to political recruitment, but for men as well as for women. Furthermore, affluence and education do not fully explain the minimal representation of women in elite politics at the state level. Similarly, the evidence seems to suggest that although fewer women possess the skills obtained from the brokerage professions, women possessing these skills are neither as fully represented as their numbers warrant, nor as fully accepted as they ought to be.

What does this research tell us then about the political recruitment of women? That women should be socialized to desire traditionally male political careers? That women should move away from what Sapiro (1983) describes as privatization? That men's socialization to sex-role-appropriate behavior needs to be drastically changed? Perhaps. But it may also be telling us something quite different. As will be discussed a little later, women may have a somewhat different notion about what constitutes the public and private spheres than men. If this is the case, their "lowered" ambition and aspirations may reflect their rational assessment of what is a useful avenue for them in achieving their goals and objectives. Improving the chances for their recruitment into the political elite may be at least as dependent on redefining the public sphere and the functions of traditional political institutions as on a crash program to heighten their ambitions to hold public office.

WOME IN THE POLITICAL ELITE— THE ISSUE OF PERFORMANCE

Before proceeding with any discussion of women's performance in the political elite, a caveat seems to be in order. Under the best of conditions, evaluating elite performance is a tricky business. Despite considerable efforts on the part of mainstream political science to define power and influence, there are still extensive differences of opinion and much ambiguity in distinguishing between the two and understanding the relationship of one to the other. This poses a serious problem for evaluating effective performance, since performance is most often equated with the ability to produce a desired outcome—that is to say, with power or influence. A lack of consensus on definitions of power and influence, in turn, prevents the emergence of any universally accepted measurement device for assessing the amount of power or influence an individual or group exerts. In the case of women, the problem is further compounded by the fact that those measuring devices for determining power or influence that have been proposed are predicated on the assumption that all individuals and groups are equal in their potential to affect policy outcomes by virtue of their capacity to bargain pragmatically.

Successful bargaining, however, implies the existence of several preconditions: an ideological neutrality that permits individuals and groups to participate in a wide range of coalitions, the individual or group's acceptability as a coalition partner, and the clout to enforce mutually agreed-upon bargains. In the case of minorities in general, and women in particular, these preconditions do not usually exist. It the first place, in most state legislatures women constitute only a small percentage of the overall membership.[4] As a consequence, their significance as a swing vote in any but a closely divided contest is minimal. While it is true that in some states women have organized themselves into a caucus in order to maximize their strength, even here their numbers are usually too small to threaten the outcome of most votes. Thus, women's support is generally not viewed as critical to the success of an overall legislative program.

Second, although on occasion their support may be eagerly sought after on close, critical votes, female state legislators do not seem to be able consistently to translate their support and votes for one set of policies into support and votes on issues of particular concern to them.

Game theory, perhaps, offers some explanation for this phenomemon. In game theory outcomes are affected by whether the game is a single-shot one or ongoing. If the game were perceived as ongoing, women in the political elite might be able to force coalition partners into honoring mutual agreements. If the game were defined as a single shot, coalition partners might well believe that there is no necessity to live up to their commitments in subsequent games. Possibly because of their limited numbers, their lack of representation in legislative and party leadership positions, and the tendency to define women as less than serious, hard-nosed, professional politicians, their male peers may well be inclined to define women's support and votes on critical close votes as a single shot rather than an ongoing game; with the result that the women are unable to enforce agreements that they have negotiated with their coalition partners.

Third, women's acceptability as equal coalition partners tends to be eroded by the perception that they primarily represent a distinctive but peripheral set of concerns, such as women's rights and social welfare. Such topics often tend not to be considered prime subjects for public policy. Indeed, some do not even view them as areas for governmental intervention at all. As a consequence, whenever possible, coalition arrangements with women are avoided, and when women's support must be obtained, there is little sense of obligation to honor previous commitments made to women.

Finally, women, like most minorities, are not ideologically neutral, especially on issues relating to social change and sex equity. This limits the range of coalition partners available to women and weakens their bargaining position.

Given the absence of these preconditions for successful pragmatic bargaining, it is no wonder that the application of existing measures for determining power and evaluations of their performance based on such measures have found women wanting. Using power to measure the performance of women in the political elite is analogous to using winning as a measure of performance in a race between an olympic runner and a person with one leg; regardless of practice or effort expended; the legless runner is bound to lose the hundred yard dash.

Yet, the significance of women in the political elite for public policy outcomes cannot be entirely ignored; especially given the initial impetus to do research on women in politics. Despite the problems involved, research attention has been directed toward the impact of women on policy outcomes, particularly in the area of women's issues, their articulation of feminist concerns, their overall effectiveness as legislators in terms of getting their bills passed, and their efforts to carve out an appropriate and effective leadership style. The findings of these studies have, in turn, contributed to the emergence of several explanations of the roles women play as members of the political elite.

The majority of studies focusing on female officeholders' sensitivity to women's issues and expressions of commitment to feminist concerns indicate that at the state level, at least, most women running for or holding public office scrupulously avoid any public identification with feminism or the Women's Movement. They run for public office neither as feminists nor on a platform that is predominantly concerned with women's issues. Nor once elected, do they often publicly describe their role as that of representing women's issues in particular or as that of serving as a role model to inspire other women to seek public office (Carroll, 1979; Githens, 1983; Githens and Prestage,

1980, 1981; Mezey, 1978b, 1978c; Carver, 1979). To the contrary, they emphasize their concern for all people—men as well as women, and for a broad range of issues that extends well beyond traditional women's issues (Gehlen, 1977b). This has led many to conclude that feminists and women in the political elite are two distinctive and highly differentiated groups.

The behavior of women in the political elite often contradicts their feminist disclaimers, however. For example, women public officeholders are more likely to credit women than men with encouraging them in their electoral bid (Currey, 1977; Githens and Prestage, 1978, 1979). Furthermore, they are often likely to act on and support feminist concerns. For instance, Cook (1981b) reports that in simulated cases, while male Democratic judges expressed similar views toward women's issues, their behavior was less positive than that of the female Democratic judges. Elsewhere, she found that female judges are more conscious of institutional constraints and more favorably disposed toward new social roles for women who demand them than are women in the general population (1980b). The development of women's caucuses in state legislatures also belies an absence of concern with women's issues. In Maryland, for example, at the beginning of each session the women's caucus develops a specific agenda for action, and largely through its efforts a number of bills specifically addressing issues of concern to women have been introduced and subsequently enacted into law.

These contradictions between descriptions of themselves and their behavior have prompted Carroll (1979) to argue that the neutrality or negativism of women in the political elite to feminism may be more apparent than real. In her view, it is the structure of elite politics that gives rise to this appearance and that forces women to "stay in the closet." If Carroll is correct in this assertion, and the evidence suggests that she is, negative evaluations of women's performance based on their failure to proclaim feminism publicly or to run on a feminist platform fail both to take into account their very real actions to advance the cause of women and to understand the effects of political structures on women's overt roles within them.

As was discussed earlier, effectiveness is most often equated with power. Since power is an attribute that few women in the political elite possess, evaluations of the effectiveness of their performance poses serious problems. Even so, some effort has been made to assess women's performance in terms of the standard criteria—the number of bills introduced or sponsored, the number of sponsored bills passed, the relationship of committee assignments to bills introduced and sponsored and the general range and scope of legislation initiated or sponsored. For example, using these criteria, Gehlen (1977b) studied women in the Ninety-third Congress along with a sample of their male peers. Her findings characterize the congresswomen as being no more independent than men in their support of the president or their party's legislative program; they were only slightly more likely than men to cosponsor bills rather than initiate them on their own, and even here gender differences declined with length of time in office; as likely as men to introduce legislation in nontraditionally female fields such as business, the economy, defense and the armed forces; and no less effective than their male peers in getting their bills acted on. But others argue the contrary (Barber, 1965; Soule and McGrath, 1977). Even the data presented by Gehlen raise questions about the accuracy of her conclusions, for while her data show that the percentage distribution of female single-sponsored, first-name cosponsored, and non-first-name cosponsored bills approximates that of congressmen, the men who constitute two-thirds of the total number of respondents introduced about four-fifths of the total number of single-sponsored bills, somewhat more than three-fourths of the first name multiple-sponsored bills and about three-fourths of the non-first-name multiple-sponsored legislation. The similarity between men and women in the percentage distribution of bills that they sponsored in each category would seem then to be offset by the greater legislative activity of the men. Furthermore, even if Gehlen is correct in her interpretation of the data, one still wonders about the validity of using power as a standard for judging the performance of any minority in the political elite.

Other proposed alternatives for evaluating performance do not appear to be any more promising. Contrary to what some have hypothesized, female state legislators do not seem to have a unique or different perception of their role. Githens and Prestage (1980) did not find women state legislators to perceive their primary role as that of serving as either an ombudsman for women's issues or a role model that would inspire other women to enter the political elite. Instead, their data show women most likely to choose the role of delegate and to define their function as that of representing the interests and general welfare of all. Although this role predilection may be as reflective of the forces that contribute to women's reluctance to be publicly identified with feminism as anything else, it does, nonetheless, mean than an alternative scheme for measuring effectiveness based on either feminism or a specifically defined, unique role is inapproriate.

Evaluations based on female legislators' perception of themselves as influential or successful is equally problematic. For one thing, the vast majority of female state legislators view themselves as both influential and successful, but their lack of representation in legislative and party leadership positions casts some doubts about the objective reality of this assessment (Githens and Prestage 1978, 1980).[5] Second, it would appear that the female legislators' perception of their success and influence is based on their sense of achievement in having made it into the political elite rather than on the traditional notions of effectiveness and power.

Studies of gender differences associated with power seem to support the idea that women use different criteria for determining their success and influence. For example, McClelland (1975) reported that men find power in strength and external action whereas women find it in internal sources. Similarly, Polk (1974) found that men are interested in action and things, women in self and other people. These differences have led Van Wagner and Swanson (1979) to conclude that the democratic coaching style rather than an authoritarian or coercive one is more consistent with women's socialization experiences and with the development of negotiating skills that grows out of their roles as wife and mother.

The criteria on which women base their perceptions of success and influence probably have some potential for developing an alternative standard for judging women's performance. However, a serious rethinking of a number of assumptions current in political science is first required. For instance, a special paradigm for minority legislative behavior needs to be developed. The Wahlke et al. (1962) legislative role typology needs to be reformulated to include advocacy and the notion of service to the community that current role types ignore. The latter is particularly critical since female state legislators are most likely to select the role of delegate as best describing them; yet the essential passivity and reactiveness conveyed by the present definition of that role do not seem to reflect accurately the women's conception of their role or function. The output emphasis of the legislative function also has to be rethought because its emphasis on external action is too oriented to male power models. While a fundamental restructuring of our present understanding of legislative behavior would make it more multidimensional and thus more useful than the present conceptions, the effort involved is very considerable, and one wonders if other aspects of minority behavior might not be more profitably explored first.

In order to get at the basic problems inherent in being effective—in exercising power—in a less complicated way than a restructuring of legislative behavior demands, some attention has been directed toward the question of women's leadership style. Those efforts have been characterized by an attempt to explore both the restrictions imposed by current stereotypes of women leaders and the efforts on the part of women to carve out an appropriate and effective role style for themselves.

Some literature in the field of organizational behavior has pointed to the prevalence of gender stereotyping of leaders with women being perceived as too focused on people, too emotional, not assertive enough, too critical, too ambitious, too stubborn, domineering or bitchy and possibly antimale as well. Boverman et al. (1972: 75) found that "women are perceived as relatively less competent, less independent, less objective, and less logical than men." These characteristics are also reported by Schein in her study of male and female leaders (1975). A typology of these stereotypes of women's leadership style— mother, pet, sex object, and iron maiden developed by Kanter (1976) also points to the association of specific negative characteristics with female leaders.

Interviews of female state legislators suggest that these negative stereotypes concern them. The women frequently refer to the necessity for limiting the number of issues on which they will take a stand; for always being very well prepared—"doing one's homework"; for carefully choosing the topic on which they will speak; and for making sure that their relations with their male peers are good (Kirkpatrick, 1974; Mandel, 1981; Githens, 1977). Is this because they fear being perceived as too emotional, too illogical, too ambitious, too domineering, too scattered in focus, too assertive, antimale? Perhaps. If their behavior is being continuously self-monitored to avoid the pitfalls associated with the negative images of female leaders, as their responses seem to indicate, the female legislators must perpetually find themselves in a position where the dynamism of leadership must always be kept under check. In such a situation, a vital leadership role is a virtual impossibility for them. Perhaps Kanter (1977a: 230) sums up the situation of female state legislators when in writing of women in corporations she says that "stereotypic assumptions about what tokens 'must be like,' such mistaken attributions and biased judgements, tend to force tokens into playing limited and caricatured roles."

The difficult situation in which female leaders find themselves is supported by other studies as well. Deaux (1979) reports that male managers perceive their jobs as more difficult than women and claim both more approval for their work and better relations with their coworkers and subordinates. Heller's (1982) study of men and women leaders found that the women's greatest support group was their superiors, while the men's was their subordinates and peers. In contrast, the women's most critical groups were their peers and subordinates. If these findings are relevant to women in the political elite, especially those serving in state legislatures, establishing an effective leadership role must be particularly frustrating.

Pertinent to the issue of women's leadership role is the literature on sex stratification. Studies of sex stratification have found that low-status people gain legitimacy by being assigned to leadership positions or by proving their interest in a group's welfare by providing encouragement or approval to others (Meeker and Weitzell-O'Neill, 1977). One is tempted to attribute the preponderance of female state legislators with only a high school degree in the few state legislative chamber and party offices held by women to the dynamics of sex stratification. As dual members of two peripheral groups—women and the less solidly middle class—these women may have higher legitimacy needs than their more middle-class female peers. As a consequence, they may be more active in seeking out positions that confer legitimacy than do other women. By the same token, their vulnerability as authoritative leaders stemming from this dual group membership may make them less threatening to the male legislators. Although this explanation is, at best, highly speculative, one thing is certain; female state legislators allude so often to the importance of the group's welfare that one strongly suspects that it is a crucial component of their behavior and influences their choice of leadership role.

Given the initial reasons for studying women and politics, the issue of women's performance is important. However, the research on it has shown the matter of performance to be much more complicated than anyone anticipated. Getting some women elected to public office is clearly not the pancea for rectifying the problems women face in society. Unless enough women get into public office to change the present political ground rules applied to women in the political elite and to alter stereotypes about women, the nature of power and appropriate leadership roles, their recruitment into the political elite cannot be expected to produce any profound changes. At the same time, the existing conditions militate against women's recruitment into the political elite. In other words, women face a classic Catch 22. As things stand now, women, at least in state legislatures, are hamstrung in what they can accomplish; any minor concession that they can wrangle is truly a major victory.

NEW RESEARCH DIRECTIONS

The research on women in the political elite at the state level has certainly been important insofar as it has indicated that factors affecting the recruitment and performance of women are highly complex. It has shown that a number of factors interacting with each other constrain the recruitment of women. Simply urging women to enter traditional politics will not change things, nor will charges of sexism fully account for women's lowered political aspirations. Similarly, an alien and somewhat hostile environment restricts women's role and performance once they have entered public office. Unrealistically high expectations for the performance of women in the political elite, in fact, fail to acknowledge the very severe institutional constraints under which they operate and undoubtedly obscure these women's valiant efforts. In addition, these unreasonable expectations may well serve to discourage the self-recruitment of women into traditional politics.

Of course, if the gender gap translates into votes for female candidates, the present conditions governing women's recruitment and performance may change. That the gender gap will mean this is uncertain, however. The range of issues reflected in the gender gap may instead mean a change in the definition of what are genuinely women's issues and who are acceptable candidates, with the result that some women, as well as men, may be rejected by women voters.

At the same time that research on women in state politics has contributed to our understanding of the complexity of factors involved in recruitment and performance, it has also artificially narrowed and distorted our understanding of women's role in the political arena. The equation of women in the political elite with officeholding has obscured the nature and scope of women's political activity and leadership and has tended to reinforce the stereotype of the politically passive woman. Few women are in the traditional political elite, and, vastly outnumbered, their effect on governmental policy is limited. Yet, women are involved in a wide variety of nontraditional political activities. These women, who by virtue of their leadership roles in a host of organizations and social movements with specific political goals and objectives, ought to be included in the political elite. Yet they have been omitted from much of the research on women, even though they have often been quite successful in achieving change in public policy. At the state level, for example, one has only to look at an organization such as Planned Parenthood and at the women in it to see the extent of the role women have played in the public policy arena. These women have managed to get significant policy changes in areas such as the introduction and funding of sex education programs in public schools, the liberalization of legislation on abortion and family planning services, the continuance of state medicaid funding for abortion, and the defeat of legislation requiring parental consent for abortions for adolescent young women. Should not these kinds of politically active women be included in research on women in politics? Similarly, at the state level the League of Women Voters has often been able to make and break candidates for public office by their efforts to publicize candidates' positions on key issues. Ought not these women be included in studies of women in the political elite? The same is true for women leaders in community activist groups, neighborhood associations, environmentalist groups, and the like. If women such as these who have often wielded considerable political power and who have affected both legislative policy outcomes and executive policy implementation are included in the study of women in the political elite, would it still be appropriate to worry about why there are so few women in politics?

A second problem associated with much of the research on women in politics to date has been the acceptance of existing definitions of what political issues are important to women. The current work on the gender gap suggests what women's issues are not necessarily the only areas of concern to women. Women, it would appear, have a much broader range of concerns than has been previously acknowledged. The almost exclusive emphasis on matters relating to sex equity and on the significance that women in the traditional political elite attach to societally defined women's issues has distorted our understanding of women's political activity as a whole.

Closely related to this is the distinction women make between the public and private spheres. Gilligan (1982) contends that women view the world and its moral dimension somewhat differently than men. Women's political activity seems to support this thesis. If one looks both at the configuration of issues that concern women as evidenced in the gender gap data and those with which women have been involved in the past, one can see that women have had a fairly consistent agenda of concerns. These concerns have continuously fused a number of issues, some of which fall within the traditional public sphere where government action is seen as appropriate, and some of which have been traditionally identified as properly falling within the private sphere and as therefore being outside the legitimate scope of public policy. Women, however, do not appear to accept these prevailing notions about the parameters of the public and private spheres (Elshtain, 1981; Diamond and Hartstock, 1981). To the contrary, women's political activities in a host of social and political movements ranging from abolition, peace, progressivism, trade unionism, and working conditions to suffrage, domestic violence, child welfare, infant and maternal health, food adulteration, and sexual purity attest to the eclecticism of their concerns and the overlapping of the public and private spheres. For women, all these areas are proper subjects for public policy.

Recently Congresswoman Barbara Mikulski commented in a public address that for women the political is private insofar as women are finally attuned to the effects of political action on individuals; the private is political insofar as women are acutely sensitive to the plight of individuals and seek public policy solutions that will remedy individuals' problems. In this Mikulski mirrors an attitude long held by women. Women cannot seem to justify the abstract merits of a public policy when it has negative effects on specific individuals. Instead, their policy concerns reflect a simultaneous concern with the well-being of the one and the many, with the abstract and the concrete. Policy in the abstract and the reality of an individual's situation are not separate. They see policy as continuously affecting individuals, specific individuals, and individuals, again specific individuals, define for women the merits of public policy. For women the casual relationship between abstract policy and individuals in concrete situations is symmetrical.

The range of women's concerns, their position on the relationship of and distinction between the public and private sphere, and their mixture of traditonal and nontraditional political activity all seem to suggest that past research efforts to investigate women's political behavior at the elite level have been far too limiting. The focus must be expanded, for it is only by broadening research to include women's diverse public/private concerns that there can be some real understanding of their participation in both traditional and nontraditional politics. Without this expanded context there can be little realization that sometimes women's concerns require their involvement in traditional elite politics and in existing political institutions, while on other occasions their objectives may be most effectively achieved through nontraditional political activity. Indeed, it may well be that being in the narrowly defined political elite of public officeholders where prevailing definitions of public and private spheres are dominant, women are less free to work on behalf of those things that realy matter to them.

The other essays in this volume represent explorations into this newer and potentially more useful way of looking at women and politics. Equally important, this new research direction will also probably enrich our discipline's understanding of the multivaried nature of political behavior.

NOTES

1. One outstanding example of this is, of course, Robert Lane's treatment of women's political participation in *Political Life* (1959).

2. The fourth constraint of biology identified by Kirkpatrick has been so thoroughly dismissed by all, including Kirkpatrick, that it has received no further serious consideration by any except polemicists like Edgar Berman.

3. Not only have a number of subsequent studies reported few, if any, significant gender differences in socialization, but some have also argued that the earlier data did not support the conclusions drawn.

4. Overall, women constituted 13 percent of all state legislators at the end of 1982. The New Hampshire legislature had the largest number of women members (28.4 percent) but many states had considerably smaller female representation.

5. In 1978, for example, female state legislators held less than 1 percent of all legislative chamber leadership positions, including committee chairs.

II

WOMEN AS POLITICAL ACTIVISTS AT THE STATE AND LOCAL LEVELS

The three case studies in this section focus on female activists in three arenas: city, county, and state.

In Atlanta, Georgia, Diane L. Fowlkes interviewed female activists for her article, "Conception of the 'Political': White Activists in Atlanta." Fowlkes argues that these activists' understandings of the nature of politics both reflect and go beyond traditional formulations in four ways: They link people through education and action; advocate causes; govern and develop power; and work to develop power for social change.

I focus on countywide politics in my article, "Filling the Party Vacuum: Women at the Grassroots Level in Local Politics." I argue that in nonpartisan Santa Clara County, California, female activists are performing five partylike functions: They are ward heelers; informal and ad hoc networkers; political educators; political recruiters and endorsers; and campaign fundraisers and workers. I conclude with an assessment of women's power in partylike coalitions.

And the state arena is the object of Edmond Costantini and Julie Davis Bell's attention. In their "Women in Political Parties: Gender Differences in Motives Among California Party Activists," they interpret surveys of California party activists (convention delegates) conducted between 1964 and 1981. They discuss gender differences in political motives and ideology and how these differences have changed over time.

3

CONCEPTIONS OF THE "POLITICAL": WHITE ACTIVISTS IN ATLANTA

Diane L. Fowlkes

When feminist criticism of political science began to emerge in the early 1970s, one of the key issues raised was the definition of politics itself (Iglitzin, 1974; Shanley and Schuck, 1974; Bourque and Grossholtz, 1974; Boals, 1975). If political science restricts itself to a definition of politics as "the activities of recruiting, replacing, and opposing public officials for and in the exercise of their official duties," which activities occur in "a legitimate system of public order or rule in which the authority of public officials is limited and restrained" (Leiserson, 1983), then the objects of study in such a narrowly defined political science continue to be supposedly legitimate and democratic white male-dominated national, state, and local governments; the slowly increasing numbers of white, Hispanic, and black women and black and Hispanic men gaining elected office notwithstanding (Johnson and Stanwick, 1976; Johnson and Carroll, 1978; Barker and McCorry, 1976; Coleman and McLemore, 1982; Fessler, 1982). As Iglitzin (1974) suggested ten years ago, such a definition of politics is sexist because it focuses our attention on the public and institutionalized aspects of the "political," from which most women have been excluded by law or ideology (e.g., Amundsen, 1971, 1977; Eisenstein, 1981) for most of American history.

But the problem runs deeper. Bourque and Grossholtz (1974) have demonstrated that the message of much of the political behavior literature has been that the political is whatever men do in seeking public office and governing and whatever women do to help political men, and this is the way it should be. As long as these assumptions

Author's Note: I wish to thank Janet Flammang for her cogent and constructive criticisms of earlier drafts of this eassy.

persist, implicitly or explicitly, then one is caught in a trap of having to argue that if women are to become truly political, women can and must act "like men."

To get out of that trap we should restate the problem by asking: What is the political? Do people in different parts of the polity, which is structured by sex, race, and economic class into hierarchies of differing resources and opportunities, see the political differently from one another? What are those differences? Are there similarities? What is the significance of these differences and similarities? In moving out of the trap, we should be careful not to fall into another trap of assuming that what women see and do politically is different from what men see and do politically. We may find that this is true in part, but we cannot assume it until more evidence is in. Clearly women and men are doing many of the same things—holding office, being involved in party and campaign politics, being chief or sole breadwinner for the family, being directly responsible for the care of children, working in movements—though, quantitatively, different proportions of men or women may be found doing different things and receiving varying forms and amounts of recognition or nonrecognition for what they do. Those quantitative differences are significant for what they tell us about the relative value of women and men in the polity. Given these differences, do women and men also differ qualitatively in how they conceptualize the political and in why they are political? To put it another way, does being political mean different things for women and men? Much qualitative research is called for before we can answer these questions.

The crux of the argument is that political science has defined the political in a sex-stereotyped way and from a white masculine viewpoint that precludes our learning much of what else there is to know about the political. The political should not be sex-typed a priori. Many women have been as political as many men, but political science has tended to see and rank as most important what white men of property have done and said. Feminist theory suggests that we begin to unravel the contradiction that political science constructs through sex-typing the political by asking what is political from women's points of view. Note that I use the plural because there is no monolithic woman's perspective. What Leiserson (1983) considers an unsatisfying "parade of definitions—taking controversial positions on public policy issues; running for elective office; who gets what, when, and how; and manipulating people"—is quite significant from a feminist theorist's viewpoint because it indicates the diverse realities of people's lives as they go about their daily struggles to survive or their daily attempts to improve or maintain the conditions of their own, their families', and other women's and men's lives. Few if any general statements can be made about women because they are a multiracial, multiclass, multi-age, multi-sexual-identity group. While all women share the biological condition of being female, what it means to be a woman—and a political woman—varies from individual to individual and over time for any particular individual. Much of the variation in meaning is tied to the different conditions and cultures in which different races and different classes live and die in different polities. But we should not be surprised to find that even within one group—white, lower-to-upper-middle class, female activists—a whole parade of definitions comes in response to a question: "Moving into a somewhat philosophical realm, could you say how you define the 'political'? To you, what is political?"

I asked this question, among many others, of twenty-two white female Atlanta activists—Democratic and Republican party precinct officials and state legislators and leftist community and student activists—during 1982 and 1983.[1] The responses of these women represent their conceptualizations of the political in their lives, what we call first-level conceptualizations. The purpose of this eassy is to develop from these first-level conceptualizations a second-level conceptual analysis of the political, which is thus grounded in the women's particular understandings.[2] Such woman-centered research (cf. Gordon, 1975: 563-564) brings questions from feminist theory to political science and thus begins to enlarge the boundaries of political science to include conceptions of the political from perspectives other than those of white masculine culture.

Before proceeding with the analysis, I should point out some limitations of my study. In this essay I will explore the rich variety of meanings that emerge in asking a small number of just one grouping— white lower-to-upper-middle-class female political activists—what "the political" means to them. I cannot extend the examination to a group of comparable men; to women of other racial, ethnic, or economic class groups; or to women or men not involved in political parties, public office, or movement politics. The comparative scope of my study thus is limited, and I cannot draw any conclusions about similarities or differences between the sexes and/or races. What *is* significant, however, even from this small sampling of women, is that some use concepts that political scientists use to define the political—notions of governing, using power, and electing representatives—but some also interpret the political to mean actions outside the traditional conceptual framework of political science—educating, raising consciousness, building new institutions, *changing* the status quo. The conceptual language of political science would be enriched immeasurably if future studies extended our questioning about the political to members of groups noted above but not included in the present study.

EXTRINSIC AND INTRINSIC CONCEPTIONS OF THE POLITICAL

In my first analysis of these white female political activists (Fowlkes, 1983), I focused on four women who represented four types of political activists: ambitious and unambitious feminists and antifeminists. The purpose of that analysis was well within the bounds of the narrow concern of political science with governance by public officials. My purpose was to understand how those who were ambitious to hold elected public office came to be that way and how their development differed from those who had no interest at all in seeking office. One of the differences that emerged in my analysis of those women's first-level reports and conceptualizations of their lives was in how they defined the political.

They almost all defined the political in relation to themselves in that their definition included some conception of themselves inside or outside one or another aspect of the political. My second-level conceptualization of their responses was that the ambitious women, whether feminist or antifeminist, Democrat or Republican, defined the political *intrinsically*, while the unambitious women defined the political *extrinsically*. In an *intrinsic* view of the political, one sees the political as including oneself as an active agent; in an *extrinsic* view, one sees the political as outside oneself or as "happening to" one's self. For example, one ambitious woman's conception of the political placed her in the middle of fashioning coalitions and using power to accomplish the possible. The unambitious women's conceptions of the political placed them outside the official centers of power. For example, one woman, rather fed up with compromising politicians, saw the political as everything affecting our whole lives both public and private. She placed herself outside the conception of the political but very much inside the women's movement, trying to change the ways government and society in general treat women.

The approach of the latter woman, whom I called Ella Washburn, provides the thread that leads beyond the political as governance by public officials into a larger understanding of the political, which will be explored in this essay. By following that thread through twenty cases,[3] we will begin to see, in the words of the women themselves, the first-level conceptual complexity of the political from women's perspectives that has been posited by feminist theory. From there we can elaborate the initial second-level conceptualization of extrinsic and intrinsic for understanding the political and its significance in women's lives. As we shall see, the extrinsic-intrinsic distinction holds; but Ella Washburn represents the proposition that an extrinsic conception of politics that places one outside of officeholding or using power may also be accompanied by another, intrinsic conception of the political as advocacy for unrepresented groups or philosophies or as party-building or as keeping informed so as to be able to educate others. In other words, if we begin by looking at the political from women's perspectives, we will see that it involves more than the political science conception of the political as officeseeking or holding and the process of governing legitimately.

Specifically, I argue that these activists' understandings, while in part based in traditional definitions, go beyond them in four ways:

1. linking people through education and action;
2. advocating causes;
3. governing and developing power; and
4. working to develop power for social change.

What follows is a consideration of these four kinds of conceptualizations and the preliminary construction of a second-level conceptual framework grounded in these understandings.

LINKING PEOPLE THROUGH EDUCATION AND ACTION

Seven women conceptualize the political in ways that involve their linking public officeholders with themselves or with other people in families and communities. The first woman draws a "fine line between politics and statesmanship." For her, the political involves public officeholding, and ideally officeholding as service, but she places herself outside that. She says she is political to the extent that she stays aware of what is going on in government by reading "the newspaper cover to cover and a number of magazines." She keeps files, and when any of their grandchildren in high school need help on that kind of homework they "always call Mamaw because if anybody has it, she does. The other day I got a call from a friend of mine . . . and one of her children was having to name the cabinet officers. So she called me to find out who they were." For her the political is keeping informed about government so that she can pass information on to grandchildren and friends' children, and she is aware that she is known in her community for that.

The second woman has dropped out of her party for the present because she is disgusted with the sexist behavior of the party activists and elected officials for whom she has been working. For her the political is definitely not what she was taught as a political science major:

> Do you mean as a process, or the issues? What a question. That is a hard one. My degree is in political science . . . and I know what it's supposed to be, and I don't think it's that at all. I'm very cynical about it. . . . I had illusions of democracy, and anybody can get involved. I think that part is true . . . that if you're willing to work hard enough and stick it out, you'll get involved. That's the only democracy I see in it. I think a few people make the decisions for everybody based on, usually, what's best for them . . . for the person making the decision.

She believes that "power corrupts, not necessarily in the sense of money . . . but in terms of principles." She even admits that if she were in that position, "I'd do the same thing if I had the power. So I can't even necessarily condemn these people for their kinds of decisions."

At the same time that she can place herself in the shoes of politicians wielding power and corrupting themselves, she also can see the value of her own position outside all that. She believes she has a better view of what is desirable and possible from the average citizen's point of view. She gives two examples of local officials who were certain that their pet bills would pass, but who were "slaughtered" in the final votes. She knew the bills had no chance, but the politicians would not listen to her.

> I'm in this community, and I talk to people all the time, and I was real interested in it. And you hear what the average person thinks. And you don't get the tunnelvision of professional politicians who spend their whole life with politicians. . . . You know, they're very isolated.

She is a bridge between the people and the politicians, if the politicians will only listen. She is outside the ranks of the politicians but inside the community of opinion and an agent for ordinary citizens.

A third woman approaches the extrinsic part of her conception of the political obliquely. Does she consider herself political?

> Not really. I mean just ordinary, really. Of course, my interest has always been in politics, even when I was a teenager. But back growing up in Chicago, you only had one mayor, one president, and one governor. And they were in from the time I was a small child until I became almost an adult.

She explains the political to which she is intrinsic as follows:

> There's so much going on, and people are not aware of what is happening. . . . If somebody doesn't do it or try to inform other people, I'm afraid we're going to lose the little bit of freedom that we have unless people really get interested in it. [So the political is] getting other people involved, and I want a better world for my kids. . . . Even with my own children, well, you have to start with that they talk with their own friends. And the next thing you've got families [of her children's friends]. Their parents voted Democrat. They're turning around now and voting Republican. And then I have taken some of them to some of the parties and introduced them to the elected officials. And they find that they're not villains or people off in space some place.

In other words, the political in her past was the Chicago party machine, which was impermeable. Today she sees herself as an "ordinary" mother-citizen gathering in her political flock and bringing them into contact with the elected officials of her own party.

Four other women voice what traditional political science has long considered the political for women in the United States: working for candidates for public office. But these women do not see themselves in what political science considers service-oriented "women's work." Rather, they are linking themselves to "right"-thinking officials or to power through political parties; or they are trying to get the community back on the "right" religious/moral track. One states it quite succinctly: "As far as I'm concerned, it would be trying to elect somebody and work for the election of somebody who I thought was a good, upstanding person, honest person, and basically, would think politically the way I do. Which I think is the name of the game, really."

Two others add the idea of the two-party system. One explains in more detail than the other:

> Oh my goodness. Politics. Well, politics runs this country. We have a two-party system which is a beautiful system. Other countries have many parties, and it's chaos. . . . The Republican party now stands for freedom of the individual in a free enterprise system and less government and more personal responsibility. The Democratic party has become a party of socialism over the years. They now believe in strong government control, strong government regulation. They do not believe in personal responsibility.

This woman goes on to elaborate on party government and power, thus linking herself to those in power through her campaign work:

> Politics is a way of governing, and politics is power. And many get in it for power. Many get in it for a way of running a country, a philosophy

of government. . . . The idea is to get your party in power so that the country is run the way you feel it ought to be run. And many get in it for the power that it gives them . . . for themselves, and because they see a way of gaining control over other people, which is, I don't deny, is part of all politics. But then there are many people in political office and many people who work behind the scenes of politics that do it because they want to have that philosophy for there. [That sounds more where you fall.] That's where I fall. I have no ambition to be in political office myself, but to elect those people who believe as I do.

The seventh woman adds a religious dimension to her rather holistic conception of the political. She, too, links herself to the system of power in the sense that she sees herself as having a hand in determining the direction our collective life takes. She also echoes the women who conceptualize the political as linking people to or educating people about the politicians who run for office.

From a religious standpoint, I think it is a commitment to a way of life. It is determining the direction that we would like to see life go in, other than religiously. And I don't really think you can separate the two. I think those who have a moral commitment should stand up for what is going on in the world that's right and wrong . . . through the caliber of persons that we put in office. . . . [We need to be] constantly educating people, making people more aware of who and what they're voting for.

These last four women may play what many would consider peripheral roles in electoral politics. But these women see electoral politics as their link to power and right thinking in office, and they assert a positive view of themselves in their conception of the political.

ADVOCATING CAUSES

Three women conceptualize the intrinsic aspect of the political as some form of fight for a cause. The first woman conceptualizes the political as a process within which she has long fought the powers that be.

I've always been interested in politics. In the long run, you know, ideas about doing things are, like somebody said, like fire balloons in the night that go out among the stars. Until you get them into politics. Eventually everything—people talk about politics being dirty and all that stuff—but it all gets into politics before it's done. [How would you define the political?] It ends in getting laws passed and implemented and executed. It's part of the things that we're obliged to live by. But it starts down with people being elected and what people demand of government, what they want—the grass roots and the special interests and the lobbyists, and all that.

She goes on to tell about how she fought for honest government in a southern city run by a political party machine. In more recent years she could have run for a seat in the state House, but she chose to stay out of electoral politics so she could "raise hell" on "what she believes in." Over the years she and a very small group have been slowly educating those in office to the advantages of a special form of tax in the hope the officeholders will be won over and write it into law. Thus, she has placed herself outside officeholding but inside an advocacy relationship with officeholders.

The other two women define the political as "everything," though one perceives it as less hostile than the other. One says:

> I guess politics, strictly speaking, is the art of getting along with people, so that in a broad category, politics is involved with everything. But I think of politics also in two other ways. One would be party, which is political and specifically defined. Then there's also issue politics.

The other says:

> Everything, just about everything in your life is affected by politics. [Examples?] There's so many rules and regulations about everything anymore that your home life's affected by politics. What you have and don't have is affected by politics. And a lot of things you are *totally* against were brought about by politics—the present administration, that sort of thing.

Both of these women reject running for office because it requires something else they reject—compromise. One even says she is not political in terms of her general definition of politics as "getting along with people":

> I think I'm pretty unpolitical. I'd like to be able to speak more cir- cumspectly and not go dashing out and making very wild statements. But I don't want to be more of a politician. I don't have any aspirations to run for a public office, not that kind of politics I don't. . . . I'd rather do my own thing and not have my job depend on it.

Her "thing" is being an "advocate" for the unrepresented, the "people who I feel don't have enough voice, and maybe who don't know *how* to get into the act, who need a representative." Presently she is working with a program designed to get young mothers-to-be in touch with county health departments in order to learn about their own and the fetus's nutritional needs.

The other woman sees herself as very political, which involves "my strong support of and work for ERA. That's the main thing in my life lately." Holding public office is not appealing to her because she could not do the things required to stay in office—swapping favors and trading off on her beliefs. But in working for the ERA she does not have to compromise. She ends with a description of and explanation for her kind of politics: "For the first time in my life I demonstrated. And it was for ERA." She has also participated in the AFL-CIO Solidarity Days in Washington, DC, and in Georgia and in numerous other ERA demonstrations.

> I'm afraid I've become very biased. If somebody's running and they don't vote for ERA, I'm afraid I have to say I can't vote for him. . . . But I decided a long time ago the only way to get anything is just to be very very adamant about it. And the labor movement probably sets the best example. If they want anything, they strike for it, or they go out and fight for it. And of course that's the way we did with the Woman Suffrage, isn't it? That's what we had to do way back then. . . . You have to almost get obnoxious about it.

These women, then, focus on a concept of the political that is intrinsically cause-oriented, advocacy-based. Their view of the political acknowledges officeholders, compromise, and policy making but only in the extrinsic sense that those people and that process are the causes of the problem at issue and the targets of their advocacy.

GOVERNING AND DEVELOPING POWER

Six women, four of whom were state legislators when interviewed, conceptualize the political in terms of governing; and three of these also speak of power and power structures within government. The three women who conceptualize the political as governing nonetheless focus on different aspects of governing. The first one begins by saying that "everything in this *life* is political" and goes on to say that it involves differences of opinion, such as liberalism and conservatism, selfish motives, greed, and human nature. Her disgust with this sort of politics is apparent, and she also is disgusted with people who do not understand "the seriousness of government." Her example of a businessman dumbfounds her. He wanted her to sign a petition against a tax assessment, but he did not even know his commissioner's name. She told him, "'You should've gotten concerned when you went to the ballot box the last two years.' I said, 'Has anyone in the neighborhood called Bob Jones?' He said, 'Who?' Bob Jones is his commissioner. So, what do you *do* with people like that?" Though *she* sees the political intrinsically as inherent to life and human nature, she recognizes that others are not as attuned as she to how government is set up. Thus, she tries to educate those less aware than she to what government is about.

Another woman speaks of the political as "an individual who works with a group to take care of the business of the people." Sometimes the group is her colleagues in the legislature. Sometimes it is particular constituencies, such as a neighborhood experiencing a problem with an expressway interchange. "We are the designated or the elected people to look after the business of everybody else. . . . You say politics, but let's call it government, the process of governing." For this woman who calls herself a "political animal," there are no ifs, ands, or buts. The political is governing, and she is political to the core.

Still another woman sees the political as building her party so that the state will have two-party politics and as a result the electorate and the legislature will be faced with important issues.

> Basically I ran for the first time . . . on the Republican ticket because I felt strongly we needed to have a two-party system and that the two-party system in Georgia certainly was not effective at that point. . . . And I think that it's important for us to address some of the issues. We have to educate the people before we get the legislators to address the issues.

In other words, she is another political educator. Her purpose in two-party politics is to raise issues and educate the people and the officeholders.

Since this woman has been in the legislature, she has come to see the political also as involving reform efforts inside the legislature. Through two-party politics, the minority party eventually will gain enough seats in the legislature to effect reform of the dominant party's leadership, which is entrenched and not receptive to questions raised from within that party.

> When I first went down there, I didn't consider myself just political [party-affiliated]. I was willing to work with anybody who I basically identified as working for the good of the cause, and I still will do that. But I will say *now* that I do, will become more political because I see the people in the Democratic party whom I've identified as working for the good of the cause say, "We cannot reform the legislature from within. The Republicans are going to have to do it." There is no way that they can get rid of [the leadership]. And it's a long haul for us to do this. . . . But that'll come. . . . I'm patient. See, I think women have learned patience because we have had to. In the first place, we have dealt with children. And you don't raise children unless you learn patience. And you learn you just have to inch along.

This woman takes the long view, a developmental view, of the political, of which she has been an integral part. She does not speak explicitly of power, but she is quite aware that there is a legislative leadership entrenched in power. On one level she continues to work with whomever she indentifies as supportive of her issues, but on a more recently added level, she has taken up the challenge of reform, which will come out of ever more successful Republican party-building.

Two other women in the legislature echo her conceptualization, but both go on to talk about power explicitly. The first one says:

> What I see as politics is a proliferation of ideas. And everyone in this house has an idea from their own background of what they think bills should be and what ideas should be. We have people in here who are prolabor,who are antilabor. We have some that are in the middle. Conservatives in both parties, liberals in both parties. But I would say that the political process—you know, put the campaigns behind you and everything else—is the coming together and working together and hopefully coming up with laws or lack of laws that will protect the people of the state, that will serve the best interest of the people of this state, and also future generations. Because that's what politics evolves down to—the laws that are voted on, the reds and greens on the board up there that become part of the permanent journal, that affect the daily lives of the people in this state. . . . So politics boils down to power and how you use it or misuse it. And hopefully, most of us use it positively rather than negatively. I guess that's it. Positive or negative use of power is what politics is all about.

The second woman says that the political is "power—getting and using power." She is aware that she is outside the legislative power structure, because as a very contentious women's rights bill, which she cosponsored, made its way through the committee system and received a do-pass, she began to receive verbal threats from the leadership's "boys." The leader himself would not confront her directly. Thus she is a living example of what her Republican colleague noted: Democrats who go against the leadership get nowhere on reform. Since her party is not a vehicle for change, she is working quietly with other women of both parties in the legislature to form a women's caucus that can coordinate priorities and rally support for bills addressing a variety of women's concerns.

The last woman in this group touches on governance and on power in her conceptualization of the political, but she also gives a particular feminist version of power as the ability to accomplish certain goals.[4] She says:

> Well, gee, there's so many facets of it. I think most people have the mistaken impression that it's nothing but a power struggle. And in some ways, it is. It is a power struggle, but it's that because there are people

who feel that they see things that need to be done, and they're willing to go through those struggles in order to get in a position to do those things. . . . I really see it as people who think that they can administer the government in the best way, and they're willing to go through all the hardships to get to that place to be able to do it, because it's really not easy at all. [Do you consider yourself a political person?] I'm probably much more one now than I was in 1977 because I've learned that politics is the art of the possible. You really have to become a realist. You have to see what *can* be done, not just feel like, "Well, this is what ought to be done, and I'm going to see it done." It's that, "This is what I think ought to be done, and here's the piece of it that I can get done." And that's politics. You have to learn to mediate, to spend time with the people that you really don't like at all, and try to see their point of view. And I think that that's what it's all about. It's very psychological.

WORKING TO DEVELOP
POWER FOR SOCIAL CHANGE

The last four women place themselves outside conventional electoral politics and governance and very much inside movement politics, even revolutionary politics. Their language as they talk about the political is strikingly different from even the most disaffected of the other women.

The youngest of the women is wrestling with how the political fits with the various parts of her life (compare Valian, 1977), which is becoming more and more politicized. As a student activist, she was instructed by the school administration "specifically not to be political." She thinks that meant to be uncontroversial, especially not to address issues that women should decide for themselves, "like abortions and everything that stems from that . . . lesbianism . . . hair under my arms" or not to attack a sexist poster put out by a fraternity. At work, as a secretary,

> I think about being active at work because I work with people who consider themselves communist or, in some cases, just very, very, very liberal people. . . . But in my work place, like these guys are real pro-labor, but they have this really funny idea about their secretaries. I mean, my consciousness has just really been raised about what I am to the office. So my political view has really expanded to include the whole economic sphere. . . . Sometimes I get really overenthusiastic. I do it to myself like, I burn out fast. But I think what I'm doing now is just trying to find out where it does fit into my life. How can I be political without losing myself in it or something.

And finally as a musician,

> I was talking to a friend who said I don't have to separate my other life from being political, that being political doesn't mean that you have to

separate the two. So, I see fusing my music with issues and ideas and things. I'm not going to produce music in a vacuum.

And so how would she sum up her definition of the political?

That's really hard, because I'm not quite sure of it, you know. I want to say that the political is being active with, working with other people. I mean, other people have to be there because you can't be political on your own to make any kind of dent. I see being incorporated in the idea of political as making specific advances or developments or changes in society in the political system. . . . I am trying now to work to the point where I can really feel very comfortable and very natural with incorporating in my life politics and all of these other things and to understand that they are in fact inseparable. And I've found that notion of the personal being political and political being personal, that they are interpenetrating. . . . I think that working with other women and working on projects dealing specifically with women's issues to me is more essential to what it means to me to be political. But there are these other things which seem to be penetrating that idea now. . . . [for example, getting involved with Atlanta Working Women] I think that just working with other women who are struggling with the same kind of crap that I'm putting up with in my office is one step to building a stronger base for some definite changes in how clerical workers are viewed by men and by the women themselves. . . . Then there's all these other issues, you know, nuclear power is a very pressing issue. . . . I was just thinking how the word "political" is really tossed around now. It has grown to mean so many things. And, you know, it makes me wonder now if there really is any kind of all-inclusive definition for political.

I quote her at length because she vividly portrays her thought process as her political consciousness is raised first by one experience and then by another until it encompasses her life.

The other three women have been involved in radical movements—labor organizing, student organizing, women's liberation—for several years. All cite examples from their personal lives in talking of the political. All conceptualize the political as a process for social change. But each one emphasizes a different dimension of the process.

One woman focuses on social change through consciousness-raising, confronting and resolving contradictions:

I really have embraced the idea that it's our responsibility to create a better world, and it's through Marxism as one of the guideposts to do that. . . . Everything in your life is related to a certain political way you have of looking at the world, and you have to think about what you're doing in trying to help. It comes up in raising kids all the time, you know, what kind of consciousness you want to teach them. Regular people do it, too. It's just that the Left made it so conscious from the beginning. Everything was so talked out that you had to change—your ideas about women, about relationships, about power structures, about Black people—the kind of consciousness changes that you were forced to go through as you went through different processes [trying to mesh how you act politically theoretically with how you believe]. You have to be open when people say, "Hey, that's a contradiction when you *do* this and you *say* this."

Another woman focuses on power struggles of groups:

I think it has to do with struggles for power. But at the same time, I think that it can't be removed from the economic sphere of society. . . . Struggles for power occur in the marriage, in the bedroom, in communities, in City Hall, in the Capitol, all those places. [What do you mean by struggles for power?] I think it means the ability to mold your interests, to see that your interests are met. And I think of it not in terms of individuals but in terms of groups. Like when I think of it in the bedroom, I think of it as women versus men. And when I think of it in the communities [it's] struggling for power as a poor person, as a tenant, as a Black, as a woman, as a worker, as a teacher, as a student—your role in a grouping in society. You're struggling for recognition of your interests and for the actualization of your interests.

The last woman expands upon the idea of empowering people through revolutionary organization and movements. What is the political?

The political quest for me is to be part of creating institutions and organizations and movements that affect the balance of power in this country. When that's important to you, politics permeates everything, really, everything. Like, for instance, I noticed the fact this year that the school where I have my four-year-old, and I chose it very carefully, didn't do a program on Martin Luther King's birthday. Now that's a small thing. But, you know, we're a generation down from where I was when I grew up, and we're in Atlanta, Georgia, and I expect, just like I expect my child to learn to read and do math, I expect him to have some knowledge of Afro-American history and some respect for Afro-American culture. And I expect the school that I send him to, for that to be an integral part of their program.

She has more to say on "creating institutions and organizations and movements." She is as political to the core as are the state legislators we heard earlier, but she is acting from an entirely different perspective outside the bound of their political—outside but not disengaged from their world. In her past, her "politics of social change" has included Ralph Nader-like actions—"monitoring and trying to get the capitalists to behave themselves." But mostly she has been involved in more "radical" politics:

I've been involved in trying to build organizations where people have power, and through their organizations they assert their power and assert their influence and attempt to bring about change for themselves and their families but also gain through organizations and movements a sense of what they can do and a sense of the importance of being organized and in a movement.

In the future, after reflecting on the lessons she has learned from past struggles:

> I think one organization that's desperately needed in this country is a third political electoral party. . . . I don't think it's the only institution that's needed, but there is a tremendous need for it so that people can go to the ballot box and vote for something that has the capacity to deliver to them and have a program that they can genuinely believe. I think it's an important tool because this is a country where the right to vote is ingrained in our culture . . . I hate to say something that sounds so simplistic and rhetorical, but the small people need their own party, their own organization, their own voice. They need a vehicle, an electoral vehicle to fight through. I still think they need other organizations, too. I mean I think they need radical women's organizations and farmers' organizations and the trade unions. I also think they need their army. They need an organization of trained leaders with a revolutionary strategy. I haven't given that up yet. But I do think this electoral thing is one thing that needs to be built in this country

And so we hear again that the political involves party-building, this one to empower the "small people."

TOWARD A SECOND-LEVEL CONCEPTUAL FRAMEWORK OF THE POLITICAL

We have seen initially that some women conceptualize the political holistically as "everything" and go on to explain what that means, while others see the political as more specific to working for causes or to governing. They place themselves in varying degrees of closeness to their conceptions of the political. They distinguish among types of politics and place themselves in one in relation to the other; or act as a link between the two. In addition to this intrinsic/extrinsic, almost spatial, conceptualization of the political we can add other dimensions of content and process (see Figure 3.1): groups, values, power, education or consciousness-raising, change, and construction or deconstruction of ideas and institutions.

McWilliams (1974) suggests that the *content* of the political includes personal issues, women's issues, women's activities, power relations, and community values. We do find some of the women in the study defining the political in these terms as well as in term of groups generally—political parties, workers, Blacks, women, pregnant women. One woman specifically sees the political as working with other women to address women's issues—abortion, lesbianism, body hair. Another is organizing a legislative women's caucus, while still another legislator works with groups to "take care of the peoples' business." Some women include or imply various community values in their ideas of the political: standing firm on principles rather than compromising, bringing moral/religious values to the attention of the voters and lawmakers, making the capitalists behave themselves.

These women activists talk about power relations in a variety of ways. Government controls and regulates our whole lives. People seek power through parties to run the country according to their philosophies, which may be liberal, conservative, socialist, or capitalist. Some people seek power for themselves in order to get personal payoffs. Some legislators use power negatively; others use it positively. Some develop it by working to build parties either to reform the power structure of the legislature or to change the balance of power in this country and empower the people. People engage in power struggles to accomplish worthy goals or to actualize group interests.

But the political as *process* involves more than power relations. McWilliams, as well as Boals (1975), suggests that the political also involves consciousness-raising and change-oriented actions. The leftist activists are the only ones to talk explicitly about consciousness-raising and radical change. Consciousness-raising, as explained by two of these activists, occurs when people experience and/or perceive contradictions between what they or others think/believe and what they or others do. From a raised consciousness flows the need to act in order to change the thoughts or actions that are now understood to constitute the contradictions.

Whereas consciousness-raising and explicitly change-oriented actions may be conflictual in style, another process that can create an atmosphere for change, education, is similar in intent but more concensual in style. Noninstitutionalized education as a political process runs as a theme through many of the women's notions of the political. Mamaw collects information about government for her grandchildren and friend's children. The disgusted cynic tries to make the politicians understand what the voters want. The citizen-mother educates experientially by bringing her children and their friends and families into contact with real officeholders to show that politicians are not villains. One woman tries to educate her neighbors about the seriousness of government. Others try to educate the voters about the quality of candidates or the issues. Still another tries to convince officeholders of

FIGURE 3.1 A Conceptual Framework of the Political, Based on Views of White Atlanta Activists

	Linkage	Advocacy	Governance	Social Change
Groups	political parties	standing up for women	working with and for groups, organizing women's caucus	actualizing group interests: women, Blacks, workers
Values	religious	standing firm, no compromise	mediation two-party system	anticapitalism
Power	aware of power of officials for selves, for party principles	aware of control — rules and regulations	getting and using power, positive and negative power	empowering common people, power struggle
Education/ Consciousness-Raising	staying aware, educating voters, children, friends and neighbors, decision makers	educating decision makers	educating constituents, legislators, the people	raising consciousness of self, others
Change	change direction of collective life religiously	work for ERA, new tax structure	work for reform of leadership	work for social change, to create a better world through Marxism
Construction and Deconstruction: Ideas and Institutions		making ideas into laws	making ideas into laws; party building	resolving contradictions between ideas and actions; party building

the value of a special kind of tax. The change that some seek through education includes returning religious morals to community life, the Equal Rights Amendment, a new form of taxation, or reform of the legislative leadership.

One other process that emerges from the women's responses is the construction or deconstruction of ideas and institutions. Several speak of the importance of ideas in politics and making these ideas into law. One of the movement activists also speaks of challenging people to resolve contradictions between ideas and actions. Two in particular see the importance of building political parties, though one is building the Republican party while the other wants to build a revolutionary peoples' party and new societal institutions.

A final observation can be made on the relationship between where one stands in relation to the political and how one conceptualizes the process and content of the political. My analysis is not designed to trace out causal relations between action and thought, but my analysis does suggest that where one plays out the political appears to be very much related to how one conceptualizes the political. The state officeholders and those ambitious for state office tend to see the political intrinsically from the viewpoint of the governors and to conceptualize the political in the language of traditional political science, speaking of governing and the uses of power. The leftist activists speak in distinctly different but still intrinsic terms of consciousness-raising and developing and using power to change present exploitative political and economic structures and conditions. Both officeholders and leftists are concerned with building political parties. The local party activists vary more in their language, some focusing on linkage through various forms of education, others on advocacy for a cause. Most women, regardless of arena and conceptualization, speak of groups, values, some degree of change, and somehow bringing family or larger community concerns to the attention of all.

CONCLUSION

Iglitzin (1974) charged that political science, reflecting society, has made women apolitical by definition because the political defined as power and governance has been sex-stereotyped as belonging in the masculine domain. Clearly, many of the activist women in my study can in no way be considered apolitical, even if we accept the narrow definition of the political as power and governance. Their conceptions of the political, which place them in the center of power struggles and governing, do not make these women "masculine"; these women are "political."

Bourque and Grossholtz (1974) charged further that political science, reflecting society, has set up a masculine standard for political behavior so that women who do become political in ways not growing out of women's societally prescribed roles of wife and mother are dubbed unnatural. According to Bourque and Grossholtz, the consequence implied is that political women, to be considered "natural," must continue to nurture leaders, not be leaders. Not stated but also implied is that because society types service-oriented political roles as "women's roles," service roles are not as valuable as leadership roles. Again, clearly, some of the women activists in this study, whether they are ambitious for legislative office, are legislators already, are revolutionaries, or are service-oriented grassroots volunteers, link their conceptions of the political to their children's needs as they the mothers see them. These women do not convey the sense that they believe their political actions are valueless to themselves or to society. Their conceptions of the political, which grow out of the stereotypical feminine private domain, do not restrict these women to the nonpolitical "eternal feminine"; these women, too, are "political." There are other women in the study who do seem to devalue their actions because their actions do not fit them for the political to which they are extrinsic. They are referring to the politics of compromise and bargaining, and they characterize their own politics as "obnoxious" or "wild"; still, they are political beings.

The critiques of Iglitzin and of Bourque and Grossholtz, together with the women activists' own conceptualization of the political, point to two contradictions that can be resolved by moving to a woman-centered analysis of the political. First, what political science, reflecting society, has assumed about women as a sex-class is that they through biology or socialization are incapable of being political in terms of engaging in processes of power and governance. The reality for many women is that they nevertheless are political animals in these terms. Second, what political science, reflecting society, defines and values as political behavior is different from what many women define and value as political behavior.

The "parade of definitions" given by these white activist women expands the definition of the political far beyond but still includes governance and power. We need further studies of Black, Hispanic, Asian, and American Indian activist women, and we need studies of activist men of different races and national origins. We also need similar studies of people who are not political activists but who nevertheless can contribute their conceptualizations of the political to our common and complex understanding of this pervasive and important phenomenon.

NOTES

1. The data for this study come from a study-in-progress of activist women of various types. The party precinct officials and some of the state legislators in this study were chosen by type—ambitious and unambitious feminists (all Democrats who favored the Equal Rights Amendment) and antifeminists (all Republicans who opposed the Equal Rights Amendment, with two exceptions)—randomly from lists generated from the Atlanta Area Party Study, which was conducted by myself and Jerry Perkins in 1977. Other state legislators were chosen to achieve some party balance. The leftist and/or student activists were known by me through my own various political involvements. I included Black women on my original lists but was unable to schedule interviews with them because of their crowded work schedules, their own sickness, or their responsibilities for other sick family members. All the women reside in the Atlanta area, but they come from all parts of the country. Most of the Democrats and some of the Republicans and leftist activists were born and grew up in the South. The other women come from the Far West, the Midwest, and states in the north central, upper, and middle Atlantic regions.

Most of the women were contacted first by letter and then by telephone to arrange interviews. The leftist activists were contacted personally by me. All were informed of the nature of the research—structured interviews consisting of open-ended questions designed to study political activists' life histories and political development. I personally conducted and taped the interviews. Jakki Gaither transcribed the tapes, and I thank her for a painstakingly accurate job.

2. For a thorough discussion of grounded theory, see Glaser and Strauss (1967). See Bernstein (1978, pp. 139-40) for a discussion of first-level and second-level constructs developed through a phenomenological approach to political science.

3. Of the twenty-two women initially included in this analysis, two gave exclusively extrinsic conceptions of the political and are not included in the rest of the analysis. One saw the political affecting our everyday lives "more than we realize . . . an encroachment by the federal government . . . and sometimes you just feel helpless because of the restrictions, of control." The other saw the political as "dirty" and as different types of governments and economic philosophies—socialism, communism, capitalism—that still cannot solve the problems we face. "I worry about what is happening to this country. [But] I don't know a solution."

4. On the various feminist definitions of power, see Flammang (1983).

4

FILLING THE PARTY VACUUM: WOMEN AT THE GRASSROOTS LEVEL IN LOCAL POLITICS

Janet A. Flammang

When I was a young lad in Chicago, I decided one day to visit the local party headquarters and offer my services. "Who sent you, boy?" asked the cigar-chomping ward heeler, peering at me over his newspaper. "Nobody sent me," I responded. He took out his cigar and said, "We don't want nobody that nobody sent." [Judge Abner Mikva, U.S. Circuit Court of Appeals[1]]

The League of Women Voters is one of the most powerful groups around and I owe my reelection to them and other women's groups. [Supervisor Rod Diridon, Santa Clara County, California[2]]

At the turn of the century, Progressives introduced electoral reforms to reduce party bosses' stranglehold on local politics. They envisioned a "clean government" with citizens bypassing the party apparatus through nonpartisan elections, direct primaries, initiative, referendum, and recall. The demise of local parties would create a power vacuum to be filled by an active and informed citizenry. One group that sought to produce just such a citizenry was the League of Women Voters, founded in 1919, just before the Nineteenth Amendment granted female suffrage. The league was particularly interested in educating women to put their newfound power to good use.

Most studies of local politics since the Progressive era have emphasized how the party vacuum has been filled by economic elites (e.g., Lynd and Lynd, 1937; Hunter, 1953; Vidich and Bensman, 1958), or voluntary associations (e.g., Banfield, 1965; Banfield and

Author's Note: I wish to thank the University of Santa Clara for the President's Research Grant, which was an enormous help in the conduct of this research project.

Wilson, 1966), or the mass media (e.g., Press and Ver Burg, 1983). Economic elites, voluntary associations (especially labor and minority groups), and the media are portrayed as educating and mobilizing voters, providing umbrella organizations for like-minded groups, and supporting sympathetic candidates. However, little attention has been paid to how grassroots women activists have been filling the party vacuum.

The focus of this essay is on the ways in which grassroots women have performed party functions in the nonpartisan local arena of Santa Clara County, California. While these women belong to diverse groups with somewhat different purposes, they recognize some common values and a bond between them that has not yet been fully developed. They share a common concern that women's needs be taken seriously and that their interests be represented in the polity. Just as political parties have been vehicles for newly mobilized collectivities in the past, so are women as a collectivity becoming empowered by performing partylike functions.

Specifically, it is argued that they have served in five partylike capacities: as ward heelers, informal and ad hoc networkers, political educators, political recruiters and endorsers, and campaign fundraisers and workers. To a large extent, these women are delivering on the Progressive promise of an informed and active citizenry. Furthermore, as an advance over their Progressive counterparts, today's female activists are less nativist and more inclusive of a constituency across lines of race, class, and sexual preference.[3] However, they are still searching for more effective ways to bridge these gaps with other women. Lessons in coalition-building drawn from this case study can be applied to other communities as well.

After a brief overview of Santa Clara County politics, we will consider the evidence for these five kinds of party activities. This evidence is drawn primarily from intensive interviews conducted during 1982 and 1983 with local activists and officials. The conclusion will discuss the significance of women's partylike power at the local level of government.

THE CASE OF SANTA CLARA COUNTY

The county of Santa Clara, located on the southwest edge of San Francisco bay, and its major city, San Jose, were chartered in 1850 and benefited from their strategic location on a supply route to the California gold mines. San Jose became a major food processing center and by 1880 it was dominated by a Republican political machine that granted franchises to utility companies and streetcar operators, provided subsidies to canneries, and protected the interests of the Southern Pacific Railroad. In the first two decades of the twentieth century, Progressive reformers succeeded in replacing San Jose's mayor with a city manager and introduced competitive bidding, civil service, initiative, referendum, and recall into the electoral process. A 1911 amendment to the California constitution made all local elections nonpartisan to reduce the power of Southern Pacific machine politics. Local business and professional men and women carried the clean government banner in groups like the Good Government League, the New Charter Club, and the Women's Civic Study League (Trounstine and Christensen, 1982).

The county provides a good test case for studying how women have filled the party void not only because of the county's Progressive history, but also because in recent years it has gained a reputation as the "feminist capital of the nation." This reputation stems from the area's record number of female elected officials. The 1980 elections produced female majorities on the Santa Clara County Board of Supervisors (three women to two men) and the San Jose City Council (seven to four). Among those in the council majority was San Jose Mayor Janet Gray Hayes, the first woman mayor of a major city, who was elected five years before San Francisco's Dianne Feinstein or Chicago's Jane Byrne. In 1982, fourteen of the fifteen cities in the county had women in their councils and four cities had female mayors. These were impressive achievements in a nation where only six percent of the county officials and thirteen percent of municipal officials were women (San Jose Mercury News, 1982; CAWP, 1981).

During the 1970s, the confluence of two developments made Santa Clara County fertile soil for the success of female candidacies: environmentalism and district elections.[4]

Environmental concerns resulted from two decades of rapid unplanned growth, which transformed the prewar agricultural Valley of Heart's Delight into the postwar electronic Silicon Valley. By 1980 San Jose was the fastest-growing major U.S. city, with 630,000 residents. The area's economy created some 40,000 new jobs yearly. Unemployment rated well below the state average, and the county's median income, $23,370, ranked highest in the nation (Sharpe, 1983). But local services—sewers, parks, schools, libraries, streets, fire protection—could not keep pace with the rapid growth, leapfrog annexation, and increasing traffic congestion and air pollution in the area.

Among those championing the environmentalist cause was a high proportion of female homemakers and volunteers whose husbands had secure professional careers. One reason why environmentalism led to female victories in Santa Clara County was that many of the male candidates were associated with the "growth machine" of a booster political elite, which had spearheaded the postwar economic boom to the benefit of developers. Economically secure, these women were viewed as beyond developers' reach, and they called for managed growth.

Many women first tasted electoral politics by bringing neighborhood concerns before their city councils. What cinched their decisions to run for office was the advent of district elections in 1980, which lowered the effort and cost of seeking office. For over a decade, a coalition of minority, feminist, and labor groups had sought to convince voters that the high cost of at-large campaigns in San Jose had resulted in two affluent neighborhoods producing nearly eighty percent of all councilmembers since 1950. By 1978 neighborhood groups joined the coalition's efforts and voters approved district elections (Trounstine and Christensen, 1982).

Districting proved crucial to the success of women running in the 1980 elections. Each of the five women who joined the San Jose City Council for the first time in 1980 told me that she would not have run in at-large elections, which seemed too costly and time-consuming. Districting reduced candidates' reliance on developers' contributions and enabled them to rely instead on mobilized community groups. These groups included not only neighborhood associations, homeowners groups, and ethnic affiliations, but also women's organizations like the League of Women Voters and the National Women's Political Caucus, which provided crucial support by networking and walking precincts.

Local women's groups went well beyond getting women elected to office. Their efforts also produced impressive programs and agencies, like the county Commission on the Status of Women, child support collection, access to abortions, a comparable worth settlement for San Jose city employees, and three battered women's shelters. Thus, the area's reputation as a feminist capital was due not only to its many female officials, but also to its grassroots female activists. In order to get a more detailed look at the precise nature of their influence, we examine the various ways in which they performed partylike functions in the county.

WARD HEELERS

In the nineteenth century, urban political machines provided services in exchange for votes. These services were vital to the welfare of ethnic groups who were vulnerable to the exigencies of a market economy and the dominant Anglo-Saxon culture. Ward heelers served immigrants from Ireland, Italy, and Eastern Europe and expected party-line votes in return.[5] while female service providers of today do not collect partisan votes, their services are nonetheless political in that they enable service receivers, who would otherwise remain isolated from each other, to join around an issue. This increases the likelihood of their becoming politically active in defense of that issue.

The parallel between female activists and ward heelers most certainly does hold for providing services not offered elsewhere. Probably the most impressive example is the provision of services for battered women and their children. San Jose's Woman's Alliance (WOMA) is a case in point. In 1974, a group of women from a service agency for low-income persons, Economic and Social Opportunities (ESO), decided to open a women's center to provide services to all women in Santa Clara county, especially low-income and minority women, who were seen as having access to fewer services and fewer alternatives. "We put in a phone and 99 percent of the people who called us were being beaten up. They needed help and there was really nothing available for them. And so our services developed along those lines."[6]

The center was initially funded by donations, followed by county-supplied CETA workers, a state grant, and United Way funds. In 1977 WOMA opened its shelter facility, the second shelter in the state of California. It was originally located in a building rented from the city, until local residents sued to have it removed. Two women came to the shelter's rescue with a low-interest loan for the down payment on a new facility. The loan was soon repaid with funds from the Hewlett Foundation and a city block grant.

WOMA served as many as 900 people a year, both by housing them at its thirty-bed shelter and by helping women obtain temporary restraining orders against their batterers. Once assisted by the shelter, women helped each other both directly, through support groups, and indirectly. Here are two examples.

Not too long ago I talked to a woman who had just gone through her temporary restraining order court hearing, and she took a couple of friends with her from the shelter. Throughout the entire hearing her husband was praying out loud and telling her that he was going to change and that it would never happen again, and so on. She told me that she was just beginning to believe him and think she ought to give him a second chance, when she heard her two friends laughing in the back of the courthouse. Just laughing their heads off! They told her later that they had heard the exact same things from their husbands a couple of weeks earlier! So she was able to maintain what she felt she had to go through because of them.

One woman is active in the _____ Opera and tries to get free tickets for current shelter residents whenever she can. Or another woman, who is back with her husband, and everything seems fine, whenever anything is on sale she buys two and give us one. We get boxes of Tide and so on from her.[7]

WOMA received assistance from just about every women's group in the area: from the San Jose Junior Women's Club, to women's church auxiliaries, to the local chapter of the National Organization for Women, which completely furnished the shelter when it first opened up. Even the Girl Scouts pitched in. They provided child care at the WOMA-sponsored Women's Unity Day at a local park in July 1983. The shelter had its own Girl Scout troop, the first of its kind in the country. It was organized by Laurie Escobar, who had worked with migrant labor camps.

It is kind of unique because the girls are there for what may be a very brief period of time: one meeting, maybe three or four. But it's not like a traditional troop. Laurie has a lot of experience working with migrant camps, where it is also very short-term. So she helped us set up our troop at the shelter and supplies us with pins and uniforms and craft items. They also give a certain number of scholarships to Girl Scout camps every year.[8]

Another form of indirect service was WOMA's assistance to and through local police officers, who responded in kind.

Just recently we did a training again with the San Jose Police Department, and I think those kind of things help. We've noticed a recent upsurge in the number of police officers calling us for assistance while they are at the scene. Sometimes they put a woman on the phone right then to discuss her alternatives. . . . If we can intervene in a situation, if a woman can call us, and we can take some kind of action and be supportive, maybe then the police don't have to return to a potentially really dangerous situation.

Occasionally we have a batterer show up at this office. This is our published address so a lot of times they think the shelter is here. So they will come her looking for women. Sometimes they are high, and you really don't know how they are going to respond. We've gotten real good police response over to this office. And on the rare, rare times when batterers have shown up at the shelter, the police are there very quickly. That's important because none of us has a black belt in karate. And we don't have guns. We don't know what could happen. So far there have been no deaths or injuries here or at the shelter. But clients have been killed in the past.[9]

WOMA was not the only women's group in the county to provide women with potentially life-saving services. Another such group was the Chicana Coalition, which worked with local Gray Panthers and Chicana nurses to pressure local hospitals to improve services for Hispanic patients. The Chicana Coalition was established by Chicana feminists in 1979 to advocate the interests of Chicanas "in the educational, political, economic, health, social, and cultural areas."[10]

In the last three years we have had an ongoing struggle with the 16 or 17 local hospitals in the area. We have been addressing the lack of bilingual services, sliding-scale fees, and access. We have very convincingly used the government watchdog—the Health Services Administration's certificate of need process—to address these issues every time a hospital comes up to ask for permission to grow or add equipment. They have to hold a public meeting and our expert members come with their statistics. I look at their affirmative action plans and bilingual staffing.[11]

In addition to the health care and domestic violence services already discussed, local women's groups responded to threats to women's economic security: employment discrimination, sexual harassment, and pension denial. These complaints were handled primarily through the county's Commission on the Status of Women, created by county ordinance in 1973 with indirect subpoena power (through a supervisor) and the ability to conduct investigations and hearings with testimony taken under oath. The commission's charge was to eliminate sex discrimination in housing, employment, education, and community services.

Throughout the 1970s, the commission mediated an average of five hundred sex discrimination complaints a year. Two things were noteworthy about how it handled complaints. The first was its one-on-one resolution of problems over the telephone. This method was used in order to meet the needs of low-income women who could not afford to take off work, come to the office, fill out a form, and wait a week for a response. Commissioners knew this was a rather expensive way of dealing with women's needs, but they felt it was worth it.

Perhaps there were other ways to reach larger numbers of people more
directly. But we got all these calls from women at the end of the line.
Calls that simply touched the heart. What were we to do? I have attended two conventions of the National Association of Commissions on the
Status of Women where there were roundtable discussions of what other
commissions were doing. I discovered that no one else was doing this
kind of complaint resolution.[12]

But complaint resolution did not stop at this one-on-one level. A
second notable feature was pursuit of the issue within the organization
until a policy change resulted.

Somebody in a position to change policy learned what sex discrimination was, what they were doing, and how it needed to be corrected. In
particular, there was a local hiring person at a national fast-food chain.
He thought women should not be cooks in hot kitchens lifting heavy
pans. Which of course gave women a great laugh! We reminded the
franchise that women had been engaging in such work for quite awhile!

In a number of companies, once an individual complaint had been
resolved, the manager would ask someone from the commission to
come out to the company to give a presentation on sex discrimination.
Then this company passed information along to the personnel division
or vice presidents of other companies. And it got to the point to where,
when our calls came through, instead of the first response being,
"What's the Commission and why should I talk to you?," it was, "Just
a moment, let me close the door. Now what do you want."[13]

Frequently the complaints of local women caused the commission
to turn to higher levels of government to seek redress.

Like the exwives of military men who were dumped with nothing and
got no pensions. They were destitute; mostly older women without
careers because of constant moving. They were divorced and left with
nothing. We did not know about this issue until they came to us. We
pressured Congress member Pete McCloskey and wrote to Congress to
change laws on pensions for military wives. We have both a local and
national focus.[14]

This discussion of service provision is not meant to imply that local
female activists are always successful in producing comprehensive services. Many times what women want is beyond the ability of these
women to deliver. As one National Organization for Women activist
put it:

We have an answerphone and for the last year or so I have answered the
messages. We get a constant flow of people who have problems. In
some ways, the question, "How can I prevent discrimination against me

at work?" is getting replaced with the question, "Do you know where I can get a job?"[15]

Nevertheless, an impressive number of women's groups are visible to women in the community and called upon by them daily to meet heretofore unaddressed needs relating to domestic violence, health care, employment discrimination, and military pensions. These are issues of economic and physical vulnerability as serious as any addressed by nineteenth-century ward heelers.

INFORMAL AND AD HOC NETWORKERS

Today's female "ward heelers" may not make a response to "who sent you?" a precondition for rendering services, as Judge Mikva's politico did. But they do have their own informal networks that are significant in developing women's political power. Three types will be examined here: those enabling women to enter and move up the ranks of government and business, those giving women problem-solving skills, and those mobilizing women around an issue on an ad hoc basis.

When Supervisor Susanne Wilson was president of California Elected Women, she set up a file of Santa Clara County women called GOG, or "Good Old Gals." As one of her aides described it:

> It is the equivalent of the old boys' network. If someone comes into town, at a moment's notice we can pull together a luncheon to hold in two weeks. Over a hundred women usually come. Everyone pays for her own meal. It is mainly informational and a good networking tool. And it is all different kinds of women: different levels of government, business, and industry. It is very informal. Of course, every now and then some fundraising is done informally. You are sitting around a room and someone says, "Hey, this person is going to run for office and needs some money." And they all pull out their checkbooks.[16]

While professional women have informal networks for climbing up the ladder of success, many of them both question what it means to "make it" and try to lower the ladder for nonprofessional and minority women. As one high-level administrator put it:

> Yes, they want to climb the ladder and "make it." But at what price? And what does it mean in terms of integrity and personal fulfillment? I think that if you imitate men you end up with pretty hollow feelings. It is interesting. I hear this kind of talk more in professional women's settings. But for most minority women, the issue is still, "How do you get in?" For most nonminority women, the issue is more, "We are in, but

how do you climb up?'' We have got to form some kind of partnership, some link. Those who are in should say, "This is how I got in and I think this is how you can get in. And once I am in, I will be your support system." When you do that, you also get support. When you mentor someone, you get something from mentoring.[17]

In addition to career advancement connections, local informal networks also provided women with problem-solving skills. For example, attorneys who had served on the Commission on the Status of Women remained on the commission's referral list for women calling in with legal questions. In the words of a former commissioner:

A number of women called me through referral from the commision to say, "What can I do about this?" The answer has been, "Well, okay, the first thing you do is talk to your supervisors." "I have already talked to them." "What did you say?" So we narrow down specifically what is wrong. Usually it is not just one thing; or it is one thing but they cannot identify the legal problem. So you narrow down to that in relatively short order and say, "Okay, try this, this, and this. And if it works, great. If it doesn't work, call me back." You do that a couple times just to see if the matter can be resolved internally. A lot of times it works. That's really exciting because first of all that person has gotten the whole thing resolved in probably a week or two; and second, they are all excited about their power and they have learned to use the process. And then they can pass that on to other people. That's part of the network which I think really makes this the feminist capital of the nation.[18]

These networks were also called into action on an ad hoc basis when a pressing issue with a deadline suddenly arose. Such was the case when the community mobilized to support congressional extension of the deadline for state ratification of the Equal Rights Amendment. This mobilization was spearheaded by the local chapter of the National Organization for Women (NOW), which used both traditional and innovative networking techniques.[19] Among the traditional techniques were using Congressmember Don Edwards's office to keep track of local congressmembers' votes; assigning someone to shadow local congressmembers and watch them in committee; and phone-banking. Among the innovative techniques were the ways in which names were secured for the phone-banking and what was requested of the people telephoned.

For example, then-Congressmember Leo Ryan opposed ERA extension. So NOW got ahold of a list of his contributors.

We went through the list and said, "Well, there's X, occupation flower grower." And somebody would say, "My Dad used to know somebody who was a flower grower." Eventually we were able to track down his contributors. We worked with the League of Women Voters, with Business and Professional Women's Clubs, and other groups. We called them and either got their membership lists, or got, "Oh, I'm sorry we can't give out the membership list. But I think I might have one in my mailbox if somebody happened to come by." When we ran out of traditional lists of supportive groups, we turned to things like the Stanford faculty list and picked out the ones who sounded like they were in more liberal departments. We finally hit upon some woman who said, "Oh, you mean to tell me Leo is not supporting that?" And it turned out we had run across an ex-South San Francisco city councilmember who had served on that council with Leo. "Let me call him and check that out." Well, I don't know which of these things did it, but Leo voted for it.[20]

When people were contacted on the phone, they were presented with alternative things they could do and a filing card was kept on each person.

I've done party phone-banking and somebody handed you a list with a bunch of names and phone numbers, which you call up with one simple message, "Are you coming to the Edwards dinner? Thank you very much." You went on to your next one and that was that. But we made filing cards on these people and gave them a series of things they could do: write a letter, make a contribution, come down and phone-bank, and send a Western Union public opinion message. We'd say, "There are thirteen critical congresspeople and it costs two dollars per public opinion message. How many would you like to send out?" We read them the messages that said, "I urge you to support ERA extension and to vote against recision." We called in the messages and billed them to their numbers. We sent out hundreds and got zero complaints from people wondering, "Hey, who put this charge on my bill?" We sat in this office night after night after night sending out hundreds of public opinion messages.

We kept records on these people and got future commitments from them. "Can we send one now, one later?" "Send ten now and ten later?" "Can we call you back?" "Do you know anyone else who would be interested?" We got our best lists from women who said, "Sure, let me get my address book." So we had people on the phones; people transferring information to three-by-five cards; people looking up numbers in the phone book; and people on the phone to Western Union, whose operators would say, "Oh, do you know Laurel from New York?" And then you'd find your friends from across the country were doing it too. I always joked that the only people in the world who knew how to spell "recision" were Western Union operators![21]

Informal networks, like these generated on an ad hoc basis for issues like the ERA extension, those spun off from the Commission on the Status of Women, and those produced by state associations such as Good Old Gals, are in place in Santa Clara County, ready to be tapped when needed. While individual women may receive tangible benefits (like clients or career advancement) from pouring their energies into these networks, it is also true that they are forging both a sisterhood and political alliances. Local women's groups work well together, even though they are not joined in an explicit coalition. As one NOW activist described the situation:

> Everything in San Jose tends to be low-keyed compared to other cities. But you have to remember that San Jose has the highest median income of all cities over 500,000. So everything here tends to be not quite as desperate and angry as it is elsewhere. It is a little more muted here. But it's all there. It's all sitting out there.[22]

POLITICAL EDUCATORS

Like political parties, women's groups seek to educate their own members, other groups, local influentials, neighbors and coworkers, and the community at large. Santa Clara County women were political educators in each of these arenas.

The first task was educating their own members. Probably the ideal-typical model in this regard was the League of Women Voters. The local chapter carefully studied issues before taking positions on them. And it produced a local television public affairs talkshow, "Left, Right, and Center." Member education is particularly difficult in a fast-growing area such as Santa Clara County. For example, even though the 200-member local chapter of the National Women's Political Caucus (NWPC) was the second-largest in the nation (with neighboring Contra Costa County chapter ranking first), its membership turnover was frustrating to some long-standing members.

> When I first came to the caucus ten years ago, many of the women were activists. They helped elect Janet Gray Hayes mayor. They were very active politically. I have seen a real change. The politically active women are still there if we need them, but they do not come to meetings, which is very frustrating. We've gotten a whole new kind of woman who is a little bit more politically naive and there to learn, so it is hard to pull them out to get real involved.[23]

Membership education was also difficult around controversial issues that had the potential to divide a group. A case in point was the Chicana Coalition's consideration of the abortion issue.

About two years ago we had a debate on the abortion issue. It is very divisive and, as president, I don't think I'd entertain such a debate again. We brought in someone from Planned Parenthood and a right to life speaker. The coalition heard both sides and voted to support abortion, the right/freedom of choice. But it is not that clear-cut. If you talk about some issues like fetal experimentation or the family, you find a very conservative bent in Hispanic women and the coalition. They really still believe that, although we should have a right to choice, every child is a blessing to be nurtured principally by the mother. A lot of Chicana Coalition members would rather not talk about it. But one of the reasons we debated it was because state funds were going to be cut off and it became an issue. We voted to send a mailgram in support of abortion along with other women's organizations in the county.[24]

In addition to educating their own ranks, grassroots women activists tried to raise the consciousness of other groups regarding women's issues. For example, staff members from the Commission on the Status of Women went out into the community and attended meetings of groups that were not specifically directed at women's issues:

For instance, there was an Asian-American Concerns group, and other ones like that. When staffers went out to these groups, they simply monitored women's issues as they came up. Or perhaps even pointed them out as they came up when other people did not notice them, did not say, "Well, that's a women's issue." They raised people's consciousness about what were women's issues.[25]

Grassroots women were particularly interested in reaching local influentials. Activists found themselves in varying degrees of proximity to the thrones of wealth and power. One reproductive-rights activist described herself as quite proximate: "I meet the heads of corporations at dinners. I was even on Queen Elizabeth's yacht in San Francisco as a guest of President Reagan. So I can discuss things on the quiet. I am grateful for my husband's money!"[26]

Those who were less proximate used academic channels, such as Stanford's Center for Research on Women (CROW), to reach local influentials. CROW's director described how the center had ripple effects on local corporate and individual donors.[27] Some two dozen corporations, which had donated $1000 or more to CROW, participated in annual Corporate Associates Seminars, where the center's research relevant to the business community was presented. The hope was to affect corporate policies toward women regarding such things as child care, stress, the problems of dual-career couples, and occupational segregation. The corporations typically sent women to these seminars, many of whom wrote to CROW detailing how their views were affected, how they created support groups at work, or how they obtained larger contributions for CROW from their firms. Among the men frequenting the seminars were a NOW member and feminist from a major "headhunting" agency with contacts in local personnel departments, a public relations director from a major electronics firm, and a corporate president who had sat in on a meeting of women at his firm and was so taken aback by what he heard that he became a CROW associate.

CROW had over 100 individual donors who attended programs updating them on a range of research broader than that presented to corporate sponsors, encompassing areas such as art, literature, and religion. Most of these donors were women, who included their friends in CROW functions. To one program, "The Effects of the Women's Movement on Men," many brought their corporate-executive husbands.

About five years ago, a retreat was held for these donors, along with faculty, staff, and graduate students.

> We broke down into several small study groups, one of which was on fundraising. Most in the group were our associates, joined by one radical lesbian graduate student. When the question "What is feminism?" was raised, I thought, "Here comes the fireworks." The graduate student said, "It is two things: putting women first, and, with respect to any topic, asking how it affects women." The associates said they agreed with her. I thought this was an incredible bridging of class and sexual preference gaps. It was the sort of thing that if these wealthy and powerful women read about it in the paper, they would say, "Oh, she is just not my type," and dismiss out of hand.[28]

Such one-on-one education, while not newsworthy enough to make its way into the media's coverage of the women's movement, is, nonetheless, the day-to-day stuff of political change. Feminists are on call daily with neighbors and coworkers to defend themselves. A university administrator described two such examples.

> The hard part comes when your colleagues say, "Are you really a feminist? What does that really mean?" A good example of that happened a couple of months ago with a faculty woman who is very active in feminist studies here. We were out to dinner with some of her male colleagues. I sat at the dinner table and watched them ask her, "What is

feminist studies? What does it really mean? You couldn't possibly mean so-and-so!" There is this constant justification, explanation, and education.

But you know the hardest part, and each of us faces it, I think, is with next-door neighbors. "Joe Jock" lives next-door. A couple of months ago I'm in my house on a Saturday and all of a sudden, "Hey Cecilia, I want you to come over because I have this guy who has never met a feminist." Right? So I go over because I thought we were friends, and there is this guy saying, "Hey, I understand you're a feminist. Want to hear the latest joke?" And then it begins. And your next-door neighbor just sits there and watches you. "Come on, Cecilia, defend yourself." And you think, "Why do I need this?" But it happens all the time and you find yourself justifying and explaining what it means to men.[29]

Community education also took the form of conferences, marches, and picketing. CROW sponsored conferences on topics ranging from careers of corporate women, to women writers, to divorce and midlife crisis.

These conferences are emotionally draining and uplifting for everyone, especially the one on midlife, which, it was joked, lasts from ages 25 to 65! I noticed this woman who sat next to me was getting more and more excited as the conference went on. At the break I talked to her. She was a local school teacher who said, "It is sad because I'm not able to share any of this with my husband. I didn't tell him I was coming. I said I was going to a school event. He gets anxious about anything with women." I tried to imagine what all of this must mean for her.[30]

One conference aimed at educating both the community and feminists was the National Hispanic Feminist Conference held in San Jose in March 1980. As conference organizer Sylvia Gonzales described these two goals:

Anglo women have been included from the start and in leadership roles with Latinos. . . . We are reaching out to non-Hispanic feminists. It is not enough to talk to ourselves. . . . It is unique in that it is dealing with theory and research, but we will also include community women. We are providing the mental tools for action. We're trying to bridge an educational gap that would normally take a generation.[31]

Some 900 women attended over 100 workshops. While Gonzales said the conference provided "an opportunity for Hispanic feminist leaders to form a much-need national network,"[32] she added that "the community women were the ones who benefited most. They were the ones who were so excited. They were the ones who for the first time were hearing things they had never heard before. They were the ones attending the workshops where the majority of work was going on."[33]

Finally, community political education also occurred during public demonstrations and rallies. The local NOW chapter was often at the forefront of such events. For example, in July 1983, NOW, the San Jose State University Women's Center, and the San Jose Peace Center cosponsored a protest at the third annual Ms. Nude America contest held at the San Jose Center for the Performing Arts. Of the seventy demonstrators, six were arrested after they spattered blood on the center's entrance. They said the blood was drawn from rape victims.[34] The purpose of this act was to dramatize the relationship between rape and the objectification of women's bodies as instruments of male pleasure.

NOW was somewhat less successful at getting local members to turn out in support of the August 1983 March for Jobs, Peace and Freedom in San Francisco, commemorating the twentieth anniversary of Martin Luther King's March on Washington.

> The local chapter pushed it at meetings and organized carpools. We made available information on busing. We hyped it on the front page of our newsletter over and over again. We phone-banked a few nights before and asked, 'Are you going to be there? Get your body there." Well, we just didn't get the people there. Maybe five or eight of us, some of whom came with other groups. And those who went are the same old standbys you can always count on. We didn't get a single body there who wasn't going to be there anyway. My view is that if you say you oppose racism, get your bodies out there.[35]

For all its frustrations, political education is percolating in Santa Clara County in settings as diverse as demonstrations and League of Women Voters study groups. Just as a political party encourages its members to understand the relationship between issues in order to advocate and defend the party's issue positions, so do grassroots women use various fora to educate themselves and others about the myriad forms of male domination: from denial of reproductive choice, to male bias in academe, to occupational segregation, to sexist jokes. This education has many political implications, not the least of which bear on electoral politics.

POLITICAL RECRUITERS AND ENDORSERS

The political recruitment function of local women's groups was for the most part performed indirectly. Their newsletters routinely announced openings for local appointive offices. NWPC, NOW, and the League of Women Voters provided women with contacts, information about the position, and experience in public speaking. For example, in July 1983, NWPC sponsored a public workshop on communication, described in its brochure as teaching "the fine art of political communication. That is, communication with intent, clarity, impact. This workshop is ideal for women in all ranks of leadership."[36]

These groups encouraged their members to run for elective office as well. One San Jose City Council member told me that the League of Women Voters provided her with her main organizational experiences for the post. "A former president of the league was my mentor. She never ran for office herself, but she helped many other women. To this day I ask myself, 'Now what would Margie do in this situation?'"[37] NWPC scouted for new talent to support. While most of the time women came to them for endorsement, occasionally they reached out to women who had never heard of them. One NWPC member recounted the story of how she struck up a conversation with a woman in the parking lot of a local community college. This woman turned out to be a candidate in a local school board race. "She had never heard about us. This was her first time running. She was a Republican with very definite ideas about what she wanted to do on the school board. We endorsed her and she won out of a field of eight candidates. She is one of our bright shining stars in recent years! She was very thankful for our endorsement and funds."[38]

Local talent was pooled at the annual Women of Achievement Awards Dinner, sponsored by the League of Friends (a support group for the Commission on the Status of Women) and the *San Jose Mercury News*. Any individual or organization could submit names of outstanding women in any of five areas: government, business/professions, arts, education, and volunteerism. A panel of judges selected an award winner from each category. The first awards dinner was in 1978. In 1980 there were forty-two nominees; by 1983 there were close to one hundred. The dinner raised funds for the commission and provided an occasion for activist women to meet one another and local influentials as well. For example, included in the 1980 program were Dr. William Miller, president of Stanford Research Institute, and Halsey Burke, a San Jose businessman listed among the city's top ten powerholders (Trounstine and Christensen, 1982: 114).

Through this dinner, the League of Friends provided nominees with visibility: to the general public (as the local newspaper was a cosponsor), to local businessmen (some of whom purchased blocs of $40 seats for the dinner), and to other women. The bringing together of a critical mass of female talent was an inspiration to women activists. As one guest described the evening:

At the banquet there is a wonderful program with a paragraph about each nominee. The thrilling thing is the breadth of achievement. I mean it is all races, all ages; people whose work has been exclusively with poverty-level clientele and people who have risen to the top in a profession or business or as educators. It is the whole gamut of human achievement. These women are everywhere. You just sort of float out at the end of the evening.[39]

In addition to informally recruiting and grooming women for public office, grassroots women's groups had formal endorsement processes. NWPC, NOW, and the Chicana Coalition employed similar procedures. Of course, each organization had its own issues of central concern. Following is a brief description of the endorsement process of each.

NWPC[40] sent out questionnaires to all candidates. On the basis of their responses, they were screened with respect to five bottom-line issues: right to abortion, public funding for abortion, child care funding, the ERA, and opposition to sex and race discrimination. After this screening, candidates were interviewed by three or four NWPC members in teams asking questions designed for each office: city council, county supervisor, school board, and so on. NWPC took over a law office on a weekend and ran candidates through every twenty minutes. Interviewers' recommendations were published in the newsletter prior to the meeting. Endorsement meetings were the best-attended of the year, especially when there were contested races. Sometimes men were endorsed over women; sometimes two good candidates were both endorsed. And incumbents' records were scrutinized before reelection support was granted. For example, several people told me off the record that many NWPC members were disappointed with Mayor Hayes's lack of feminist leadership during her first term; she only narrowly carried the reendorsement vote.

In Santa Clara County, NWPC endorsement was sought by both radical and mainstream candidates. They liked to include it in their advertisements. "They have bought the idea that 'feminist capital' means that there is a bloc of women voters out there."[41] "We were surprised. Someone in a recent election did a poll and in fact an endorsement from women's groups came out very high in the poll."[42] However, archconservative candidates from the county's Bible Belt (south, southwest Santa Clara County) did not seek NWPC support. And school board candidates were not as likely as others to seek it. One member speculated that this may have been because school races were associated with the family, which many voters feared was threatened by the women's movement.[43]

Like NWPC, NOW[44] had bottom-line issues for endorsement. These were the ERA, reproductive rights, lesbian rights, and antiracism. In fact, some San Jose chapter members fought unsuccessfully to have state and national NOW endorsement committees adhere to all four criteria before backing any candidate. "We felt that those were four basic issues and that no matter how good a politician was on three of them, if they were not at least consonant with us on the fourth, we should not endorse or give money to that person."[45] Other members of the San Jose chapter were more inclined to support Democratic candidates, even if they did not meet all four criteria. But, given this division in the local chapter, Democratic candidates could not assume they had the NOW endorsement in their pocket.[46]

Local officials also sought the endorsement of the Chicana Coalition.[47] Candidates were invited to come before a political involvement committee, which made recommendations to the general membership. Members were polled both to develop the questions to ask candidates and to make the final vote. Unlike NWPC and NOW, there was no bottom-line checklist. Rather, questions were different for each office. The Coalition endorsed in several ways: use of its name, monetarily, and with volunteers.

All three women's groups have had their share of difficult cases. When two Hispanic women were up for the same San Jose City Council seat, the coalition endorsed only one of them. The woman who was not supported (a former coalition officer) has since not returned to the group. A hard case for NWPC was that between two candidates for county supervisor. It endorsed the man who had been very active in NWPC over the woman who did not yet have a track record on women's issues, but who subsequently won the election and proved to be generally supportive of NWPC positions. The next time a case arose where both a male and female candidate were popular with the group, NWPC decided to endorse both, but give money to neither. NOW's experiences served as a reminder that feminist support was not a necessary condition for victory. In the 1980 election, it endorsed only one of the nine women who made it to the fall ballot for city council or county supervisor.

While endorsement procedures were complicated and potentially divisive of women's groups, it was a tribute to them that their support was so widely sought by local candidates. In most areas, it was an asset to have women's groups listed on your campaign literature. Equally important to endorsement were the fundraising and precinct-walking support provided by grassroots women.

CAMPAIGN FUNDRAISERS AND WORKERS

While local women's organizations had nowhere near the monetary resources of groups like developers or labor, they nonetheless contributed to races of sympathetic candidates. The NWPC distributed between $3000 and $5000 per race, depending on the type of race.[48] Supervisorial candidates were given over $1000. San Jose had a limit on donations for council races—$500 per candidate per political action committee. NWPC contributed to school board races as well, but had to be selective since the county had so many of them. It raised funds through events such as the annual Celebrity Spaghetti Dinner, where men, including county firefighters, the San Jose Peace Officers' Association, and elected officials, cooked and waited on tables.

These funds were helpful to local candidates, but the "people power" provided by grassroots women's groups was probably even more significant. Local activist Pat Miller[49] illustrated this with the case of Congressmember Pete McCloskey's first race for Congress in a 1967 special election. He ran as an environmentalist against former movie star Shirley Temple Black. Upon learning that Black was ahead, McCloskey got together a group comprised mostly of women to do last-minute campaign work for him. He told Miller that the areas women leafleted were the areas where he won; so he attributed his victory to women's efforts. Miller added that women were more effective precinctwalkers than men because, given the high crime rate, people were often afraid to open their doors to men. Women were more trusted and had better access to voters in door-to-door work.

Finally, women had a reputation for loyalty. Women's groups did not always have the resources to monitor all the candidates they supported, but they did go to bat for their best allies when they came under fire. A case in point was public officials who supported local gay rights ordinances. In 1979 both the Santa Clara County Board of Supervisors and the San Jose City Council passed ordinances protecting the rights of gay and lesbian citizens. In the 1980 election, the Los Gatos Christian Church and Concerned Citizens (a fundamentalist religious group) spearheaded voter repeal of these measures by a three-to-one margin, and they mounted a drive to recall Supervisor Rod Diridon, a supporter of gay rights and an opponent of relaxing the environmental restrictions in county building permits. Local women's groups rallied behind Diridon against this evangelical-developer coalition. He was a strong advocate of feminist issues and held annual meetings to assess the policy needs of women in the county. As one activist described women's relations to Diridon and the rest of the board of supervisors:

> The board is kept on their toes by us. We walk the precincts for them and support them when they are attacked. Diridon may annoy me sometimes, but he is a solid feminist. He goes to women's meetings. Concerned Citizens attacked him for his stand on gay rights and feminism. He is the most visible proponent of these issues in the county.[50]

As indicated by his quote at the outset of this essay, Diridon felt indebted to county women in his electoral efforts. However, in his case, women lined up on different sides of the Progressive legacy: church women backing the (antilesbian) initiative and recall and feminists supporting women as a group (i.e., including lesbians). County women were probably more divided on this issue than on any other, a sobering qualification to the area's feminism. Nevertheless, feminist candidates like Diridon benefited from the funds and people-power of local women's groups.

CONCLUSION: POWER IN PARTYLIKE COALITION

In the absence of strong party structures in the nonpartisan local governments of Santa Clara County, grassroots women's groups have performed party functions as campaign fundraisers and workers; political recruiters and endorsers; political educators; informal and ad hoc networkers; and ward heelers. This account does not mean to suggest that women's groups are the only, or even the most effective, ones to fill the party vacuum. An equally plausible case could be made for economic elites, labor and minority groups, and the media.

Relative to these party substitutes, women's organizations are newcomers to the political scene (with notable exceptions such as the League of Women Voters). At the risk of passing premature judgment, one can provide a preliminary assessment of their grassroots activity in Santa Clara County over the past decade. What is most striking is their *potential* to forge a broad-based coalition for social change. They are not unique in this regard. Consumers and environmentalists as groups also have the potential to embrace in their respective causes more than half the polity. And many of their issues are as far-reaching and radical as women's issues. Like consumer and environmental groups, women find both a blessing and a curse in their unwieldy numbers. The blessing is a voter bloc, like the much-touted gender gap, and the numbers that can be mobilized under the right conditions. The curse is that these conditions are not always obvious to those affected. For example, the "feminization of poverty" sounds like so many statistics to affluent women. It is hard for a citizen to get moved to action around forms of disadvantage that are viewed as only indirectly accruing to oneself. And it is even more difficult to face up to how one might in fact be advantaged by what disadvantages others.

Examples from this case study are race and class advantage. White women did not turn out in the same numbers at the Martin Luther King rally, at CROW lectures on minority women's issues, or at the Hispanic Feminist Conference as they did for ERA rallies, Ms. Nude America demonstrations, or conference workshops on corporate ladder-climbing. White women tend to see racism as minority women's problem, not their problem. Chicanas formed the Chicana Coalition because they did not feel comfortable in white women's groups.

However, for their part, activists from NOW, NWPC, and the League of Women Voters all expressed to me their concern about their disproportionately white membership. They felt that their outreach attempts had not been successful. Based on my observation, I proffer two object lessons, which, while drawn from this case study, can easily be applied to other communities as well.

The first has to do with race. Initially the Chicana Coalition was adamant about retaining its Chicana-only membership. But all it took was one high-ranking white feminist, national NOW's Action Vice-President Jane Wells-Schooley, to take a public stand in solidarity with Sylvia Gonzales's National Hispanic Feminist Conference, and the Coalition opened its ranks to Anglo women. As Gonzales recounted the story:

> Jane and I were invited to appear on the "San Francisco AM" television program. At the studio, she started to notice all sorts of strange things: only her name was posted on the wall; only she was asked to sign information sheets. She got suspicious and told me so. Sure enough, a couple of minutes before air time, we were told that only she was going to go on. Jane turned to me and said, "Once upon a time I would have thought that it is better that at least one of us goes on rather than no one getting the message across to the public. But I no longer think that way." And she refused to go on alone. There was a big panic, with the moderator (a former Miss America) arguing on our behalf. Finally they decided to let us both go on. After the broadcast, we had lunch with the Chicana Coalition. When Jane told this story to them, it touched their

hearts and they spontaneously offered her a membership, even though she lives in Washington, D.C. Having admitted Jane, they then had to admit other Anglo women as well.[51]

Gonzales said she knew many Chicanas who wanted to join Anglo organizations but did not do so for fear of being rejected. Some even went so far as to ask her, "Will the League of Women Voters allow me to join?" Gonzales added that while language was a barrier for some Chicanas, like those in an east San Jose Spanish-speaking homemakers club to which she belonged, it was not an obstacle for most who wanted to join Anglo groups. She suggested that Chicana's fear of rejection could be overcome by Anglo women reaching out and joining groups like the Chicana Coalition. A lesson to white women from Gonzales's observations and from the Wells-Schooley incident is that they should take the first step rather than wait for minority women to come to them on white turf and terms.

A second and similar object lesson can be drawn across class lines. The Commission on the Status of Women waited for electronics assembly line workers to bring their complaints to the commission. While this strategy might work for women in less vulnerable positions (e.g., managers who suspect sex discrimination and have the mobility and money to take on a fight), it is of limited value to line workers. Former commissioner Ann Bender[52] agreed that company treatment of women in the electronics industry was a very important issue and said the commission had held two hearings on this subject. Women testified about exposure to dangerous chemicals, improper safety instructions and clothing, poor ventilation, and locked doors. They did not raise these issues at work for fear of losing their jobs. They knew they were easily replaceable and, in light of the strong anti-union sentiment in Silicon Valley industries, they were reluctant to get involved in union activity. Most speakers who were willing to talk about working condidtions had already left the industry. The commission never investigated the women's complaints. CAL-OSHA was supposed to do so, but the women claimed that the companies cleaned up temporarily in advance of its inspections, after which they reverted to their dangerous practices.

The same lesson is applicable here. More privileged women can hardly expect line workers to come to them on their turf and terms. Attempts could be made to obtain more information, investigate complaints, and take legal action against illegal anti-union harrassment. These line workers, mostly minority women, constitute the silent and powerless underbelly of Silicon Valley's economic miracle and cast a long shadow over the feminist capital's place in the sun. Women's groups could increase their support for attorneys who are working to organize these workers and for organizations like Economic and Social Opportunities, which are providing job training for low-skilled women workers. Most activists recognize that a considerable amount of work remains to be done across class lines. As one NOW member described her frustration at the enormity of the task at hand:

> While the commission is a good beginning, it is also the case that if I were on it and I looked out over the Silicon Valley and saw all those women working in the middle of all those chemicals, not knowing why they were getting headaches and miscarrying, I would want to get out and start educating them. I would get out and fan the flames of discontent![53]

In order to realize their full potential as a power in local politics, grassroots women see the need for a concerted effort on their part to join in a stronger coalition with other women, not only across race and class, but across organizations as well. First of all, this would reduce the duplication of effort around issues and help centralize information. For example, groups could facilitate their endorsement procedures by pooling candidate questionnaires. Their newsletter editors could coordinate a sharing of information among groups. Second, a stronger coalition would minimize competition and territoriality, which presumably feminists want to avoid. As for competition, the most common form is over scarce budget allocations. For example, one activist stated off the record that WOMA, as the largest and oldest battered women's shelter in the county, is not as willing as it could be to share funds with its two sister shelters in the county. And as for territoriality, one NOW member[54] recounted how NOW was miffed when Business and Professional Women (BPW) convinced a California legislator to introduce a state ERA without first consulting NOW about this strategy, as compared to a federal ERA approach. NOW got the legislator to withdraw the bill without an adequate discussion with BPW regarding the merits of the two strategies. Such territoriality only serves to keep women working at cross-purposes.

Probably the strongest evidence supporting coalition-building can be found in the achievements that have already resulted from informal coalition efforts: sharing group membership lists for the ERA extension mobilization; joining forces to prevent state termination of funds for MediCal abortions; launching WOMA with the help of groups as diverse as the Junior Women's Club, church auxiliaries, and NOW. Instead of continuing on an ad hoc basis, even more effective coalitions could result from each group selecting one member to serve as liaison with other women's groups.

It is not necessary to have the equivalent of a party's central committee to reap the benefits of partylike organizations. Parties in this country have been little more than umbrella organizations tenuously holding together changing arrays of voters in loose coalition. For example, in the 1930s New Deal coalition, the Democratic umbrella encompassed labor, black, urban, and Catholic voters. Today, of these groups, only blacks remain under that umbrella, as boll weevils (conservative Southern Democrats) and gypsy moths (liberal Northern Republicans) complicate the landscape of partisan politics.

Coalitions of relatively powerless majorities have heretofore used political parties to mobilize their numbers against organized powerful minorities possessing such resources as wealth and status. That is, parties have been mechanisms by which the powerless have become empowered. Political scientists who are concerned with the decline of parties in contemporary politics fear that their absence will leave the already powerful intact and unchallenged. As Walter Dean Burnham (1969: 20) puts it:

> [Parties'] disappearance as active intermediaries, if not as preliminary screening devices, would only entail the unchallenged ascendency of the already powerful, unless new structures of collective power were somehow developed to replace them, and unless America's social structure and political culture came to be such that they could be effectively used.

It is too early to tell if changes in the social structure (like women's workforce participation and corresponding changes in sex roles) and in the political culture (like women's growing perception of themselves as participants in, rather than subjects of, the political regime) are fundamental enough to result in women's organizations providing a wholly-new form of collective power to replace parties. After all, urban machines arose as a political response to the social dislocations resulting from massive waves of immigration. It is possible that the social upheaval of changing gender relations will elicit an equally novel political response in our own era. Even if women's organizations never replace parties, and it is not argued here that they necessarily should or will, they are certainly serving as a significant intermediary umbrella for organized majorites—across lines of race and class—to challenge the ascendency of the already powerful by performing crucial partylike functions.

NOTES

1. Judge Abner Mikva, address to the annual meeting of the American Political Science Association, Chicago, September 1983.

2. Interview with Supervisor Rod Diridon, July 21, 1982.

3. For a discussion of the Progressive movement's nativism, see Hofstadter (1955); for its class and race bias, see Kraditor (1971).

4. This discussion is drawn from Flammang (forthcoming).

5. It must be remembered, however, that machine politics both included certain groups and excluded others, who were viewed as ideologically or numerically threatening both to established local powers and to recently included groups. See, for example, Schefter (1983) and Erie (1983a).

6. Interview with Anne McCormac, WOMA Deputy Director, August 16, 1983.

7. Ibid.

8. Ibid.

9. Ibid.

10. Pamphlet distributed by the Chicana Coalition, San Jose, CA, 1983.

11. Interview with Kathy Espinoza-Howard, personnel division of Hewlett-Packard and president of the Chicana Coalition, July 28, 1983.

12. Interview with Ann Bender, attorney and former commissioner and chair, Santa Clara County Commission on the Status of Women, August 8, 1983.

13. Ibid.

14. Interview with Pat Miller, president of Family Planning Alternatives and former commissioner and chair, Santa Clara County Commission on the Status of Women, July 9, 1983.

15. Interview with Robin Yeamans, attorney and NOW member, August 18, 1983.

16. Interview with Sarah Janigian, aide to Supervisor Susanne Wilson and NWPC member, July 26, 1983.

17. Interview with Cecilia Preciado-Burciaga, Assistant Provost at Stanford University, August 3, 1983.

18. Interview with Ann Bender (see note 12).

19. This account of NOW's role in mobilizing local sentiment in favor of ERA deadline extension and against state recision is based on an interview with Joyce Sogg, attorney and NOW member, August 29, 1983.

20. Ibid.

21. Ibid.

22. Interview with Robin Yeamans (see note 15).

23. Interview with Sarah Janigian (see note 16).

24. Interview with Kathy Espinoza-Howard (see note 11).

25. Interview with Ann Bender (see note 12).

26. Interview with Pat Miller (see note 14).

27. Interview with Myra Strober, Professor of Education at Stanford and CROW Director, September 16, 1983.

28. Ibid.

29. Interview with Cecilia Preciado-Burciaga (see note 17).

30. Interview with Myra Strober (see note 27).

31. Sylvia Gonzales, quoted in Janice Mall, "About Women," *Los Angeles Times,* November 25, 1979.

32. Sylvia Gonzales, quoted in Robin McKiel, "Historic Hispanic Feminist Conference Establishes Network," *National NOW Times*, May 1980.

33. Interview with Sylvia Gonzales, former Professor of Mexican American Studies at San Jose State University and organizer of the National Hispanic Feminist Conference, August 16, 1983.

34. Bernard Bauer, "Promoter Sells His Naked Message, *San Jose Mercury News,* July 24, 1983.

35. Interview with Joyce Sogg (see note 19).

36. NWPC brochure for Communications Workshop, San Jose, CA, July 30, 1983.

37. Interview with San Jose City Councilmember Nancy Ianni, August 11, 1982.

38. Interview with Sarah Janigian (see note 16).

39. Interview with Ann Bender (see note 12).

40. This discussion of NWPC endorsement procedures is drawn from interviews with Sarah Janigian (see note 16) and Fanny Rinn, Professor of Political Science at San Jose State University and NWPC member, May 24, 1983.

41. Interview with Fanny Rinn (see note 40).

42. Interview with Sarah Janigian (see note 16).

43. Interview with Susan Charles, NWPC chapter president, August 13, 1983.

44. This discussion of NOW endorsement procedures is drawn from interviews with Joyce Sogg (see note 19) and Robin Yeamans (see note 15).

45. Interview with Joyce Sogg (see note 19).

46. This debate is sparked in both NOW and NWPC every time local California Assemblymember John Vasconcellos is up for reelection. He has a strong record supporting women's issues, with the exception of abortion, which he opposes.

47. This discussion of Chicana Coalition endorsement procedures is drawn from an interview with Kathy Espinoza-Howard (see note 11).

48. This discussion of NWPC campaign funds is drawn from interviews with Sarah Janigian (see note 16) and Fanny Rinn (see note 40).

49. Interview with Pat Miller (see note 14).

50. Ibid.

51. Interview with Sylvia Gonzales (see note 33).

52. Interview with Ann Bender (see note 12).

53. Interview with Robin Yeamans (see note 15).

54. Interview with Joyce Sogg (see note 19).

5

WOMEN IN POLITICAL PARTIES: GENDER DIFFERENCES IN MOTIVES AMONG CALIFORNIA PARTY ACTIVISTS

Edmond Costantini
Julie Davis Bell

The issue addressed here is how men and women party activists in California, studied over a seventeen-year period, differ in terms of what they want from politics. The central focus is upon gender differences with respect to reasons underlying political activity or declared political motives. We will also touch upon other matters—for example, male-female differences in ideology—relevant to that central focus. Further, we will consider the extent to which associations between gender and political motivation have changed over the time span of the study.

DATABASE

The data upon which the analysis is based derive from questionnaires completed by 2565 California party leaders and activists surveyed by mail at four-year intervals from 1964 through 1981. Respondents were members of the state's delegations to presidential nominating conventions or of losing delegation slates entered in presidential primaries held during this period.

Author's Note: The support of the Institute of Governmental Affairs, University of California, Davis, and the Institute of Personality Assessment and Research, University of California, Berkeley, is acknowledged. We also would like to express our appreciation to Professor Kenneth H. Craik (Department of Psychology, UC Berkeley), coprincipal in the larger study of party leadership from which this chapter originates.

Democratic participants greatly outnumber Republicans (as shown in Table 5.1) principally because California's Democratic presidential primaries have been much more competitive than their Republican counterparts, with twenty of the twenty-nine candidates slates surveyed having been entered in the former. Additionally, Democratic delegations have been consistently larger and their response rates generally higher. Note must be made of the small number of Republican respondents in 1968 and 1972. In the latter year the Republican response rate was distinctively low, falling well below the norm—over forty percent—achieved by the remainder of the two-party sample, a possible byproduct of the Watergate scandal and the attendant special reluctance of Nixon partisans to participate in a survey taken in the midst of the demise of the Nixon administration. While we report gender differences for the 1968 and 1972 Republican respondents for the sake of symmetry, the small number of female respondents (under twenty), while proportionate to those in the population, makes gender comparisons suspect for those years.

The sample has much to commend it. First, California is the nation's largest state—home of one-tenth of its population, with corresponding representation in the loci of national political power. Its size has meant that slates of would-be national convention delegations entered in the state's presidential primaries are relatively large and thus particularly suitable for survey analysis. Second, the process by which delegation slates are constructed tends to assure that each candidate faction will attempt to enlist for membership as many as possible of the men and women who "count" in the state's political scheme of things in order to maximize rank-and-file support in the primary campaign and to maintain harmony among the faithful. Indeed, in many ways delegation slate membership is the highest accolade a party or any of is various candidate factions can bestow on its active members, and it is generally understood that such bestowal should be reserved for those whose past or prospective leadership contributions are of the highest quality. In general, we have every reason to agree with Kirkpatrick's (1976: 18) observation that "the delegates to the two national conventions constitute a cross section of the effective elite of the presidential paries . . . and for this reason they are a promising perspective from which to observe the American political scene."

Third, the present sample avoids the problem that arises, particularly in winner-take-all situations, when a state's delegation to a national convention excludes significant party leaders by virtue of their serving on delegation slates pledged to presidential candidates unsuccessful in the year's presidential primary. Thus, for example, members of the

TABLE 5.1 Samples

| | Democratic Respondents | | | | | Republican Respondents | | | | |
| | Male | | Female | | | Male | | Female | | |
	%	(N)	%	(N)	Total N	%	(N)	%	(N)	Total N
1964	84	(153)	16	(30)	(183)	82	(150)	18	(33)	(183)
1968	82	(273)	18	(59)	(332)	82	(49)	18	(11)	(60)
1972	51	(361)	49	(351)	(712)	69	(22)	31	(10)	(32)
1976	51	(233)	49	(220)	(453)	49	(107)	51	(112)	(219)
1980	49	(106)	51	(109)	(215)	62	(110)	38	(66)	(176)
Total	59	(1126)	41	(679)	(1895)	65	(438)	35	(232)	(670)

1972 Muskie slate—selected when Muskie was the leading contender for his party's nomination and including a wide assortment of party notables—are part of our research population, even though Muskie had withdrawn from the race by the time of the California primary and, accordingly, received only a miniscule percentage of the vote and no delegates. This feature of the full sample takes on special significance because all major candidates are normally entered in the California primary—winner-take-all throughout the various phases of the project for the Republicans and through the 1972 primary for the Democrats—due to the size of the delegation at stake and the fact that, occurring on the last day of the primary season, it has had the potential for providing a dramatic momentum-producing climax to the preconvention campaign.

Fourth, drawing comparable samples at regular intervals over an extended period permits the search for transhistorical consistency in gender differences and the identification of evidence of political change. This feature of the database is particularly salutary since the political blossoming of the contemporary women's movement occurred within the project time frame. Its most direct manifestation is in the sharp increase in the percentage of women among Democratic respondents in 1972 and thereafter. There is little doubt that this increase has been nurtured by the affirmative action guidelines for delegate selection adopted by the Democrats in each of the three most recent presidential campaigns and assuring virtual gender equality in representation. However, substantial increases in the number of female delegation members would have very likely been achieved absent those guidelines and can be discerned among the more laissez-faire Republicans.

Whatever the explanation for the increase in female representation, we agree with Jennings and Farah (1981: 463) when they conclude from a comparison of the gender breakdown of the 1964 and 1976 Michigan national convention delegations: "To the extent that delegation membership constitutes a sign of admission to a party's elite, the statistical gain by women in each party must be viewed as a sizable incursion on traditional male dominance."

MEASURING POLITICAL MOTIVES

The motives of political leaders and activists have been an abiding interest of students of political behavior. Some have understandably focused on the desire for power, office-seeking goals, and personal political ambitions of politicians (Schlesinger, 1966).

Others—including those preferring a "system" rather than "rational" model approach to political organization (Wilson, 1973)—have been interested in illuminating the plurality of motives underlying political activity, encouraged by the fact that "empirical studies have repeatedly found that party activists and leaders seek multiple values through political activity" (Kirkpatrick, 1976: 94).

The central issue here is whether our male and female respondents differ in terms of the reasons underlying their political activity. For this we turn to two series of Likert-type questions included in our survey instruments probing political motives. The first series of seventeen items—not all of which were used in all five phases of the project—inquires into the respondent's reasons for initially becoming involved in politics. The second series of five items asks the respondents why they wished to become delegates to their party's most recent presidential nominating convention.

Factor-analytic techniques have been used to reduce those items into five underlying dimensions, the consideration of which provides the framework for the following analysis. The conceptual integrity of the dimensions—whose constituent items will be treated as comprising additive scales—permits assigning the following labels to them.

- *Self-Enhancement*. Items here embrace the desire for power, prestige, and profit—tangible and intangible rewards likely to be valued by those striving for personal political ascendancy.

- *Sociality*. Items reflect an interest in the opportunities politics offers for friendship, fun, and conviviality.

- *Purposive*. Items indicate a concern for issues and the direction in which society is moving.

- *Personalist*. Items suggest the importance of particular individuals—proximate (family and friends) or remote (candidates)—in attracting the respondent to political activity.

- *Allegiance*. Items reflect an obligation to fidelity or loyalty to party, party leaders and the general community.

The first three dimensions are substantially similar to those associated with the Clark and Wilson (1961) typology of incentives—material, solidary, and purposive—which has served as the dominant conceptual framework in this area of inquiry. The theoretical implications of the labeling changes warranted in two of them and of the full five-factor solution, as well as the procedures used to achieve that solution, are discussed elsewhere (Costantini and King, forthcoming).[1]

Analysis of the responses to the motivational items is facilitated in the following discussion by use of "motivational ratios" (or group means) for each gender calculated for each item by assigning values of 1.0 to a "not at all" response, 2.0 to a "very little" response, 3.0 to a "somewhat" response, and 4.0 to a "very much" response. "Mean ratios" (or scale scores) are also calculated for each gender for each motivational dimension based on the motivational ratios achieved on the items included in the given scale.

ANALYSIS

Perusal of mean ratios achieved by each party's aggregated respondents suggests three notable patterns. First, each gender in each party provides identical rankings for the five mean ratios, with the highest ratios achieved on the purposive scale and the lowest on the self-enhancement scale. Second, the direction of the gender difference on each scale is the same for each party. Women achieve higher mean ratios on all but the self-enhancement scale, although the extent of the differences with respect to the sociality scale is quite small. Third, the gender difference on each scale is greater in magnitude among the Democrats. Let us explore gender differences on the scales more closely, considering response patterns with respect to individual items, the time dimension, and other, nonmotivational data that may be particularly relevant to a given motivational dimension.

THE SELF-ENHANCEMENT DIMENSION: POWER POLITICS

As would be expected, our surveys indicate substantial gender differences in the public-officeholding aspect of the political careers of our respondents. In each year of the study, female respondents were less likely to be government officials, to have ever held elective or appointive office, and to attribute their selection as delegation or delegate-slate members to public officeholding status.

Four explanations are prominently offered for the underrepresentation of women among America's political elite, particularly when defined in officeholding terms. The structural explanation focuses upon the inequality of resources (i.e., differing levels of educational attainment, incomes, employment experience, and so forth) that men and women are able to bring to politics and the relative absence of women in the eligibility pool defined in socioeconomic terms from which leaders emerge and candidates for positions of power are typically drawn. The situational explanation emphasizes the way in which the responsibilities associated with homemaking and motherhood mean that women "do not have the time or energy to pursue political activities [and do not] have the political contacts to get started in the political arena" (Welch, 1978: 372). The socialization explanation focuses upon the way in which females (and males) come to believe that politics is "a man's game." The gatekeeping explanation turns to the way in which voters may tend to be less receptive to female candidates for public office and/or males who dominate positions of political power may use that domination to perpetuate their superordinate political statuses.

Somewhat less frequently explored is a motivational explanation. Put simply, such an explanation posits that female underrepresentation in positions of political power reflects the fact that they are less likely than men to value or aspire to its achievement. Women don't have power—defined in public-officeholding terms—because they don't want power. Obviously such an explanation is not incompatible with the other explanations indicated above. Women's relative lack of interest in seeking power may be a manifestation of any or all of the gender differences suggested by the other explanations. However, for our respondents such lack of interest would most likely be a direct expression of the socialization explanation and the acceptance of traditional understanding of sex roles vis-a-vis the political process (compare, Lee, 1976: 306). After all, the female respondents have already passed the threshhold where structural and situational factors might serve as barriers to political activity; their mere presence in the sample frame signifies that they have already achieved some level of political leadership and there are any number of indications in the present data file that these are persons—the women, as well as the men—who have already made a substantial commitment of time, energy, and monetary resources to politics. Further, there is considerable evidence that once women become candidates for elective office they are as electable as men (Karnig and Walter, 1976; Darcy and Schramm, 1977; Deber, 1982; Hedlund et al., 1979; Welch et al., 1982). A recent study of Georgia party activists finds female respondents less politically ambitious than men and concludes "that the underrepresentation of women in elective office is more the result of a paucity of women candidates than discrimination against them at the polls" (Fowlkes et al., 1979: 779). Finding no female disadvantage at the polling place in 1975 through 1980 races for the legislatures in six midwestern states, Welch and associates (1982: 17) also question the gatekeeping explanation and observe that "the lack of female legislators can be attributed mostly to the paucity of candidates. Our findings do not support the argument that political party elites work against females once they have become candidates."

The California data provide powerful confirmation for the motivational explanation for the relative absence of women in positions of political power. As shown in Table 5.2, male respondents achieve higher self-enhancement motivational ratios in all but one of the sixty-four year-by-year gender comparisons. In only twenty-two of these (including the single counterindicative case and twelve of the comparisons for the small 1968 and 1972 Republican samples) does the male-female difference fail to meet the standard of statistical significance (p < .10) we have set for ourselves. Considering the aggregate sample for each party, all seven items comprising the scale produce motivational ratios indicating that male respondents are significantly more self-enhancing than female respondents. In general, the gender gap found in our motivational data is nowhere clearer and more consistent across parties, across time, and across items than on the self-enhancement dimension.

The findings take on special significance when we consider that the items in this scale and the gender differences obtained for them extend beyond the matter of a desire for public office and political power narrowly conceived and embrace other considerations likely to be valued by those seeking personal ascendancy through political activity. If politically active women are relatively uninterested in the achievement of public office or political power, this lack of interest may be indicative of a general disinclination to use political activity as a vehicle for self-enhancement, including, for example, in terms of social or community prestige.

With respect to changes over time, there has been a marked narrowing of the gender gap over the life of the project. This is particularly evident among the Democrats. Thus, for example, Democratic mean ratios, whether calculated for each year for all items in the scale or only for the four items included in all five survey instruments, show that the male-female difference declines rather precipitously across the years through 1976 and then essentially remains unchanged in 1980. If the problematic 1968 and 1972 Republican samples are overlooked, mean ratios for this party also reveal an overtime reduction in male-female differences in self-enhancement, although those differences remain substantially larger in 1976 and 1980 than for the Democrats.

Further, the data for both parties suggests that the closing of the gender gap on this dimension results from an increasing interest in self-enhancement among female respondents rather than from any clear male trend in the contrary direction. Indeed, the Democratic female mean ratios increase monotonically over time, just as they do among the Republicans if the two years with such small numbers of

TABLE 5.2 The Self-Enhancement Dimension

	1964 M	1964 F	1968 M	1968 F	1972 M	1972 F	1976 M	1976 F	1980 M	1980 F	All Respondents 1964-1980 M	All Respondents 1964-1980 F
Democrats												
Seek elective public office	2.21 *	1.48	2.11 *	1.34	2.24 *	1.85	2.34 *	1.90	2.33 **	2.04	2.24 *	1.85
Seek appointive public office	NA		1.69 *	1.29	1.67 *	1.48	1.75	1.72	1.92	1.88	1.72 **	1.62
Search for power and influence	2.18 *	1.22	2.07	1.60	1.87 *	1.55	NA		2.38 *	2.02	2.04 *	1.64
Make business/professional contacts	1.72 *	1.11	1.46 ***	1.24	1.49 *	1.29	1.72	1.75	1.88	1.80	1.60 **	1.50
Be close to influentials	2.21 *	1.37	1.99 *	1.54	1.96 *	1.73	2.10 ***	1.95	2.21	2.05	2.05 *	1.81
Enhance social prestige	NA		1.88 *	1.48	1.78 *	1.48	1.88 ***	1.73	2.20	2.01	1.88	1.64
Enhance prestige[1]	2.55 **	2.00	2.03	1.93	1.92 *	1.60	2.07	2.04	2.13	1.92	2.08 *	1.81
Mean ratios	2.17	1.44	1.89	1.49	1.85	1.57	1.98	1.85	2.15	1.96	1.94	1.70
Mean ratios/Four common items	2.17	1.49	1.90	1.51	1.90	1.62	2.06	1.91	2.14	1.95	1.99	1.74
Gender difference	0.68		0.39		0.28		0.15		0.19		0.25	

Republican

Seek elective office	2.03 *	1.14	1.60	1.37	2.28 ***	1.33	2.23 *	1.55	2.27 **	1.80	2.11 *	1.57
Seek appointive office	NA		1.31	1.12	1.50	1.00	1.68 **	1.42	1.84 ***	1.61	1.67 **	1.46
Search for power and influence	1.59 **	1.19	1.37	1.25	1.72 **	1.00	NA		2.17 **	1.79	1.78 ***	1.57
Make business/professional contacts	1.56 *	1.05	1.56	1.50	1.50	1.00	1.96 *	1.49	1.90	1.70	1.75	1.50
Be close to influentials	1.80	1.50	1.79	1.62	2.06	1.33	2.13 *	1.72	2.41 *	1.92	2.05	1.74
Enhance social prestige	NA		1.61	1.25	1.82	1.33	2.01 *	1.62	2.18	1.95	2.00	1.71
Enhance prestige[1]	2.03 *	1.44	1.76	1.56	1.75	1.33	2.04 **	1.68	2.18 **	1.78	2.03	1.66
Mean ratios	1.80	1.26	1.57	1.38	1.80	1.19	2.01	1.58	2.14	1.79	1.91	1.60
Mean ratios/Four common items	1.86	1.28	1.68	1.51	1.90	1.25	2.09	1.61	2.19	1.80	1.98	1.62
Gender difference	0.58		0.17		0.65		0.48		0.39		0.36	

NOTE: For this and other tables where data are motivational ratios, significance levels are established by a t-test of the gender differences, where * = p < .01, ** = p < .05, *** = p < .10. Given the mode of calculation, applying tests of significance to differences with respect to mean ratios is not appropriate. The t-test of significance is used throughout in the consideration of motivational ratios.

1. This item is in the series involving reasons for wanting to be a delegation member. Other items are in the series involving reasons for initial involvement in politics.

female respondents are removed from consideration. The female motivational ratios reach their high point in 1980 on six of the seven items for the Democrats and on all seven for the Republicans.

Self-Enhancement and the Feminist Impulse. Needless to say, the increase in self-enhancing predispositions among female respondents—particularly among the Democrats—has occurred simultaneously with the emergence of the contemporary feminist movement. Indeed, that increase may well serve as a measure of the success of the movement and the challenge it presents to traditional understandings of gender roles in the society. The present data indicate that the simultaneity of the two developments is not coincidental and in the following four ways they support the notion that the feminist impulse has contributed to the closing of the self-enhancement gender gap.

First, in 1976 and 1980 respondents were asked if they were members of feminist organizations. The mean ratio on the self-enhancement scale achieved in each year by women claiming such membership is significantly higher than that of nonmembers. (In contrast, among male respondents, membership in feminist organizations is unrelated to self-enhancement.) Second, in 1980 respondents were asked about the extent of their support for the Equal Rights Amendment. Again, feminism measured by this indicator is positively associated with self-enhancement among female, but not male respondents. Third, feminism—as measured by the foregoing two indicators—has clearly had a stronger impact on Democratic than Republican women respondents, and it is among Democratic women that there have been especially precipitous increases in self-enhancement scale scores. The relative imperviousness of the Republican leadership cadre to women with feminist perspectives may well explain interparty differences in the self-enhancing predispositions of female respondents.

Fourth, we have inquired into the age of our respondents. The feminist movement's impact is likely to be strongest among younger women and, indeed, female respondents under 40 years of age prove more likely to belong to feminist organizations and to favor ERA passage than those over 40. As it turns out, interest in self-enhancement comes distinctively into play among the under-40 women in the more recent phases of the present project. Younger male and female respondents in each party consistently achieve higher mean ratios on the self-enhancement scale than the older same-gender respondents throughout the life of project. Additionally, male respondents in each party in each of the two age groups achieve higher mean ratios on self-enhancement than female counterparts at each phase of the project. However, it is among females under 40 that self-enhancement mean ratios increase across decades most precipitously in each party, and it is among the younger group in each party that the gender gap is narrowest.

"Why can't a woman be more like a man?" In terms of self-enhancing predispositions among party activists and leaders, our data suggest that she can. And, further, they suggest that closing the gender gap in this respect is most likely to occur where the feminist impulse is strongest.

THE SOCIALITY DIMENSION: PLEASURE POLITICS

For Eldersveld (1964) the critical distinction in considering the motives underlying political activism is between those which are personal and those which are impersonal in nature. The sociality dimension, as in the case of the self-enhancement dimension, involves a personal-serving explanation of such activism. If the female respondents are relatively uninspired by the possibility that political activity may provide personal fulfillment in power, profit, and prestige (i.e., self-enhancement) terms, are they more likely to be attracted by its social, presumably more pleasureful rewards? The data offer scarce support for such a conclusion. As Table 5.3 shows, there is very little consistency in the findings, either across time or across items. The few gender differences of notable magnitude differ in direction.

Impact of Political Activity on Personal Life. While our female respondents do not appear to be distinctively attracted to political activity by its more personal rewards, defined in sociality or self-enhancement terms, this does not mean that political activity is less personally satisfying for them than it is for their male counterparts. Our 1980 survey instrument probed the matter of the impact of political activism on nine aspects of personal life, asking the respondent to indicate such impact on each aspect in terms of a five-point scale ranging from highly beneficial to highly detrimental. Women in each party are decidedly more likely than men to feel that their involvement in politics is personally beneficial, including in such areas as family life, personal growth and psychological well-being (compare Sapiro, 1982). In seventeen of the eighteen gender comparisons for the two parties' respondents, including the thirteen instances where the gender difference is statistically significant, women are more likely than men to indicate that their activism has a beneficial impact on their private lives.

It is possible that these gender differences reflect the fact that female respondents have spouses who are more understanding and

TABLE 5.3 The Sociality Dimension (Motivational Ratios)

	1964		1968		1972		1976		1980		All Respondents 1964-1980	
	M	F	M	F	M	F	M	F	M	F	M	F
Democrats												
Fun and excitement	2.37 ***	2.03	2.33	2.22	2.30	2.33	2.51	2.49	2.77	2.70	2.41	2.42
Social contacts and friends	1.93 **	1.52	1.81	1.80	2.07	2.08	2.19	2.13	2.29	2.31	2.04	2.09
Enjoy social occasion[1]	2.71 **	2.32	2.07 ***	2.43	1.96	1.98	2.40	2.43	2.22	2.37	2.20	2.20
Mean ratios	2.34	1.96	2.07	2.15	2.11	2.13	2.37	2.35	2.43	2.46	2.22	2.24
Gender difference	0.38		-0.08		-0.02		0.02		-0.03		-0.02	
Republicans												
Fun and excitement	1.94	2.05	1.80 ***	2.44	2.06	1.67	2.34	2.31	2.62	2.61	2.22 ***	2.36
Social contacts and friends	1.76 **	1.67	1.71 ***	2.37	1.83	1.71	1.97	2.08	2.10	2.26	1.90 **	2.09
Enjoy social occasion[1]	2.07	2.04	1.95 **	2.75	2.13	2.50	2.21	2.20	2.47	2.50	2.19	2.30
Mean ratios	1.92	1.92	1.82	2.52	2.01	1.96	2.17	2.20	2.40	2.46	2.10	2.25
Gender difference	0.00		-0.70		0.05		-0.03		-0.06		-0.15	

1. This item is in the series involving reasons for wanting to be a delegation member. Other items are in the series involving reasons for initial involvement in politics.

supportive of their political activity than male respondents (Sapiro, 1982; Mezey, 1978a) and/or that the self-enhancing careers pursued more frequently by the latter entail especially high personal costs (Sapiro, 1982). We will now show that our female respondents are more attracted than male respondents by the impersonal, more public-serving aspects of political activity. It is possible that these entail activities and rewards which are more personally satisfying, even though less tangible than a public office and less seemingly pleasureful than the interpersonal relationships associated with political involvement.

THE PURPOSIVE DIMENSIONS: ISSUE POLITICS

Female respondents prove notably more purposive in their political motivations than their male counterparts. Of the thirty-two gender differences in the year-by-year comparisons shown in Table 5.4, only nine do not conform to the general pattern and four of these (including the two where the counterindicative differences achieve statistical significance) appear in the problematic 1968 and 1972 Republican samples. Women are particularly more likely than men to have aspired to be convention delegates in order to participate in the process of considering policy issues and defining the programmatic posture of their party. Their greater purposiveness is reflected in the various mean ratios, with the exception again involving the 1972 Republicans. Further, there are no clear indications of changes over time in gender differences with respect to this scale or in the degree of purposiveness of either gender in either party.

Issues and Ideology. If female activists in both parties tend to be more purposive in their political motivations and more issue-oriented than their male counterparts, do they bring correspondingly different ideologies to politics and want different policy responses to the issues of the day? Such questions may bear upon the consequences of enlarging the role of women in political decision-making arenas, although Hershey's (1980: 196) admonition is indisputably valid: "It is risky . . . to try to predict the characteristics, policy preferences, and effect of future women political leaders by making a linear extrapolation from the findings of current studies. . . . We might expect to find different distributions of attitudes and behavior among women in politics when political leadership is no longer an unusual role for women." More clearly, a consideration of such questions may disclose a possible source of tension within the activist stratum of one or both parties during the period covered, and may illuminate a possible source of interparty ideological conflict.

The relatively low levels of support among the nation's women for Ronald Reagan as candidate and as president has, of course, attracted

TABLE 5.4　The Purposive Dimension (Motivational Ratios)

	1964 M	1964 F	1968 M	1968 F	1972 M	1972 F	1976 M	1976 F	1980 M	1980 F	All Respondents 1964-1980 M	F
Democrats												
Concern for issues	3.85	3.87	3.89 **	3.96	3.74 *	3.84	3.81	3.82	3.84	3.90	3.81 ***	3.85
Desire change in society	NA		NA		3.49 **	3.70	3.59	3.52	3.69	3.63	3.61	3.63
Indignation over state of affairs	NA		3.22 ***	3.49	3.29 *	3.53	3.26	3.20	3.29	3.39	3.26 **	3.41
Develop party program[1]	3.25 **	3.57	3.26 **	3.52	3.36 ***	3.47	3.32 **	3.48	3.21 *	3.53	3.30 *	3.49
Mean ratios	3.55	3.72	3.46	3.66	3.50	3.64	3.50	3.51	3.51	3.61	3.50	3.60
Mean ratios/Two common items	3.55	3.72	3.58	3.74	3.55	3.66	3.56	3.65	3.52	3.71	3.56	3.67
Gender difference	-0.17		-0.16		-0.11		-0.09		-0.19		-0.11	
Republicans												
Concern for issues	3.83	3.81	3.94	3.80	4.00 **	3.60	3.86	3.85	3.71 ***	3.83	3.83	3.82
Desire change in society	NA		NA		3.42 **	2.29	3.46	3.40	3.34 ***	3.55	3.40	3.41
Indignation over state of affairs	NA		3.33	3.78	3.71 ***	3.00	3.45 ***	3.66	3.27 ***	3.49	3.38 **	3.58
Develop party program[1]	3.36 ***	3.62	2.82 **	3.64	3.28	3.33	3.05 *	3.63	2.97 *	3.39	3.12 *	3.54
Mean ratios	3.60	3.72	3.36	3.74	3.60	3.05	3.46	3.64	3.32	3.56	3.43	3.59
Mean ratios/Two common items	3.60	3.72	3.38	3.72	3.64	3.46	3.46	3.74	3.34	3.61	3.48	3.68
Gender difference	-0.12		-0.34		0.18		-0.28		-0.27		-0.20	

1. This item is in the series involving reasons for wanting to be a delegation member. Other items are in the series involving reasons for initial involvement in politics.

considerable attention among political practitioners, journalists, and scholars alike. (See, for example, Blydenburg and Sigel, 1983; Erie, 1983b; Frankovic, 1982; Lake, 1982.) The phenomenon is particularly notable because public opinion research has generally found that America's men and women are essentially similar in their views on policy issues and in ideology. As Perkins and Fowlkes (1980: 146) note: "Existing studies have found few differences between the sexes in opinions that could be ordered on the modern liberal-conservative dimension." On the other hand, scholars approaching the matter from a comparative perspective have generally found that women are politically more conservative than men (Almond and Verba, 1965: 325; Lipset, 1960: 221; Goot and Reid, 1975: 21-25). As Baxter and Lansing (1980: 146) conclude: "Social science has generally described women as being more conservative than men in their choice of candidates and political parties." Still other researchers—including those seeking to illuminate the Reagan gender gap—have focused on the relationship between gender and opinions on particular sorts of issues. Thus, for example, women have been variously characterized as more "pacifist-minded," more "humanitarian," and more "moralistic" than men.

Of course, patterns of gender differences at the public level may be no guide to patterns at the activist level. Other studies of delegates suggest a general pattern of similarity in the ideologies of the sexes—except perhaps in terms of opinions on military policy (Kirkpatrick, 1976: 439-442; Jennings and Thomas, 1968: 488-489; Jennings and Farah, 1981: 473-474). However, the greater purposiveness of the female respondents studied here signals the possibility of a pattern of *dis*similarity, one in which men and women will not differ in parallel ways in each party but rather in which the two parties will cast mirror images of each other in terms of the gender-ideology relationship, with women less centrist in each, or more to the left among Democrats and more to the right among Republicans.

Out data indicate that the latter is the case. Respondents have been asked in each year of the study to place themselves along a five-point liberal-conservative continuum. In the aggregate, Democratic women are significantly more liberal and Republican women significantly more conservative than their male copartisans, although gender differences in no way approach in magnitude interparty differences in ideological self-identification. The same pattern emerges in each of the five years for the Democrats and for all but the problematic 1968 and 1972 samples for the Republicans.

A series of four-point Likert-type issue items included on each year's questionnaire permits us to probe more deeply into the matter of ideology. Thirty-four different items appeared over the life of the project, most being included in more than a single year's question-naire. Responses to each item prove to be significantly associated with ideological self-identification and with party, confirming the judgment made on substantive grounds that they serve individually and in the aggregate as liberal-conservative measures. Again, female respondents tend to be less centrist than men and to accentuate the already substantial and unrelenting interparty difference found among the latter. Among aggregated partisans, Democratic women are more liberal on twenty-seven of the thirty-four issues, and Republican women are more conservative than male copartisans on the equivalent number. The mirror-image pattern holds for the major-ity of issue questions asked in each year, and for the great majority of comparisons in which gender differences achieve statistical significance. Of the 127 year-by-year comparisons on individual issue items over the life of the project, Democratic women are more liberal in 104 and Republican women more conservative in 85 than their respective male counterparts. Positions on a number of specific issues having broad substantive range illustrate the general pattern in a marked and rather consistent manner over time, with Democratic women being relatively more liberal and Republican women more conservative on such matters as universal federal health insurance, cracking down on welfare recipients, combatting domestic com-munism, government regulation of business, and measures to ensure racial equality.

There are exceptions to the general pattern. On some matters Republican women join Democratic women in being more liberal than their male counterparts. These do not include the two items included in the surveys most central to the feminist agenda: Republican women, in contrast to Democratic women, are more opposed to the ERA and to abortion rights than their male counterparts. If male party activists turn to their female copartisans for a better understanding of the wants of women with respect to issues most distinctively affecting them, they are likely to turn in opposite directions and to receive substantially different messages. The issues on which both Republican and Democratic women are relatively liberal do not reveal the sorts of broad dispositional gender differences suggested elsewhere. For example, while Republican women are somewhat more favorable to anti-poverty programs, on other measures of humanitarianism or wel-farism they differ from Democratic women in being more conserva-tive than male copartisans. Both Democratic and Republican women are significantly more likely than their male copartisans to oppose the development of nuclear power as an energy source, as is apparently the case at the general public level (Kay, 1983). However, this opposi-tion does not seem to reflect a general female disposition toward either environmentalism or pacifism which some students of the subject have linked to gender differences on nuclear energy (Nelkin, 1981; Merchant, 1980). In neither party do significant or consistent gender differences emerge regarding pollution control or wilderness preservation. While women in both parties are more favorable to American withdrawal from overseas commitments and to normalizing relations with the People's Republic of China, on other foreign policy/national security issues Republican women prove to be more divergent from the Democratic posture, especially that of Democratic women, than Republican men; for example, they are more favorable toward enhancing the nation's military preparedness, ABM deployment, and withdrawal from the United Nations.

Democratic women join Republican women in being more conservative than their male copartisans on some issues, notably those involving antipornography, antimarijuana, and anticriminal measures. Here such conservatism is suggestive of the moralist posture generally ascribed to them (Erikson, Luttbeg and Tedin, 1980: 186-87; Gruberg, 1968: Ch. 1).

In any event, notwithstanding exceptions with respect to specific issues, the pattern is quite clear: Intraparty ideological differences are gender-related; while there are cross-sex differences within parties, they pale to insignificance when compared to cross-party differences; and interparty differences are accentuated by our women respondents, attenuated by the men.

THE PERSONALIST DIMENSION: CANDIDATE POLITICS

The early survey-based voting and political socialization studies noted the greater propensity of females than males to personalize politics, that is, to weigh more heavily the candidates and their personalities in the equation of factors leading to an election-day decision (Campbell et al., 1954: 155; Campbell et al., 1960: 492; Greenstein, 1965: 107-108; Hess and Torney, 1967: 203-209). As Shabad and Anderson observe (1979: 18): one of the received understandings "concerning women's political orientations and behavior . . . is that [they] tend to personalize politics and politicians. Women, it is said, are more likely than men to be interested in a candidate's personal attributes, style, character, looks, and family background—and to evaluate a candidate on the basis of such personal qualities rather than on issue positions."

The motivational ratios presented in Table 5.5 provide support at the leadership level for the notion that females tend to be more personalist than males—although the gender differences are, as in the case of the 1952 through 1975 voter data reported by Shabad and

TABLE 5.5 The Personalist Dimension (Motivational Ratios)

	1964			1968			1972			1976			1980			All Respondents 1964-1980		
	M		F	M		F	M		F	M		F	M		F	M		F
Democrats																		
Attraction of a particular leader	2.81	*	2.54	2.72		2.91	2.74	**	2.96	2.88		3.03	2.64		2.79	2.76	*	2.92
Influence of friend(s)	2.10		2.04	1.96		2.11	1.99		1.98	2.06		2.16	1.90		1.83	2.00		2.02
Friendship with candidate		NA		2.13		1.89	2.01	**	1.81	1.65	**	1.86	1.78		1.85	2.06	*	1.82
Active family		NA			NA			NA			NA			NA		1.69	**	1.86
To select candidates[1]	3.35	*	3.80	3.68	***	3.83	3.72		3.79	3.69	*	3.77	3.69		3.69	3.65	*	3.77
Mean ratios	2.75		2.79	2.62		2.68	2.62		2.38	2.57		2.70	2.50		2.54	2.43		2.48
Mean ratios/Three common items	2.75		2.79	2.79		2.95	2.82		2.91	2.88		2.99	2.74		2.77	2.80		2.90
Gender difference	-0.044			-0.16			-0.09			-0.11			-0.03			-0.10		
Republicans																		
Attraction of a particular leader	2.24	***	2.65	2.28		2.00	2.50	*	4.00	2.65	*	3.21	2.86		3.11	2.51	*	3.08
Influence of friend(s)	1.97		2.14	2.00		2.00	1.72		2.17	1.94	***	2.19	1.95		1.87	1.95		2.08
Friendship with candidate		NA		2.14		1.75	2.10		2.50	1.49		1.93	1.44	*	1.81	2.13		2.12
Active family		NA			NA			NA			NA			NA		1.47	*	1.89
To select candidates[1]	3.72		3.82	3.74		4.00	3.53		3.22	3.80		3.89	3.66	***	3.85	3.72	**	3.85
Mean ratios	2.64		2.87	2.54		2.44	2.46		2.97	2.47		2.80	2.48		2.66	2.36		2.60
Mean ratios/Three common items	2.64		2.87	2.67		2.67	2.58		3.13	2.80		3.10	2.82		2.94	2.73		3.00
Gender difference	-0.23			0.00			-0.55			-0.30			-0.12			-0.27		

1. This item is in the series involving reasons for wanting to be a delegation member. Other items are in the series involving reasons for initial involvement in politics.

Anderson, modest, and not consistent across time or items. Of the thirty-eight gender differences in the year-by-year comparison of responses to individual scale items, only ten are counterindicative and these include only one of the twelve instances where those differences achieve statistical significance. Women achieve higher motivational ratios than men in seventeen of the twenty comparisons involving the two items most directly suggestive of candidate orientation, with seven of these differences achieving significance. The gender differences for each party's aggregated respondents on these two items—measuring the extent to which the attraction of particular political leaders inspired involvement and the extent to which the respondent wished to be a convention delegate in order to help select the party's national candidates—all reach statistically significant magnitudes.

The relatively low female motivational ratios on the one discordant item in the scale—regarding the importance of friendship with a candidate in initiating political involvement—may well reflect upon the way political women are located on the periphery of power conceived in office-holding terms. Indeed, factor analysis shows that this item loads quite heavily on the self-enhancement dimension, more so than any other item not included in that scale. On the other hand, an item in the personalist scale not reflecting candidate orientation where women achieve markedly higher motivational ratios than men may have its own, independent import. The fact that women in each party are substantially more likely than their male counterparts to attribute their entry into politics to the effects of having a politically active family is suggestive of the sort of compensatory background characteristic which may assist women in overcoming the traditional sex role prescriptions by which politics is considered a male domain.

THE ALLEGIANCE DIMENSION: PARTY POLITICS

The final dimension to which we turn is particularly interesting because it so heavily implicates the respondent's psychological attachment to party. Indeed, scale scores on this dimension are highly associated with a number of other measures of party attachment, loyalty, and anchorage included in our survey instruments. The fact that the factor-analytic solution emerging from our data reveals that this dimension also includes an item on sense of community obligation as precipitating political activism suggests that party loyalty for these respondents may be part of a larger sense of fidelity to one's attachments.

As is true of the two other public-serving dimensions considered here, this component of the field of motivational forces underlying political activity is more important for our female than our male

TABLE 5.6 The Allegiance Dimension (Motivational Ratios)

	1964 M	1964 F	1968 M	1968 F	1972 M	1972 F	1976 M	1976 F	1980 M	1980 F	All Respondents 1964-1980 M	All Respondents 1964-1980 F
Democrats												
Party loyalty	3.04	3.20	*** 2.50	2.79	*** 2.41	2.50	** 2.63	2.74	2.96	2.92	2.61	2.68
Community obligation	3.52	3.56	3.38	3.37	3.12	3.24	3.23	3.40	3.44	3.46	3.29	3.33
To demonstrate loyalty to party membership[1]	2.68	2.74	*** 1.77	2.07	1.72	1.73	* 1.77	2.14	** 1.86	2.20	*** 1.89	1.98
Mean ratios	3.08	3.17	2.55	2.74	2.42	2.49	2.54	2.76	2.75	2.86	2.60	2.66
Gender difference	−0.09		−0.10		−0.07		−0.22		−0.09		−0.06	
Republicans												
Party loyalty	* 2.59	3.41	*** 2.87	3.50	2.79	3.11	* 2.82	3.30	* 2.65	3.08	* 2.71	3.25
Community obligation	3.55	3.71	3.53	3.40	3.16	3.43	3.42 3	3.57	3.43	3.48	3.47	3.55
To demonstrate loyalty to party membership[1]	** 2.12	2.65	** 2.33	3.40	2.27	2.67	* 2.05	2.74	* 2.08	2.78	* 2.12	2.77
Mean ratios	2.75	3.26	2.91	3.43	2.74	3.07	2.76	3.20	2.74	3.11	2.77	3.19
Gender difference	−0.51		−0.52		−0.33		−0.44		−0.39		−0.42	

1. This item is in the series involving reasons for wanting to be a delegation member. Other items are in the series involving reasons for initial involvement in politics.

respondents. The gender difference is reflected in the mean ratios shown in Table 5.6 for each year for each party, and in the motivational ratios achieved for each party's aggregated sample on each of the three items in the scale. Of the thirty year-by-year individual item comparisons, women achieve higher motivational ratios than men in twenty-seven, including all fourteen instances where the differences are statistically significant.[2]

There are at least four general implications to be drawn from the pattern of responses with respect to the allegiance dimension. First, it suggests the way traditional gender role differences may find expression in the arena of political party activism. We have seen that male activists tend to be more self-enhancing than their female counterparts. In this sense they are more likely to pursue careers that involve specialization in the instrumental functions of political parties, functions related to the external world. In contrast, the relatively high scores on the allegiance dimension achieved by female respondents suggest that they specialize in the party's expressive functions or those related to its internal affairs and maintenance. Such a conclusion can also be drawn from other evidence in the present data set regarding party anchorage; for example, in most years for each party, female respondents were more likely than their male counterparts to hold party office, to have never supported a candidate of the other party, and to have been selected as delegation slate members because of the party office they hold, their loyal support of current party leadership, and the time and energy they have devoted to their party or its candidates.[3] In many ways the political role differences suggested by these data are comparable to those associated with traditional role differences in the family, with the males pursuing careers in the outside world and females relegated to, or relegating themselves to, more supportive careers within the organizational unit (compare Costantini and Craik, 1972; Farah, 1976; Fowlkes et al., 1979).

Second, male-female differences on the allegiance scale are markedly greater among the Republicans than the Democrats, with this wider gender gap due to the higher scores achieved by Republican women than Democratic women. In this sense, traditional gender role patterns are more deeply etched in the Republican party's leadership cadre than in that of the Democratic party (compare Jennings and Thomas, 1969: 483-484). As we have seen, the same conclusion may be drawn with respect to self-enhancement, where the relatively low scores of Republican women tend to be responsible for the greater magnitude of the gender gap on this motivational dimension among Republican respondents.

Third, there is no clear over time trend in gender differences in either party with respect to the allegiance dimension. As women acti-

vists become more impelled by an interest, traditionally associated
with male activists, in using politics as a vehicle for personal ascendancy, it might be assumed that they will retreat from the responsibilities of organizational maintenance in which they have tended to
specialize. Fowlkes et al. (1979: 779) put the deleterious effect on
parties as organizations, which might follow from increasing female interest in the achievement of personal power this way: "As women
adopt less traditional gender roles and become less responsible for performing their traditional party roles, and if men cannot be encouraged
to do the same, the party organization, which is already weak because
of other reasons, may become weaker." Our data do not indicate that
men have been specially persuaded over the life of the project to pursue a commitment to party. Nor, however, do they indicate a special
decline in the willingness of female activists to perform "their traditional party roles."

Fourth, the observed differences with respect to the allegiance
dimension are inconsistent with the conventional observation that
female activists bring a distinctively "amateur" perspective to party
politics. The relatively low scores of female respondents on the self-
enhancement scale and their greater purposiveness—combined with
the generally more extremist caste of their ideological profiles—are,
indeed, suggestive of amateurism (compare Lynn and Flora, 1977:
140; Schramm, 1981: 54). However, the question of party loyalty goes
more directly to the conceptual core of the amateur-professional
distinction, and here the findings—not only from the items comprising the allegiance scale but also from the other measures of party
loyalty/party anchorage included in our questionnaires—suggest that
female activists are less likely to be amateurs than their male copartisans.

Of course, the notion of amateur is a complex one. Different
students of the subject have emphasized different conceptual ingre-
dients while others have attempted to illuminate its multidimension-
ality (e.g., Hofstetter, 1971; Hofstetter, 1973; Soule and Clarke,
1970). Our 1976 and 1980 questionnaires included a series of items
adapted from previous studies of the amateur-professional distinction
and measuring attitudinal dimemsions associated with that distinction
beyond party loyalty. Here we find that female respondents in both
parties more readily embrace at least one component of the amateur
style than men in that they seem less comfortable with "brokerage"
and victory-oriented politics and more supportive of the "politics-of-
principle." (E.g., they are significantly more likely than male
respondents to agree with the proposition that "a candidate should
not compromise basic values in order to win.") For women, fidelity to
party may come into conflict with fidelity to principle in the everyday

life of politics, but the former may forestall an amateur response to such a conflict, namely a retreat from organizational commitment. For men, on the other hand, when faced with frustration with respect to the self-enhancement (rather than programmatic) goals most characteristic of them, the relative absence of strong party loyalty in their attitudinal profile may make such an amateur response more likely. In any event, the present data suggest the inadequacy of the amateur-professional distinction with respect to unravelling the behavioral consequences of male-female motivational differences.

CONCLUSION

The men and women party activists surveyed over the course of the present project differ notably in the reasons underlying their political involvement. Such differences emerge across time, across specific indicators (i.e., individual items) and across parties with respect to four of the five motivational dimensions into which relevant responses have been organized. Female respondents prove more likely than their male copartisans to be impelled by public-serving considerations—more purposive, allegiant and personalist in the motivational basis of their activism—and less likely to be attracted by the opportunities afforded by politics for personal self-enhancement.

What activists want from politics no doubt affects what they get, and an interest in politics as a vehicle for self-enhancement is likely to be a necessary, although certainly not sufficient motivational base from which to pursue an ascendant political career defined in office-holding or related terms. As an explanation for the underrepresentation of women in positions of political power, the relatively low scores achieved by female respondents on the self-enhancement scale no doubt implicate, to one extent or another, the various non-motivational explanations—less proximate and more remote in character than the motivational explanation—for that underrepresentation. In particular, these low scores may reflect gender differences in political socialization and the acceptance of conventional notions stemming from those differences as to what are appropriate and inappropriate undertakings for women.

While the present data may contribute to our understanding of sexual inequality in terms of political power conventionally understood, they also suggest that a preoccupation with this component of political life at the activist level may lead to an undervaluation of the distinctive contribution women make thereto. The success of a political party is understandably often measured by the extent to which its representatives successfully venture into the external world of inter-party competition for public office. Male activists may indeed tend to specialize in this form of political activity. From a system perspective, however, political parties—like other forms of social organization—require internally as well or externally oriented activities. Our data suggest that it is with respect to the internal needs of the party and to organizational maintenance—conceived both in terms of a party's housekeeping requirements and its need to maintain programmatic integrity—that women tend to specialize.

This sort of gender specialization in party functions fits quite nicely with traditional understandings of gender role differences with respect to the family unit. These understandings have not gone unchallenged. And we make no claim here that the distribution of functions within parties needs to be or should be gender-related. Indeed, we have seen how the gender gap with respect to the self-enhancement dimension has been sharply narrowing over the life of the present study, an apparent manifestation of the feminist challenge to traditional understandings.

We find no evidence that the increase in self-enhancing dispositions among female respondents has been accompanied by a corresponding dilution of their distinctively strong profiles with respect to issue-orientation and party loyalty. However, there is bound to be a lag between changes in motivation and change in patterns of achievement. If and when women reach parity with men in public officeholding and other political power terms, one unintended consequence may well be the further debilitation of political parties as organizations.

NOTES

1. There the analysis is based on the full complement of over 3000 respondents who have participated in the California party leaders project over its history—the delegation component of the date file considered here, plus supplementary samples of party and elected officials not in the delegation component who were included in the 1964, 1968, and 1976 samples. The supplementary samples are excluded from the present study to enhance the overtime comparability of the data we present. While the factor loadings for the sample subset considered here are slightly different from those obtained when using the full data file, the same factor solution emerges in that the item content and the order of the factors are no different, and the Eigenvalues and variance explained by each factor are virtually identical.

2. Gender differences in terms of sense of allegiance may be reflected at the general public level in the findings that women are more likely than men to identify with a political party (Pierson, 1983).

3. One area where female respondents apparently have made a smaller investment and are less deeply anchored in their party than men involves financial contributions. The reported money contributions to their party and its candidates in the most recent midterm and presidential election year is consistently and significantly smaller. Additionally, they are consistently and significantly less likely than male copartisans to attribute selection as a delegate or delegate-candidate to their status as major financial contributors.

III

FEMALE OFFICIALS IN
STATE AND LOCAL GOVERNMENTS

The chapters in this section discuss obstacles to women's pursuit of public office and their behavior once in office.

In their "Women as Legislative Candidates in Six States," Janet Clark, R. Darcy, Susan Welch, and Margery Ambrosius look at difficulties faced by female candidates in legislative races in New Mexico, Oklahoma, Nebraska, Iowa, Missouri, and Wyoming. They consider the effects on female candidacies of four factors: voter hostility, the targeting of women to difficult races, single- versus multimember districts, and partisan versus nonpartisan races.

Carol Mueller, in her "Women's Organizational Strategies in State Legislatures," focuses on women in eighteen state legislatures nationwide. She differentiates the contexts in which these women operate according to (1) the perception of their male colleagues, (2) the strength of partisanship, and (3) divisions from previous controversies such as ERA and abortion. She claims that in response to these contexts, female state legislators have established both informal and formal social networks, ad hoc coalitions, and caucuses.

The influence of female state legislators on their male colleagues is the subject of David B. Hill's "Women State Senators as Cue-Givers: ERA Roll-Call Voting, 1972-1979." He examines the thirty-one states with roll call votes on ERA ratification and female senators present for these votes between 1972 and 1979. He considers the evidence for two hypotheses: (1) female legislators served as one important cue in the male vote and (2) women's influence increased with their seniority and occupational status.

Finally, Beverly B. Cook looks at what helps and hinders women's access to local and state judicial posts across the nation. In her "Women on the State Bench: Correlates of Access," she reviews the literature on female judges with reference to factors such as appointment versus election, the hierarchical court structure, partisan versus professional control of nominations, party strength and competition, and interest group power.

6

WOMEN AS LEGISLATIVE CANDIDATES IN SIX STATES

Janet Clark
R. Darcy
Susan Welch
Margery Ambrosius

When the characteristics of American political leaders are examined, it quickly becomes clear that the more important the role, the more visible the office, the more influential the position, the less likely a woman is to be found in it. No woman has been a president or vice-president. Only one woman has ever served on the Supreme Court and she has only just been appointed. Fewer women have served in the U.S. Senate than have served in the U.S. House and fewer women have served in the Congress than have served in the state legislatures. Yet very few of the state legislators have ever been women and most of these have only been elected in the past few years. Even today only fourteen percent of the nation's state legislators are women.

The state legislatures are key entry points to higher elective office. They are a major source of congressional and gubernatorial candidates, which in turn provide a major source of successful U.S. senatorial candidates. Presidential and vice-presidential candidates are typically drawn from these last groups (see Jacobson and Kernell, 1981; Kiewiet, 1982). Thus, if women state legislative candidates face barriers not encountered by men, the consequences will reach far beyond the state legislatures themselves. Such obstacles will effectively limit the recruitment of female candidates for higher offices beyond whatever impediments are encountered when running for those higher offices. Hence, barriers to women entering into the state legislature are of concern both to those interested in bringing women into that

Authors' Note: We appreciate the assistance of C.J. Robinson, Timothy Bledsoe, Judy Clay, Margaret Brewer, and Cal Clark in preparing the data for analysis.

level of government and those puzzled by the paucity of women in higher office.

The present analysis focuses on two possible difficulties faced by women trying to enter state legislatures: voter hostility and the targeting of female candidates to more difficult races. In addition, we will examine two aspects of the electoral environment, the effects of single-member districts versus multimember districts and partisan versus nonpartisan races.

Data were gathered on state legislative races in six contiguous states: New Mexico, Oklahoma, Nebraska, Iowa, Missouri, and Wyoming. These states include generally Republican and generally Democratic states, states that have lower than average female representation in their legislatures, and states that have higher than average female representation. Some of the states include major metropolitan areas and others are largely rural. One state (Wyoming) elects its legislature from multimember districts and another (Nebraska) is nonpartisan in its legislative races. While no group of six states can be considered typical of all fifty states, this group represents the range of political circumstances thought relevant to the chances of a woman being nominated and elected into the legislature.

For New Mexico, Oklahoma, and Wyoming, data were obtained for every candidate declaring for the lower house of the legislature from 1968 to 1980. For Nebraska, information was gathered for 1970 to 1980 on all candidates declaring for that state's unicameral legislature. In the case of Missouri and Iowa the procedure was somewhat different. Information was gathered in these states on all candidates declaring in districts having female candidates in the years 1970 to 1980. In addition, a random sample of districts having only male candidates was gathered and information on all candidates in the sampled districts was coded. The unit of analysis, in all instances then, is the candidate and all candidates in a district are included, including candidates facing no opposition and candidates who filed but were not nominated after losing the primary. In all, information on 6339 candidates was obtained.

VOTER HOSTILITY AND POLITICAL CULTURE

The small number of female public officials in this country, even two generations after the granting of suffrage, has often been attributed to voter reluctance to support female candidates. This seems like a plausible explanation given the sexist attitudes once prevalent. In Gallup surveys since 1958, for example, important segments of the electorate report refusing to vote for qualified female candidates of their own party for president or for Congress (see Ferree, 1974). The best evidence, however, for the hostility of the electorate to female candidates is the very scarcity of female elected officials. This scarcity attracted attention to the few who seriously did run. In 1962 Stokes and Miller wrote, "One of the best ways for a Representative to be known is to be a Congresswoman. . . . The fact of being a woman may make a candidate more visible, but a woman may have to be unusually visible (as a Congressman's widow, say) before she can be elected to the House, or even become a serious candidate" (Stokes and Miller, 1966: 207). Few women challenged these arguments with their candidacies.

Yet when political scientists began systematically examining the electoral consequences of female candidacies in the 1970's, little evidence to support the idea of voter hostility could be identified. Karnig and Walter (1976), in a nationwide study of female candidates to city councils, found little voter discrimination against them. Darcy and Schramm's (1977) study of women and men major party candidates for Congress similarly found no differences in voter reaction to women and men candidates in equivalent electoral situations. Other studies yielded similar results (see Welch et al., 1982). Adams (1975) and Eckstrand and Eckert (1981) presented experimental evidence that university students did not discriminate against female candidates and Hedlund and associates (1979) found that when survey respondents were asked about their reactions to *both* women and men candidates about as many would be hostile to a male candidate as to a female candidate. Jeanne Kirkpatrick (1974) and Irene Diamond (1977) reported that female legislators indicated little negative voter reaction to their gender. These studies all point to a lack of voter discrimination against female candidates.

However, this research fails to consider two more general patterns that affect women's electoral success. First, our political system is such that there is little mobility from the local level of government, which is often nonpartisan in character, to state and national officeholding where partisan politics is typical. While it is true that women are better represented at the local levels than they are elsewhere, better representation at local levels will not necessarily be a prelude to officeholding elsewhere. Next, while it is now clear that female candidates who receive their party's nomination for Congress do as well as similar male candidates (see Bernstein, 1982), few women get those nominations. As successful new congressional candidates are most likely to come from the state legislatures, a lack of female Congressional candidates can be traced to electoral difficulties at the state legislative level. Therefore, it is necessary to consider both electoral mechanisms and potential voter hostility in an analysis of female candidacies. It is also possible that recent studies found little voter bias because voters have, since the mid-1970's, become more familiar with changing gender roles and female politicians. Hence, it is important to compare reactions of voters to new female candidates over time. Whatever voter hostility that may have existed is expected to decrease over time.

One way to analyze potential voter hostility toward female candidates is with respect to a state's political culture. In the six states examined here, female candidates are expected to do less well in Oklahoma, New Mexico, and Missouri where traditionalistic political cultures stress the maintenance of dominant political, economic, and social elites (see Elazar, 1966). Under these conditons female candidates will be seen as challenging the existing order (see Diamond, 1977: 23). Further, these states share many traditions with the South and are strongly Democratic in their politics, two additional factors associated with few women being elected to public office (Werner, 1968; Rule, 1981).

Iowa should be different. By and large it is a Republican state, in the North, possessing a moralistic political culture. This moralistic political culture, stressing the advancement of the public good and interest, is characterized by honesty, selflessness, and amateur participation in politics (Elazar, 1966). Diamond found moralistic states to have the greatest proportion of women legislators (Diamond, 1977).

Female candidates were not expected to do well in Nebraska. Nebraska's individualistic political culture, stressing as it does using politics for the self-advancement and rewards it brings will attract formidable male candidates for the legislature (Diamond, 1977: 23). Further, the nonpartisan aspect of the elections, by removing party labels, will make other characteristics such as gender more salient. Any voter hostility toward female candidates is most likely to manifest itself under these conditions. Wyoming's multimember electoral system creates unique conditions requiring separate analysis (see below).

In order to determine the effects of political culture on voters, two other factors need to be controlled. A number of studies show that two major factors influencing voting in legislative races are party and incumbency. In some states Democratic candidates generally do better than Republicans and in other states it is the other way around. In all states incumbents are in a generally strong position (see Erikson, 1971). Hence party and incumbency need to be controlled before the performance of male and female candidates can be meaningfully compared.

Table 6.1 presents the average vote for new male and female candidates (incumbents are excluded) in a variety of general election situations for the five states being examined. To gauge the relative performance of male and female candidates in equivalent situations, only cases where the candidate's opponent was male are included. Incumbents are excluded as the concern here is with those just entering the electoral system. The data are divided into two periods. The difference between the similar male and female candidates was calculated, multiplied by the number of female candidates involved, summed, and then averaged by dividing by the number of female candidates. As differences were weighted by the number of female candidates, a positive average difference indicates an overall disadvantage and a negative average difference indicates an advantage for the typical female candidate.

There is a clear difference in the performance of female candidates in the earlier and later periods. In every state their overall relative performance improved. But even in the earlier period the difference between similar male and female candidates averaged only about 2.5 percent (to the disadvantage of the women). After 1974 the difference (still to their disadvantage) was reduced to about one third of one percent. In the early period there was little difference between male and female candidates in races against incumbents where, in any case, neither men nor women had a chance for victory. On the other hand, in contests for open seats in the early period female candidates *were* disadvantaged. As open seats provided the most likely access to the legislature, voter reaction to female candidates did play a role in reducing female representation. After 1976, however, women competed equally with men in both kinds of races. While some differences persist, today there is very little difference in the voters' reaction to similarly situated candidates of both sexes.

Turning to particular states, expected patterns were not found in all cases. The most disadvantaged female candidates were found in Nebraska, with the pattern of greater male votes only slightly diminished over time. In the cases of New Mexico, Oklahoma, and Missouri, differences did exist to the disadvantage of women in the earlier period but after 1974 these had largely disappeared or even turned to their net advantage. Political culture, Democratic dominance, and southern traditions do not appear to be producing voter hostility toward female candidates. However, as expected in Iowa, they performed relatively well. In the earlier period their average disadvantage was two percent, the smallest of the states

TABLE 6.1 New Male and Female Candidates in Contested General Elections Against Male Opponents[*]

State, Party, and Type of Election	Early Period Men (n)	Women (n)	Later Period Men (n)	Women (n)
NEW MEXICO	(1968-1974)		(1976-1980)	
Republican				
Against an incumbent	38.1 (84)	40.6 (13)	39.0 (43)	42.5 (12)
Open seat	47.4 (49)	38.7 (9)	47.9 (25)	48.8 (4)
Democratic				
Against an incumbent	43.7 (47)	43.6 (4)	38.3 (35)	33.5 (4)
Open seat	52.7 (55)	43.3 (5)	51.9 (26)	46.9 (2)
Mean difference:	+3.0%		−1.0%	
NEBRASKA	(1970-1974)		(1976-1980)	
Independent				
Against an incumbent	40.0 (36)	36.7 (4)	42.7 (25)	34.6 (7)
Open seat	50.0 (42)	41.8 (3)	50.0 (42)	51.0 (4)
Mean difference	+5.4%		+4.7%	
IOWA	(1970-1974)		(1976-1980)	
Republican				
Against an incumbent	39.0 (10)	36.0 (6)	40.7 (41)	39.7 (14)
Open seat	46.2 (28)	48.5 (10)	47.0 (14)	50.5 (7)
Democratic				
Against an incumbent	42.8 (35)	43.0 (17)	39.6 (18)	35.5 (8)
Open seat	53.3 (27)	44.7 (12)	51.7 (16)	54.0 (6)
Mean difference	+2.1%		+0.24%	
MISSOURI	(1970-1974)		(1976-1980)	
Republican				
Against an incumbent	31.4 (33)	31.1 (6)	29.5 (51)	30.7 (25)
Open seat	51.5 (19)	39.8 (5)	46.1 (26)	27.3 (5)
Democratic				
Against an incumbent	43.6 (13)	41.8 (5)	40.3 (25)	36.3 (5)
Open seat	48.9 (20)	49.5 (6)	52.2 (25)	58.6 (7)
Mean difference	+2.9%		+0.93%	
OKLAHOMA	(1968-1974)		(1976-1988)	
Republican				
Against an incumbent	38.1 (73)	33.5 (6)	37.5 (38)	46.2 (4)
Open seat	44.2 (37)	52.1 (5)	43.4 (22)	44.5 (6)
Democratic				
Against an incumbent	41.4 (50)	43.1 (4)	34.1 (18)	36.8 (6)
Open seat	56.2 (38)	48.3 (6)	55.7 (23)	55.3 (7)
Mean difference	+1.3%		−1.5%	
Mean difference for all states	+2.5%		+0.2%	
Mean difference against incumbents	+0.6%		+0.2%	
Mean difference in open seats	+4.8%		+0.1%	

[*]Mean percentage of vote by state and time period.

examined, and that small disadvantage almost completely disappeared after 1974.

In addition to general elections, we can also look at primaries. In general elections, party and incumbency are major determinants of the vote, with individual candidate characteristics playing lesser roles. However, in primaries, as in nonpartisan elections, the influence of party is nullified, making candidate characteristics more important. Table 6.2 illustrates the performance of new candidates in primaries of five states. As for the general elections, the average weighted difference between the male and the female candidates is calculated for each state and for the set of states as a whole.

Very little difference is observed in the performance of aspiring male and female candidates. Challenging incumbents is generally a risky business, although the few Republican who tried it in Iowa came out well. Overall, a challenge against an incumbent produces less than a third of the vote. In the early period women were quite disadvantaged in such races compared to men; but this has been reversed and now women outperform men in these contests. Races without a party incumbent yield an average below fifty percent, an indication of several candidates splitting the vote. In the early period women and men candidates competed equally in such races but women are slightly disadvantaged today. This is a potential problem area for female candidates.

In primary elections, political culture, Democratic domination and southern traditions again fail to produce the expected patterns. In the early period, New Mexico and Missouri reveal only very small net disadvantages to women (they receive about one percent less vote than equivalent men) and in Oklahoma women have a decisive advantage over similar men, on the average. It is in two northern states, Iowa (Republican) and Nebraska (nonpartisan), where in the early period the average female candidate was most disadvantaged. Again, this disadvantage is only about three to four percent. In the later period the overall difference between entering men and women nearly disappears. Women retain an advantage over men in Oklahoma primaries and gain an advantage in Iowa. Only in New Mexico and Nebraska do meaningful differences persist to the disadvantage of female candidates. Overall, even without the structuring provided by party label, women are not disadvantaged to any meaningful degree. Primary elections are not serving to deny new women their party nomination.

In sum, there is very little difference among the states in the relative performance of female candidates trying to enter legislatures. Even in the earlier period they suffered only a small disadvantage. After the 1976 election, that small disadvantage almost completely disappeared, and, in some states, there is a small relative advantage for female can-

TABLE 6.2 Entering Men and Women Candidates in Contested Primaries Against Male Opponents[*]

State, Party, and Type of Election	Early Period		Later Period	
	Men (n)	Women (n)	Men (n)	Women (n)
NEW MEXICO	(1968-1974)		(1976-1980)	
Republican				
Against an incumbent	37.4 (6)	–	26.9 (8)	–
Open seat	43.1 (44)	46.0 (4)	45.4 (11)	49.9 (4)
Democratic				
Against an incumbent	35.1 (62)	28.9 (6)	32.9 (45)	30.3 (6)
Open seat	41.3 (80)	42.4 (11)	48.3 (31)	35.3 (4)
Mean difference	+0.64%		+3.54%	
NEBRASKA	(1970-1974)		(1976-1980)	
Independent				
Against an incumbent	23.6 (68)	17.7 (7)	27.2 (41)	22.9 (8)
Open seat	23.5 (66)	23.2 (6)	25.5 (57)	19.2 (9)
Mean difference	+3.3%		+5.3%	
IOWA	(1970-1974)		(1976-1980)	
Republican				
Against an incumbent	47.8 (13)	36.2 (2)	50.0 (2)	59.5 (1)
Open seat	45.0 (19)	45.3 (12)	40.3 (19)	50.0 (6)
Democratic				
Against an incumbent	49.7 (5)	40.7 (2)	32.2 (6)	29.2 (4)
Open seat	46.2 (42)	40.2 (11)	45.8 (32)	40.5 (10)
Mean difference	+3.8%		−0.1%	
MISSOURI	(1970-1974)		(1976-1980)	
Republican				
Against an incumbent	41.2 (8)	31.5 (1)	27.4 (10)	33.9 (2)
Open seat	50.6 (33)	45.7 (9)	40.2 (38)	38.7 (14)
Democratic				
Against an incumbent	27.2 (34)	21.3 (12)	23.8 (76)	28.3 (19)
Open seat	39.2 (84)	44.7 (14)	37.8 (49)	32.4 (18)
Mean difference	+1.3%		+0.3%	
OKLAHOMA	(1968-1974)		(1976-1980)	
Republican				
Against an incumbent	37.0 (8)	–	30.1 (12)	45.7 (1)
Open seat	39.3 (40)	53.6 (4)	43.4 (32)	38.6 (4)
Democratic				
Against an incumbent	32.0 (140)	29.5 (4)	26.5 (96)	34.5 (12)
Open seat	35.3 (141)	37.0 (6)	31.6 (114)	28.7 (9)
Mean difference	−4.1%		−2.5%	
Mean difference for all states	+1.1%		+0.05%	
Mean difference against incumbents	+5.6%		−3.2%	
Mean difference in open seats	−0.7%		+3.1%	

[*]Mean percentage of vote by state, party, and period.

didates. While political culture may have been related to voter hostility in the past, we conclude that voter hostility cannot account for the small number of female legislators today.

IN THE RUNNING—BUT WHERE?
CANDIDATE TARGETING

Voters alone do not determine composition of the state legislatures. They can only choose among those who are offered, or who offer themselves, as candidates. Women can do very well compared to similar men candidates in elections and yet the result can still be that few women are elected. Races against incumbents, for example, are almost always destined for failure. Jeane Kirkpatrick suggested the possibility of what she called a male conspiracy against an expanded political role for women. In 1974 she wrote: "This explanation of women's non-participation in power sees women as oppressed, barred from power by a ruling class bent on maintaining its hegemony" (Kirkpatrick, 1974: 19). This can be accomplished in a variety of ways. No small number of observers have pointed out that women have an easier time getting elected than they have in gaining their party's nomination (Duverger, 1955; Werner, 1968; Tolchin and Tolchin, 1976:62; Rule, 1981; Mezey, 1978a; Deber, 1982). Others assert than when women *are* nominated by parties it is only because the party's cause is hopeless and a sacrificial lamb is needed (Jennings and Thomas, 1966; Lamson, 1968; Lynn, 1975; Carroll, 1977). These same elites further diminish the chances of female candidates with lukewarm electoral support and inadequate campaign funds (Werner, 1968; Tochin and Tolchin, 1976; Carroll, 1977; Baxter and Lansing, 1980).

Direct evidence of the male conspiracy is elusive, however, and three reports indicate party elites are not hostile to female candidates (Clark, 1979; McDonald and Pierson, 1984; Welch et al., 1982). While it may not be possible to observe systematically the deliberations leading to the recruitment and support of candidates, it is a simple matter to examine the results of these deliberations. If women entering the electoral arena are more likely than their male contemporaries to be slated against incumbents or in other non-winnable races, then this will effectively keep women out of the legislatures, no matter how well they do relative to similar men. Thus, if there are differences in the conditions under which men and female candidates run, this will affect their relative chances of being elected even if voters are not influenced by candidate gender. To examine this, data were gathered concerning the sorts of races nonincumbent male and female candidates entered by party and time period. Nebraska was excluded as candidates there all run as independents and Wyoming was also excluded as its multimember district system requires separate analysis. Table 6.3 presents the results.

In primaries, new Republican candidates very rarely challenged incumbents, most of whom run unopposed. In this regard there is very little difference across either time or gender. New Democrats are about three times as likely to run against their own party's incumbents as the Republicans and less than half as likely to get through their primary unopposed. Female candidates, however, are at an advantage over new male Democratic candidates in their primaries. In the earlier period they were much more likely than males to be unopposed, and about ten percent less likely to run against an incumbent. These differences were diminished by the later period but persisted in favor of the female candidates. In primaries, then, both in the earlier period and the later, Republican and Democratic women ran in situations similar to, or better than, men.

In general elections, most new Republican candidates of both genders find themselves slated against Democratic incumbents. Only a negligible number of new Republican get through the general election with no opponent at all. This situation is the same for both time periods and there are only minor sex differences. These minute differences certainly do not support the notion that new Republican female candidates are recruited as sacrificial lambs for races that cannot be won. Both male and female Republican candidates trying to enter the legislature face a difficult situation.

Somewhat less than half of the new Democratic candidates also face an incumbent in the general election, substantially fewer than faced by Republican newcomers. Compared to Republicans, new Democratic candidates are also ten or twenty times as likely to find themselves happily unopposed in the general election. The electoral situation facing new Democratic candidates, then, is better for them than for the Republicans. Before 1976, new women Democratic candidates were about ten percent more likely to face a Republican incumbent than were the new Democratic men and the women were about ten percent less likely than the new Democratic men candidates to be unopposed in the general election. By the later period, this difference had been cut in half. New Democratic female candidates were still slightly more likely than men to face Republican incumbents and less likely than men to get through without an opponent.

The distribution of entering men and women candidates between the majority and minority parties also affects aggregate female success. If women run in a state's minority party, then their chances of

TABLE 6.3 Types of Primaries and General Elections New Male and Female Candidates Faced in New Mexico, Missouri, Oklahoma, and Iowa[*]

Party, Election and Period	Candidate Sex	Against Incumbent	Contested Open Seat	No Opponent	Total	(n)
REPUBLICAN						
Primary						
1968-1974	Male	7.7	33.8	58.5	100.0	(503)
	Female	3.1	38.1	58.8	100.0	(97)
1976-1980	Male	9.1	33.3	57.6	100.0	(427)
	Female	7.6	33.1	59.3	100.0	(118)
General election						
1968-1974	Male	57.4	41.6	1.0	100.0	(387)
	Female	51.4	45.7	2.9	100.0	(70)
1976-1980	Male	64.4	34.1	1.6	100.0	(320)
	Female	68.9	30.0	1.1	100.0	(90)
DEMOCRATIC						
Primary						
1968-1974	Male	32.8	46.6	20.6	100.0	(897)
	Female	22.6	43.5	33.9	100.0	(124)
1976-1980	Male	38.1	46.1	15.8	100.0	(733)
	Female	34.5	45.3	20.3	100.0	(48)
General election						
1968-1974	Male	42.9	42.6	14.5	100.0	(387)
	Female	52.2	44.8	3.0	100.0	(67)
1976-1980	Male	42.6	41.9	15.4	100.0	(272)
	Female	48.3	41.4	10.3	100.0	(58)

*Percentage by party and period.

getting elected will be reduced, even if they do as well as male candidates of the party. Table 6.4 presents the party distribution of all entering candidates by state, time, and gender (leaving out nonpartisan Nebraska). In the early period women are consistently more likely than men to be the candidate of the minority party. In Republican Iowa and Wyoming a greater proportion of the new women than men candidates came in as Democrats, while in Democratic New Mexico, Oklahoma, and Missouri they tend to be Republicans. These differences were about ten percent for all the states except Iowa, where the gender difference was negligible. In the later period these differences diminish by half. In Iowa women and men are almost identically Republican, while for the other states the tendency of the women to be the candidate of the minority party persists.

TABLE 6.4   New Candidates for Lower House Seats by State, Gender, Year, and Party*

State, Period, and Gender		Percentage of Gender Republican	Percentage of Gender Democratic	Total Percentage of New Candidates	(n)
NEW MEXICO					
1968-1974	Male	46.3	53.7	89.2	(417)
	Female	56.0	44.0	10.8	(50)
1976-1980	Male	41.7	58.3	83.0	(230)
	Female	47.9	52.1	17.0	(47)
IOWA					
1970-1974	Male	41.3	58.7		(196)
	Female	40.0	60.0		(75)
1976-1980	Male	48.9	51.1		(192)
	Female	49.2	50.8		(71)
MISSOURI					
1970-1974	Male	36.6	63.3		(318)
	Female	45.0	55.0		(71)
1976-1980	Male	38.1	61.9		(396)
	Female	43.5	56.5		(108)
OKLAHOMA					
1968-1974	Male	30.0	70.0	93.9	(550)
	Female	41.6	58.4	6.1	(36)
1976-1980	Male	28.8	71.2	88.7	(388)
	Female	34.0	66.0	11.3	(50)
WYOMING					
1968-1974	Male	47.1	52.9	87.9	(335)
	Female	36.9	63.1	12.1	(46)
1976-1980	Male	52.8	47.2	84.6	(265)
	Female	47.9	52.1	15.4	(48)

*In percentages.

One additional aspect of Table 6.4 can be noticed. Women represent only a small percentage of those aspiring to legislative seats. The sampling frame does not permit calculations for Iowa and Missouri, and the other states show the proportion of female candidates no more than seventeen percent anywhere. While the proportions do show consistent growth from the first to the second period, males are the vast majority of those contesting as new candidates. Increasing the numbers of female candidates will be necessary before the number of elected women will rise.

WYOMING: THE CASE OF MULTIMEMBER DISTRICTS

Almost all electoral research on legislatures done in this country deals with single-member systems or assumes our elections are of this sort (see Cox, 1983). Yet an inspection of the electoral methods of the fifty state legislatures reveals more than half in any given year employ multimember districts (Clark and Darcy, 1983). Wyoming is such a state with twelve (out of twenty-three) multiseat districts for the lower house. While there are a number of ways these districts can be organized, in Wyoming candidates do not declare for positions. Instead, all within the district run and a number of top vote-getters equal to the open seats are elected. Voters can cast several votes equal to the number to be elected.

In this situation new candidates need not consider themselves as running against a particular incumbent who may be in the race, nor need the voter. In fact, candidates need not run *against* anyone. They can run for themselves, and the voter can vote for them and someone else also. Under these conditions small disadvantages that might be held by female candidates could be mitigated against. Further, when women do not have to run against some particular candidate, either in a primary or in a general election, they may be more willing to declare as candidates.

On the other hand, multiseat systems could also work against women. The number of representatives elected must be proportional to the number of people being represented. Hence, the more representatives elected from a multiseat district, the larger the population of the district—one factor associated with smaller female representation in legislatures (see Werner, 1968; Diamond, 1977). Larger districts require greater campaign funds, mass media and other resources women may find more difficult than men to obtain. On the other hand, a number of studies have shown women advantaged by urbanization. Higher urbanization, in turn, is also associated with the need for greater campaign funding and mass media rather than personal campaigning (see Welch et al., 1982).

Table 6.5 presents the proportion of all candidates who are women by district size. As the districts become larger so does the proportion of female candidates. Districts electing four or more to the legislature draw more than twice the proportion of women as do those that are single-member. This is not a simple function of urbanization. Certainly the multimember districts have the larger populations but during the period examined Wyoming was the only state without an SMSA. The state did not contain any metropolitan areas that might create a special milieu favorable to female candidates.

TABLE 6.5   District Size and the Proportion of Men and Women
             Candidates in Wyoming*

| | | District Size | |
Election and Gender	1 Member	2-3 Members	4 or More Members
Primaries			
Men:	93.5	89.5	85.0
Women:	6.5	10.5	15.0
Total (n):	100.0 (139)	100.0 (276)	100.0 (587)
General election			
Men:	95.8	88.8	83.1
Women:	4.2	11.2	16.9
Total (n):	100.0 (118)	100.0 (233)	100.0 (462)

*In percentages

The relative electoral performance of male and female candidates
was evaluated using the MCA technique to control for possible con-
founding factors such as incumbency, time period, number of
candidates and party. Table 6.6 presents the MCA results for district
size. An analysis of variance (not presented) shows district size to
account for twelve percent of the variation in voting for female candidates in primaries and seven percent of the variation in general
elections, even after the effects of party, incumbency, number of candidates and time period are removed. In each case the variation explained by district size was significant at .002.

The unadjusted percents in Table 6.6 are the averages received by
candidates in the appropriate categories. The adjusted proportions of
the vote for women controls for the number of candidates, time
period, party, and incumbency. In both the primaries and in the
general election female candidates gain a larger proportion of the vote
as the district size increases. The analysis of seven Wyoming elections,
hence, supports the hypothesis that larger multiseat election districts
enhance the chances of women gaining legislative seats since more
women run in larger districts and women get more votes in them as
well.

CONCLUSIONS

This analysis sought to discover what happens when a woman
becomes a candidate for the state legislature. A number of different
settings were used to determine if the new female candidate would

TABLE 6.6 MCA Breakdowns of Votes Received by Wyoming Women
Candidates*

Category	Primary Unadjusted	Adjusted	General Unadjusted	Adjusted
District size				
One member	32	27	53	19
Two to three members	58	47	48	29
Four or more members	54	57	41	50
Grand mean	54		43	

*In percentages

have any disadvantage that a comparable male candidate would not.
While women once were likely to gain fewer votes than similar male
candidates, that difference has disappeared for both primaries and
general elections. Female state legislative candidates now can be expected to do as well as male candidates. Next, the kind of races new
women and men candidates entered was examined. Women, both
Democrats and Republicans, were about four percent more likely to
run against an incumbent in the general election than were men candidates. This difference is less now than it once was, but it persists to
the disadvantage of women. Female candidates were also slightly
more likely than male candidates to run under the banner of a state's
minority party. Again, this disadvantage for women is growing less
over time.

Factors relating to the electoral system itself were also examined
with regard to their effect on women's candidacies. The nonpartisan
Nebraska electoral system disadvantaged female candidates, while the
multiseat system of neighboring Wyoming proved advantageous. In
the multiseat districts more women were likely to run as candidates
than in the state's single-seat districts, and female candidates did better in the elections in the multiseat districts.

The electoral system no longer presents the barriers to female candidates for state legislatures it once may have. As more women run for
the legislature, more will be elected. As more women begin serving in
the legislature there will be a gradual increase in women elected to
other, higher, offices as more female legislators become available for
recruitment.

7

WOMEN'S ORGANIZATIONAL STRATEGIES IN STATE LEGISLATURES

Carol Mueller

Over a decade ago, when Frieda Gehlen described the eleven women of the eighty-eighth Congress, she observed that "the women seem to deliberately shun the idea of being considered a bloc" (1969). By the early 1980s, there had been a dramatic change in the way that women in Congress and the state legislatures identified with other women in public office. Increasingly, they have recognized that the experience of being a female legislator is different than the experience of being a male legislator. From the recognition of differences in experience has developed the widespread sense of membership in a minority accompanied by varying perceptions of exclusion or not being taken seriously. Where this collective sense of group membership has emerged, women no longer shun the idea of joining together as women legislators for social and/or political reasons.

The number of women in state legislatures has tripled since the advent of the contemporary women's movement in 1970. By 1982, women made up ten percent or more of state lawmakers in sixty percent of the states. In fourteen percent of the states, they made up more than twenty percent. Women are now visible collectively. No longer can they be seen as isolated tokens or as occasional aberrations in the natural male order. As the number of state female lawmakers has in-

Author's Note: This chapter is a revised and condensed version of a report of the Tenth Anniversary Conference of Women State Legislators held on Cape Cod, Massachusetts (June 1982). The report was submitted to the Center for the American Woman and Politics (CAWP), the Eagleton Institute of Politics at Rutgers University in June 1983. Appreciation is due to Ruth Mandel, director of CAWP, who made it possible for me to observe a planning session as well as the conference; to Debbie Walsh, who provided transcripts of the conference sessions; to the staff of CAWP and Alan Rosenthal of the Eagelton Institute, who provided valuable suggestions for revising an initial draft of the report and to the legislators who generously gave of their time during the conference.

creased, collective strategies have developed within legislatures to address women's shared experience of exclusion and marginality and to maximize the political influence that increased numbers afford. Informal social networking has developed and paved the way for ad hoc coalitions of women lawmakers and, in some state contexts, formal caucuses of women.

The rapid increase of women in state legislatures and the proliferation of collective strategies raise a new set of questions regarding the mobilization and utilization of power and influence by women in public office. These questions go beyond the issues faced by individual women in the early 1970s, which focused primarily on overcoming discriminatory treatment based on traditional stereotypes about the role of women in politics. Yet, the questions raised are no easier to answer than were those of the early 1970s. To a large extent they are the same issues faced by racial, ethnic, and religious minorities as their numbers have increased in positions of political office holding. These issues raise the following questions: How can women organize within legislatures without alienating their male colleagues and potential allies? How can organizations of women legislators develop in states where there are competing loyalties from strong, competitive parties? What organizational strategies will help women who are in office to develop and to maintain a sense of mutual responsibility, to pass legislation that is responsive to women's needs, and to achieve positions of legislative leadership? How successful are these different strategies in producing legislative outcomes responsible to women and in establishing a center of influence for women in state government?

In exploring these issues, this chapter focuses first on the critical factors that influence the emergences of one collective strategy rather than another in a particular state. Strategies of social networking and organizing politically through ad hoc coalitions and formal caucuses are discussed. Finally, the consequences of these strategies are evaluated in terms of legislative outcomes and collective influence.

Data for the chapter are drawn primarily from the transcripts[1] of workshops, panels, and speeches at the Tenth Anniversary Conference of Women State Legislators held on Cape Cod, Massachusetts, in June 1982.[2] Eighteen states were represented by delegations of female legislators.[3] Also included in the transcripts were the observations of two veteran male legislators attending the conference. The author attended the conference and a previous planning session as an observer. Thus, the chapter also reflects the author's personal observations and conversations with conference participants.[4]

ORGANIZING IN DIVERSE STATE CONTEXTS

As the number of female legislators has increased, three factors have been crucial in influencing the form that collective efforts take in any given state. The first factor is the perception that women have of how their male colleagues will react to an organized bloc of women in the legislature. The issue here is how vulnerable women feel and whether this vulnerability leads to a strong collective effort or to a more individualistic response. A second factor concerns the strength of partisanship in the legislature. The question is one of whether collective identification with female legislators and women's issues can coexist with competing party loyalties. This issue, in turn, raises the question of what women's issues are and whether they transcend party lines. Finally, in some states, deep divisions among female legislators have developed due to previous battles over issues such as the ERA and abortion. The question is whether strategies exist that will overcome these deep divisions. As these three issues are worked out, a characteristic collective solution tends to emerge in each state.

VULNERABILITY AND PERCEPTIONS OF MALE COLLEAGUES

Ten years ago, female legislators related primarily as individuals to overwhelmingly male legislators. They negotiated these relationships with whatever social skills and personal competence they brought to public life. If it were considered problematic to be a woman in an overwhelmingly male environment, it was a personal issue to be handled privately. Now that the number of women has increased significantly in the majority of legislatures, relationships with the male majority are no longer treated as strictly a personal or a private matter. Whether women choose to work through formal caucuses, informal networks, or personally constructed coalitions is strongly influenced by their relationships with male colleagues. The success of these collective efforts, in turn, has its own impact on relationships with male allies and the male legislative leadership.

Under these circumstances, the type of collective strategy that develops is strongly influenced by the issue of group visibility—how visible to female legislators feel they can be vis-à-vis their male colleagues in supporting women's issues and openly coordinating their efforts as a network or caucus without inviting negative sanctions. When a delegate from Arizona was asked whether her male colleagues would be threatened by a female caucus, she laughed and replied, "No, their egos are much too secure." Nevertheless, in several states, women have not organized formally because of their apprehensions about the response from their male colleagues. There is widespread uneasiness about "waving a red flag" or "ruffling too many feathers" by becoming visible as a bloc of female legislators. This feeling was expressed by several delegates from California who felt that their group should remain informal. One California delegate explained this preference as a logical consequence of their limited numbers—two senators (out of forty) and ten representatives (out of eighty). She felt California female legislators might be ready for a more visible role when their numbers got larger. Their collective solution has emphasized a low profile with informal, evening get togethers away from the capitol and an issue-by-issue approach to legislation based on ad hoc coalitions. A low profile has also been maintained in politically conservative states, although the numbers and proportions of women may be larger.

This apprehension and sense of vulnerability contrast sharply with states where there is a strong sense that women have collectively established their credibility as a political force among male colleagues. They seem to enjoy more respect collectively as women. The question of respect seems related to their willingness to become collectively associated with controversy—one of the most visible ways of attempting to exercise influence. The most effective combination seems to be one of coordinated pressure, partial victories, and growing credibility. Yet, this is not the whole picture. A male legislator from a caucus state also acknowledged that

> taking a position on controversial issues doesn't necessarily mean that you are going to arouse animosity, but I can tell you when the other side doesn't agree with you, then—people have done this in the legislature—various groups will impugn a lot of the women legislators. They impugn their motives and start going into personalities.

Willingness to withstand such animosity as well as controversy seems to be a part of winning credibility and collegial acceptance. These comments were similar to advice offered by a male leader from a northeastern state, "If you have a political force, don't be afraid to use it and don't be too concerned that you may offend a few people in so doing."

COMPETING PARTY LOYALTIES

Partisanship is the second major factor that influences the form that organizing will take in a state. It is the critical factor that inhibits the development of formal caucuses in states like Minnesota and

Maine where party loyalties are strong. In largely Democratic states like Massachussets and Maryland, which had the first caucuses, partisanship was not an issue. A founder of the Maryland caucus said, "We didn't realize we should have any difficulties. The question of parties never came up." In caucus states with strong parties, however, strict bipartisanship has been the rule. In Illinois, there are always two coconvenors, one from each major party. An Illinois delegate noted, "Bipartisanship is the glue that holds us together." A delegate from North Carolina also points out that it is the unity of bipartisanship that increases their leverage with the legislative leadership.

While bipartisanship unifies women in many states and proves an effective lobbying tool in others, in some states it hasn't worked. A Minnesota delegate felt that they were "more broken down by parties" than most of the states represented at the conference and a Maine delegate found the talk of bipartisanship "euphoric." She felt:

> You could say most issues are women's issues or you could say most issues affect the pocketbook. AFDC—you could say its a women's issue but the split (in Maine) was broken down by party lines.

She concluded, "We're not a caucus-oriented state. We're a partisan state and we love our political parties."

BATTLE SCARS OVER ISSUE DIFFERENCES

Although female legislators in most states seem to draw strength from collective identification, this is not always the case. The third factor that strongly influences the form of organizational strategy is the history of political differences between female legislators over specific issues. In a few states, like Colorado, Florida, and Nevada, the wounds from ERA battles or other differences are too deep to overcome in even informal gatherings. A delegate from Florida remembered that the only occasions for which all the female legislators in her state would come together were those held by the wives of lobbyists. If a group of female legislators called a meeting, most others would not come. In the Florida legislature, it has proved impossible to even discuss issues of wife beating or child abuse with some female legislators. Fundamentalist constituents consider the discussion of these issues an illegitimate government intrusion into private, domestic life. Although strong differences such as these prevent organizing in some states, in other states strategies have evolved for dealing with controversial issues. This is usually handled by following a consensus rule. Caucuses support only legislation for which wide support has developed among women in the legislature.

While issue consensus was widely regarded as the most effective response to controversial questions, there were a few delegates who disagreed. Delegates from noncaucus states pointed out that they were not compromised by the consensus rule and were free to build coalitions on controversial issues. Another criticism came from one of the male delegates. He felt that the women's caucus in his state had failed in its responsibility on some issues because of an emphasis on consensus. "When human social services are curtailed, it's really the women and children who get hurt." Yet, he maintained, "the women's caucus has left it to the black caucus and the urban caucus." Clearly, women in some states have chosen not to organize because of their differences over such economic issues as these while in other states organized efforts proceed on other issues.

TYPES OF COLLECTIVE STRATEGIES

Although some women in most of the states will choose to "go it alone," most female legislators have joined together for moral support, relaxation, personal development, exchange of information, and the pursuit of common political goals. A wide variety of organizational strategies have emerged to meet these diverse needs in the context of widely differing state conditions. These range from the informal networking based frequently on social get-togethers to formal, staffed caucuses. In a majority of states represented at the conference, formal and informal organizations exist side by side and reinforce each other.

INFORMAL SOCIAL NETWORKING

Informal groupings drawn together by social occasions are the most prevalent form of organizing and are not incompatible with a more formal, politically focused organization. The frequency of these social occasions ranges from the biannual socials in Minnesota to monthly dinner meetings in California, biweekly breakfasts in Missouri, and weekly luncheons in Connecticut, Illinois, and Iowa. These occasions not only provide opportunities to relax and to hear an informative speaker, but—if held frequently—also foster a sense of collective responsibility among female legislators. The bonds that develop from such occasions can help to overcome the differences that might otherwise divide women on the basis of party, geography, or seniority. The low visibility also reduces the chances of retaliation in legislatures where women feel vulnerable about collective identification.

The informal ties between women that are established through social occasions meet a variety of needs. The most general of these is the need for social support. As an Iowa delegate explained, "Very rarely do we march out and collect votes as a group, but we try to be supportive of each other." Even in caucus states, the support function remains of paramount importance. One of the founders of Women Legislators of Maryland described the importance of their caucus as a support group:

> I related very well to the other women in the Maryland General Assembly and I think it's very much due to the fact that we have a caucus which brings us together, helps us deal with each other as friends and as cohorts and as competitors, because on many, many issues on the floor, we are competitors. It's only when we're dealing with women's issues that we are almost unanimously dedicated to the result we are trying to obtain.

In a more specific way, social support can provide junior members with an opportunity to find compatible mentors.

The common denominator in all of the social occasions that bring female lawmakers together is still one of gaining some collective strength through a group identity. A delegate from Maine told of how some women in their legislature get together occasionally in "ambience oriented" gatherings just to make the point that "it's no longer an old boys' club. The women are not interested in choosing the license plate color."

Despite the occasional deep divisions that remain in some legislatures, in many states the social reasons for getting together blend into the political as information is exchanged on the status of pending bills, of committee assignments, and of shifting alliances and coalitions. In several states these informal networks have developed a more explicitly political function by taking group positions on selected bills, developing group strategies, and working out a division of labor in managing bills on the floor.

ORGANIZING POLITICALLY

A wide range of organizational strategies have evolved for passing legislation responsible to women. They essentially fall into two types—ad hoc coalitions and formal caucuses. Maryland and Massachusetts have long had formal caucuses with staff, office space, and intern programs that permit routine review of all legislation and a statewide focal point for women's issues. Both Kansas and Oregon have had formal caucuses that have recently become less active and more informal. Illinois has now had a formal caucus for four years and newer caucuses have emerged more recently in Connecticut, Iowa, North Carolina, and Vermont.

Despite the spread of the formal caucus, delegates from California, Colorado, Florida, Maine, and Minnesota argued that more legislation for women could be passed in their states without formal ties between women legislators. Some delegates from Maine and Minnesota also saw little need for formal or informal organization among women legislators as a prerequisite for passing legislation. They felt they could get stronger support from their male colleagues by taking up issues on an ad hoc basis and forming coalitions one issue at a time. An unspoken assumption in these states seems to be that there are overwhelming political liabilities when women's concerns are visibly identified as "women's issues." Thus, ad hoc coalitions are the preferred organizational strategy.

AD HOC COALITIONS

The basic political strategy for men as well as women in state legislatures is that of forming coalitions on an issue-by-issue basis. Building coalitions involves the mobilization of allies by individual women or by an informal group of women who decide to support or defeat a piece of legislation or course of action. In contrast to the caucus approach, individuals usually decide independently to sponsor a bill and develop support for it. A California representative described how they work:

> What happens . . . is that if there is a piece of legislation, i.e., rape, we then go around and say to each female, would you (support me) if I introduce a bill . . . and then the two of us will go around to our respective colleagues and say, "would you like to come. . . . We would like to have a bloc of (supporters) that would give strength to this bill when it's introduced."

In this way, she argued, no one is taken for granted and you know whose support you have. She also felt that she should approach her female colleagues on the merits of each bill without saying it is a women's issue. "She has to come to that conclusion herself." A Florida representative described a similar process that included male colleagues as well. In removing the state sales tax on women's hygiene products, she was able to get 85 House votes out of 120 without a debate. Her male colleagues were ready to cosponsor rather than have the issue brought to the floor. Final Senate passage depended on attaching her bill to another tax-exemption bill for the state's largest oil transport company. She concluded, that "we have to first be politicians and understand the political system and maybe we can get more done that way."

In some states, coalition building has been a regular way of conducting business for many years. In other states, it has begun to happen only recently. An Arizona delegate described a recent coalition including most of the women in her legislature on a bill she cosponsored to put a surcharge on marriage licenses that would fund support for battered families and abused children. It was the first action that had elicited such widespread support from female legislators.

Ad hoc coalitions frequently exist in a complex network of policy-oriented organizations both inside and outside government. Usually, this network is based on a stable support network of women's organizations outside the legislature. In Maine, a Women's Lobby has a paid, professional lobbyist who carries the ball on women's issues in Maine. Men are included as associate members of the lobby. In California and Minnesota there are strong state Commissions on the Status of Women. The commission in Minnesota provides staff support for men and women in the legislature who are part of a women's issues group. There is additional support in California from the Elected Women's Association, which includes women from every level of government throughout the state.

Coalition building is not restricted to states without legislative women's organizations. It is also a major strategy in states with formal caucuses or informal groups. Delegates pointed out that they found it was much easier to walk a bill if a division of labor was decided on at the weekly luncheon meeting. In some states, a bipartisan network among women can overcome strong partisan resistance when combined with male support from a major party. In Iowa, Republican women went to the Speaker and told him that Republicans should support funding of the AFDC-UP program because Republicans should not endorse the break up of the family by forcing husbands to leave their wives and children. Once the leadership discovered there was a coalition of Democratic and Republican women combined with Democratic men, "They moved rapidly to get to the head of the pack." Women may also fall back on a coalition strategy in states where a caucus is losing its dynamism. This sometimes takes a formal turn when issue groups are formed around women's concerns. After considerable success throughout the 1970s, the Oregon caucus has moved in this direction.

The major advantage of the coalition-building strategy is its flexibility in diverse situations where a more formal network or caucus would be politically undesirable or unattainable even if desirable. Complete reliance on individual women to take the initiative for each piece of legislation has advantages and disadvantages, however. Because it is not necessary to maintain organizational unity, an individual can take on a controversial issue or a strongly partisan issue that might divide a caucus. On the other hand, the burden of developing arguments, following a bill through committee, lining up sponsors, and building support also falls on the individual woman and her allies. When credits are built up for passing an important bill, however, it is more likely that they will go to an individual or a few women. This approach provides more opportunities for individual women to develop a reputation for leadership. Yet, it does not seem to be a strategy that can develop credibility for women collectively.

Despite the effectiveness of these ad hoc coalitions, a delegate from Kansas still felt that something was missing:

> We very much need a caucus, but we feel that we have a good thing and don't want to take a chance on disrupting it. I guess it's a more feminine diplomacy.

This feeling was also expressed by delegates from North Carolina where a caucus was formed immediately prior to the conference. One North Carolina delegate said, "We decided that we did need to come out into the open because we had met sort of behind closed doors before."

FORMALIZING COLLECTIVE STRATEGIES

The formal caucuses are distinguished from ad hoc coalitions by their overt political goals and their explicit structure. They represent a highly visible symbol of women's collective influence in state government. They also serve as pressure groups of elected public officials working within the legislatures on behalf of women's issues. Less formally, they try to increase the influence of female officials within the legislatures. The degree of formality varies from state to state.

The major question facing formal caucuses is how to establish a united group when women differ in terms of party affiliations and, sometimes, their support for issues of concern to women. If these issues are settled, there are other questions: how to handle controversial issues, how to maximize the efforts of the caucus, and how to get the resources that will permit the caucus to function effectively? A caucus's credibility as well as its legislative success will be influenced by all these decisions. Credibility and success, in turn, will be major factors influencing relationships with male colleagues and the legislative leadership. As the delegates from caucus states acknowledged, solving these problems to maintain a caucus involves some costs. There were other delegates who thought that the costs were too high.

ORIGINS

The origins of the caucuses reflect clearly the importance of the increasing number of women in state legislatures. In 1975, for instance, the number of women in the Maryland House of Delegates doubled to nineteen. This provided the impetus and the resources for forming the Women Legislators of Maryland. The precipitant in Illinois was similar. One of the coconvenors of the Conference of Women Legislators (COWL) described the reasons for its creation in the previous legislative session:

> Until that time, we felt we were small enough in numbers that we could get together on an informal basis just by going around the House and Senate floors and saying, "Come over to my apartment tonight and let's talk about this." But we now have twenty-eight women in the House and four in the Senate and so when the numbers get that large, we felt the need for something more formalized.

There is no magic number, however, that indicates a critical point for caucus formation. Massachusetts (with the oldest formal caucus) still had only nineteen women in both Houses at the time of the conference and had only half that many when its caucus formed in 1973.

In other states, a caucus was formed when significant numbers combined with a crisis regarding a particular issue. In Missouri, it was a rape law.

> It was an outgrowth of just a spontaneous get together and all of us feeling so strongly that the rape bill they were passing was not right. . . . It was literally left in our hands.

A critical mass of twenty women was galvanized by these particular challenges. Thus, threat or frustration added to the strength of numbers. The rape issue in Missouri also helped to overcome years of division and bitterness among women in the legislature over the ERA. In Maryland, also, numbers combined with a strong desire to have a collective impact on revising the state's rape laws and in bringing

Maryland laws into compliance with its new Equal Rights Amendment.

MEMBERSHIP

In states with formal caucuses, membership is open to all women legislators, regardless of party or philosophy. In Maryland, for instance,

> Membership is automatic; if you're a woman and you're elected to the legislature, you're a member of the caucus. We never even ask anybody. They're just in. A few don't participate but nobody has denied us. There is no outright opposition. . . . We have both Democrats and Republicans; both conservatives and liberals.

In most states, however, membership is optional and some choose not to join. In Massachusetts, three out of five women Senators chose not to join from the 1982 legislative session. In Illinois, there have always been three or four women who did not join. In other states, like Kansas and Oregon, it is only in the last few years that an increasing number of women being elected "were not with us." Most caucuses do not give up easily on potential members, however, and consciously try to be inclusive. In Illinois, "there is a constant struggle" to find a broader set of issues that will overcome differences on the ERA.

RESOURCES

Although committed women are the major resource needed for an effective caucus, their efforts can be extended through the availability of a staffed office, mailing and phone privileges, and interns. These resources have been mobilized through a variety of channels. The Maryland caucus began with a small grant from *Ms.* magazine and later charged each woman $100 a year from her interim expense fund. At a propitious moment, their caucus moved a desk and file cabinet into an alcove in the hall and asked the Speaker for a phone. "We were off and running," said one Maryland delegate. They also have an active program of student interns who compete for the opportunity to work with the Maryland women's caucus. In recent years, they have moved toward more independent fundraising by holding an annual reception for other legislators, lobbyists, and supporters. The first year the reception raised a few hundred dollars. In Massachusetts, the caucus also has an office and a paid staff including an executive director and secretary. Funds come from the Speaker.

In most states, it is women's volunteer efforts and personal resources that keep a caucus running. In states like Massachusetts, a paid staff and office come at the price of a sense of obligation to the legislative leadership. The most successful funding seems to tap a variety of sources as in Maryland where an "office" and phone are supplied by the Speaker but staff and interns are funded through the independent efforts of caucus members.

REACHING CONSENSUS

To overcome the diversity of women's beliefs and other political commitments, most caucuses have developed a consensus rule for supporting issues. The process of arriving at consensus differs from state to state. In some states, there is a simple discussion of pending bills; in other states, the process is more elaborate. An Illinois delegate described as intensive process of holding hearings throughout the state, finding the areas of consensus within the caucus, and then drafting appropriate legislation. An intensive process for selecting caucus issues is also a way of locating supportive constituents, isolating trouble spots, and building support for the issue once it gets to the floor. In addition to the consensus rule, Illinois and Massachusetts have found that their legislative efforts are more successful if their caucuses focus on a few, selected issues. One year the major issue in Illinois was strip searching; another year it was teenage pregnancy. In Massachusetts one issue was rape staircasing.

ISSUE SELECTION

All caucuses face the issue of deciding how they should distribute their energies and resources among competing pieces of legislation. An Illinois representative summarized the arguments for limiting the number of issue positions taken by a caucus:

> I think the question becomes, if your caucus simply is becoming a rubber stamp for any issue that any woman member wants to present, it does lose its credibility. . . . Be a little choosy and your credibility will increase.

This point was underscored by a representative from Vermont: "when we talked about narrowing our focus on issues, the number of issues we could take on, it was because of credibility." The Vermont caucus didn't feel that they could come in again and again and say, "Here we are again. Women, women, women on everything that they generally assume women are interested in."

COORDINATING CAUCUS EFFORTS

Once issues are selected that have gained caucus support, three major strategies are used jointly for bringing the resources of the caucus to bear on pending legislation. These time-honored strategies of covering the major committees, handling bills on the floor, and building a base of support in the community are greatly facilitated by a collective approach.

Covering the major committees works more effectively as the number of women increases. In Vermont, this works particularly well in the House where there were thirty-five women out of one hundred fifty in 1982. A Vermont delegate felt "there has been relatively little difficulty getting through the House major pieces of women's legislation." She attributed this to the fact that most committees in the House have several women and the caucus works to make sure that when a bill is before a particular committee, "all of the women are aware of exactly what the legislation entails. . . . what the hidden factors are." Despite greater difficulty in the Senate, where there were only four women out of thirty members, the Vermont delegate reported that they had been successful in passing legislation on violence, on sexual assault, on funding for women's shelters, on credit, on discrimination in housing and employment—with very little debate.

In addition to effective committee work, there is no substitute for "working the floor" or "doing your homework." This point was underscored by a delegate from Illinois. After describing the extensive hearings that COWL conducts before approving an issue, she observed that

> it doesn't mean that you can do away with that basic thing of going around and getting additional sponsors and working the House floor. You still have to do that.

In a state with a less formal caucus, like Iowa, the same homework is perhaps necessary, but resources are stretched thin in order to be effective.

Building political support is not restricted to committee work or working the floor. Maryland representatives were emphatic about going out into the community.

> We have a network of women we invite to our fundraiser, who are on our mailing list, and whose phone numbers we have, and when there is a tough issue that we are not certain we can get the votes for, we go out into the community and say, "You tell your legislator that you want this

bill passed." And that has been very significant on some very hard issues in Maryland.

Maryland representatives also noted a potential source of support that might be ignored—"the wives of the male legislators get involved because they feel very strongly about the issue." The wives, it was suggested, can be "the ultimate weapon."

SUSTAINING A CAUCUS

Resolving the questions of numbers, partisanship, and controversy is not sufficient, however, for sustaining a caucus—even if it has been very successful. In Kansas, Democratic women had no trouble joining with Republican women in 1976 when women from both parties numbered only eight. Yet, now that there are eighteen women in the legislature, one delegate found:

> We're seeing the women that are getting elected primarily who are not at all interested in being identified with other women and it has been very difficult to hold that caucus together.

In Oregon, decline in the dynamism of the caucus was attributed to success rather than size and diversity. In 1982, there were nineteen women in both houses making up twenty-two percent of the sixty-member legislature. Women there have been very successful in winning top leadership positions.[5] Instead of operating as a formal caucus, the Oregon women now meet socially. To some extent this is an attempt to regain the momentum of the mid-1970s. To develop women's issues in the legislature, however, a Women's Issues Forum has been started for all interested legislators. Most of its members are still female legislators who work closely with the Women's Rights Coalition, a lobbying group.

EVALUATING COLLECTIVE STRATEGIES

No universally acceptable criteria exist for evaluating whether an organizational strategy has been successful. Nevertheless, two alternative ways of viewing success are held by female legislators. The first is an assessment of the amount and type of legislation that a caucus or coalition has been instrumental in passing. The second—limited to formal caucuses—is sometimes called the "credibility" issue. It focuses on whether the caucus has become a "presence" recognized by the legislative leadership, male colleagues, lobbyists, and outside organizations as a source of power and influence in state government.

Although the two types of success frequently occur together, sometimes they do not. It also seems unlikely that ad hoc coalitions can gain collective credibility given their fluid organizational structure.

The contrast between the two types of success was posed most dramatically by one of the veteran male legislators. In his observations, he noted, "I've never been that conscious of our women's legislative caucus," and "I've never looked upon the women's caucus as an important political force in our state." Because he was unaware of the work of the caucus, however, he interviewed some of its members before coming to the conference. He reported,

> What I found was that our caucus has been really quite successful and in a rather low key, bipartisan manner has really gotten a very strong program that was initiated by the caucus enacted into law. Actually, in the last two years they have really had an important impact on women in [the state].

He then went on to itemize the caucus's legislative achievements: an objective job evaluation study of all classifications of state employees; medical support for handicapped adoptions; tax credits for industries to set up day care operations; additional funding for abused spouse centers as well as new centers; mandated rape crisis training for police officers; a red shield bill; and collective bargaining for part-time state employees. He also indicated that he knew of no major legislation supported by the caucus that had been defeated. Despite these achievements, the senator felt the caucus had failed by not becoming a visible political force. This, he felt, was essential for women to win positions of legislative leadership because, "That's where the action is."

The female legislators present were more impressed by the accomplishments of the women's caucus in his state. A representative from Oregon suggested, "I just want to say . . . if your women's caucus got 'comparable worth,' they did something very significant." A delegate from Florida also commented, "it seems to me that they operated very well." Nevertheless, the senator's comments focused attention on the possible incompatibility of the two different criteria for success. A low-key, bipartisan style may be more successful in holding women together as a united force and in leading to success in passing legislation but fail in giving them public recognition as a force to be taken into account.

Success is even more difficult to identify in noncaucus states where women sometimes run into conflicts with their male colleagues over who gets to define legislative solutions and who gets to take the credit. A California assemblywoman maintained that "most of those issues that have to do with women are preempted by men." Sometimes these are legislative proposals that the women in the legislature can't support. A representative described a situation in the previous session where male members were pushing for lay midwifery with a high school education equivalency. The female legislators couldn't support the bill for a number of reasons, most notably that they preferred a nurse midwifery. They confronted the bill's male author and had it dropped. In another case, a representative reported that the Business and Professional Women had gone to a male member during the 1982 session and asked him to carry a state Equal Rights Amendment. Meeting informally with other women's organizations in the state, the women in the assembly decided they wanted to wait for a decision on the federal amendment due in 1982. Unified on the issue, they went to the Speaker and got him to have the bill dropped.

In other states, frustration was voiced because of not having enough collective credibility. A delegate from Massachusetts noted, for instance, that many members of their caucus had not wanted to go as a united group to the Speaker and request committee assignment and committee chairs. For this delegate, "That's the number one frustration for those of us who aren't really power hungry, but who at least want the women to be taken seriously, individually and collectively." Similarly, a delegate from Iowa said, "I am afraid there is a tendency for the male legislators not to take it (the caucus) seriously; to view it as, well, those are the women talking over there."

How to be taken seriously has been approached in a variety of ways. In several states, it was felt that credibility would be enhanced if the caucus successfully pursued a legislative agenda in an area other than women's issues. In Florida, there was one attempt to create credibility and to organize a caucus by working together as women on high automobile insurance rates, a serious problem in the state. Their amendment was defeated, however, and they failed to establish a good track record. Since then they haven't met together formally. In Vermont and North Carolina, female legislators also felt they should "not limit ourselves to the so-called women's issues." A representative from North Carolina noted that their caucus has decided

to just go out into the ballfield and try to approach those same topics that men were interested in many cases but that we felt we could have some direct impact on, maybe changing them a little bit more so that the impact on women would be more favorable while it still affected the broad citizenry.

The question of credibility was also at the heart of the discussion about limiting the number of issues endorsed by a caucus. As a Vermont delegate argued, "in order to increase the power, we have to narrow the focus and not make ourselves so goody goody on every issue." The payoff comes when a caucus can claim, as they did in Vermont, "when we do come in with issues and we're together on them, we don't lose too often." When women do lose repeatedly on the issues, it doesn't seem to matter what the subject of the legislation is. They lose credibility as well.

CONCLUSIONS

Women in public office, as elsewhere, have diverse goals. For some, their primary commitment is to the needs of women. For them, all issues are women's issues. Others deny that any women's issues remain to be addressed legislatively. For them, the major priority is economic inequality, protection of the environment, or the threat of nuclear war. These priorities outweigh women's concerns. The majority fall in between. Women's issues compete with other legislative priorities for their time, energy, and commitment.

Regardless of a woman's legislative priorities, however, she must contend with the fact that she is herself a woman. To some extent she will be perceived and evaluated, included or excluded in terms of prevailing stereotypes about the appropriateness of women generally in positions of power and influence. Her advance into the ranks of legislative leadership and the success of her legislative priorities will be influenced by the collective status of women legislators as well as her own efforts.

As the number and proportion of women in state legislatures have grown, both the legislative agenda of women's concerns and the status of women as public officials have been increasingly addressed collectively. New strategies have been developed by women for passing legislation of concern to women and for supporting women in positions of legislative or party influence. These collective strategies reflect the number and proportion of women in each legislature; the strength of partisanship as parties provide alternative definitions of issue priorities and collective identification; and the history of past issues that have divided or united women in the state. From the diverse strategies discussed at the conference, a composite picture of caucus formation emerged that encompasses issues of when a formal caucus of female legislators might develop, what factors inhibit formation, what are the advantages and disadvantages of developing a caucus and what are the alternatives.

Assuming that the number of women continues to grow in state legislatures, an increasing number of states will reach the critical stage where a more formal collective strategy is feasible. Informal, but regularly scheduled social occasions seem to offer the best way of exploring issues and finding the common ground for collective action. Undoubtedly, leadership is important in finding this common ground and making the transition to a more formal organization. Yet, leadership does not seem to be in short supply among the new women office holders.

Lest the importance of numbers be underestimated, a representative from Oregon told the following story from the 1981 session of the legislature:

> On International Women's Day, our one woman senator invited all the women members of the House over for a little ceremony. We went to the Speaker to tell him that we wanted to be excused to go over to the Senate side.
>
> He said, "No, we are just going to continue with business and you'll just have to miss those votes and there's nothing important coming up."
>
> The representative told him, "Mr. Speaker, I don't think you can do that. I think you are going to have to recess."
>
> The Speaker said, "No, no. We have a heavy calendar."
>
> The representative replied, "When the women in the House leave, you will not have a quorum."
>
> The Speaker finally announced it from the podium, because men members of the House were saying, "Well, why don't we just continue?"
>
> And, finally, the Speaker had to say, "We cannot continue when the women leave the House because we will not have a quorum."
>
> And the rest of the session, that was really recognized. That was the first time men ever knew we could take the quorum away from them.

Lest the value of numbers be overstated, it should also be recognized that the women from the Oregon House had to walk out together to take the quorum with them.

APPENDIX A   Characteristics of States with Delegations at the Cape Cod Conference

Sta States	Size of Legislature	Women in Legislature (July 1981) Number	Percentage	Women's Legislators Collective Strategies (June 1982)
1. Arizona	90	17	18.9	United on a legislative issue for the first time in the last session.
2. California	120	12	10.0	Meet informally on a regular basis. Ad hoc coalitions on issues.
3. Colorado	100	23	23.0	Ad hoc coalitions on issues.
4. Connecticut	187	44	23.5	Formal caucus; ties with Order of Women Legislators'
5. Florida	160	17	10.6	Informal group works on legislation.
6. Illinois	236	32	13.6	Formal caucus, Conference of Women Legislators.
7. Iowa	150	18	12.0	Meet informally on a regular basis.
8. Kansas	165	22	13.3	Original caucus was more social and cultural. Want to revitalize.
9. Maine	184	42	22.8	Get together occasionally. Some work with Women's Lobby.
10. Maryland	188	28	14.9	Formal caucus.
11. Massachusetts	200	19	9.5	Formal caucus.
12 Minnesota	201	24	11.9	Loose coalition on issues. Work with Governor's Commission.
13. Missouri	197	22	11.2	New caucus (2 years old).
14. New Jersey	120	8	6.7	No form of organization.
15. North Carolina	170	22	12.9	New caucus (this session).
16. Oregon	90	20	22.2	Former caucus; less formal than in the past. Issues group.
17. Vermont	180	39	21.7	Caucus is a loose coalition that meets regularly.
18. Washington	147	35	23.8	Met recently to consider forming a caucus.

NOTES

1. The conference was sponsored by the Center for the American Woman in Politics (CAWP), Eagleton Institute of Politics, Rutgers University. This was the second major conference for women held by CAWP. Interviews conducted at the first conference, held in 1972, formed the basis of the book *Political Woman* by Jeane Kirkpatrick.

2. Because of the unsystematic nature of these data, the generalization to follow should be regarded as tentative.

3. There were two principal criteria for selecting states. States were included that had ten percent or more women in their legislatures and either had an organization of female legislators or seemed likely to develop one. (New Jersey, with 6.7 percent women in its legislature, was included because it is the host state of CAWP.) Criteria for selecting delegates were determined by the women in each legislature. Although individual women legislators attended the conference from four other states, the generalizations reported here are based on the eighteen states with formal delegations.

4. Although direct quotations are used to let conference participants speak in their own words, the sensitive and personal nature of the discussions has led to the omission of individual names.

5. Attending the conference, for instance, were Norma Paulus, former three-term representative and presently in her second term as secretary of state; Mary Burrows, the ranking Republican woman and vice-chair of the House Revenue Committee; and Barbara Roberts, favored to be the next majority leader. There was also a female speaker pro tem.

8

FEMALE STATE SENATORS AS CUE GIVERS: ERA ROLL-CALL VOTING, 1972-1979

David B. Hill

Studies of legislative behavior have consistently shown that legislators often rely on a variety of cues when deciding how to vote on controversial, mundane, or unfamiliar issues.[1] Legislators may hold strong pre-existing feelings about a proposed law and not feel the need for the advice of others; lacking such internal guidance, however, legislators turn to sources including standing committee members, chamber and party leaders, the governor and other executive branch officials, personal friends in and out of the chamber, and constituents. This study examines the possibility that female state senators functioned as an influential source of cues for their fellow state senantors considering the proposed Equal Rights Amendment to the U.S. Constitution between 1972 and 1979.

EXPERTISE IN LEGISLATURES: WHAT ROLE FOR WOMEN?

Most state legislatures are severely understaffed despite recurrent reform efforts to professionalize the state houses. As a consequence of inadequate staffing, legislators themselves often are expected to function as experts or specialists in one or more fields of policy making. This expectation is manifest in several ways, including the tendency of legislative leaders to appoint members to committees and subcommittees that reflect members' special interests and knowledge. For exam-

Author's Note: I'd like to express my appreciation to Mark Stubbs, Kathy Jewell, and Cathy Covington, all graduate students in the Department of Political Science at Texas A&M, for their assistance in the research reported in this chapter.

ple, a lawyer might be routinely assigned to a judiciary committee or a school teacher to an education committee. Because of their supposed special understanding of their own vocational fields, members become influential advisors to their colleagues, both formally (as a committee member) and informally (in casual conversations) about the desirability of proposed legislation (Wahlke et al., 1962: Chs. 9 and 10).

Vocation is not the only characteristic that legislators take into account, however, in seeking out informed advice. Factors such as seniority, geographical location of district, district urbanity, electoral success, or race might prove to be important in the choice of advisors. And given the increasing number of women in the legislatures, gender may be emerging as a factor that influences the credibility of a cue giver. In short, many legislators may purposefully seek out the views of female legislators when evaluating the merits of certain classes of legislation.

When women are elected to the legislature they bring with them many characteristics other than their gender, but gender is a critical factor in determining how they are perceived by male legislators. For one thing, there are so few women in many legislatures that their very presence creates a certain curiosity among male legislators. But it is also significant that many more women than men come to the legislature without a formal occupation. Many female lawmakers make their way into the legislature after homemaking, raising children, and participating in volunteer work, frequently leaving little time for formal education and a prestigious professional or business career outside of the home (Kirkpatrick, 1974; Diamond, 1977; Dubeck, 1976; and, Constantini and Craik, 1972).

Given the perceptions of male legislators and the background of many female legislators, most women are likely to be seen as specialists in matters that are *stereotypically* assigned to the purview of women. Female legislators, therefore, might be considered experts in education (as teachers of children), cultural affairs (as participants in artistic and historical activities), domestic relations (as caretakers of the family unit), and human services (as charitable humanitarians), among other areas.[2] We might also expect women to be regarded by some male legislators as experts in areas that are commonly perceived as "women's issues," including abortion, equal employment and affirmative action policies, and the subject of this study: the Equal Rights Amendment. While female salons may not approve of such stereotyping of their legislative roles, such deference may actually work to their advantage in influencing legislative decisions. As Harris and Hain (1983: 277) have observed, expertise, or at least the reputation for expertise, brings with it power in the legislative process.

WOMEN VERSUS OTHER CUE GIVERS

A perception of subject-matter expertise may have made women important cue givers regarding state ratification of the ERA. But whatever the influence of women, other cue givers doubtless exercised control over the outcome of ERA roll call votes, too. Hill (1983) has demonstrated that political parties often served as influential sources of cues, with Democratic legislative parties most often in favor and Republicans in opposition. Many governors lobbied the legislation, with most being supportive (Boles, 1979). Several presidents and first ladies spoke out in favor of ERA and contacted key legislators to seek their support.[3] Newspaper editors and authors of countless letters to the editor expressed their views.[4] Public opinion was expressed through active interest group lobbying on both sides of the issue. And several male legislators even reported being lobbied by wives and daughters.

Despite the large number of cues available to male legislators seeking guidance on this controversial proposal, it seems possible that their female colleagues might have served as a cue of more than average influence. Given that female legislators might be perceived as having expertise in some aspects (legal, political, historical, and social) of the ERA, and given the importance usually attributed to colleagues as a source of cues, this seems a distinct possibility.[5] It is not reasonable to suggest that male legislators would seek out and follow the advice of any and all female colleagues, however. We would expect personal characteristics of each woman to affect her perceived credibility and utility as a cue giver. And of course not all female legislators in each chamber voted for ERA, forcing male legislators interested in the advice of female colleagues to choose between the advice of two or more women cue givers. In this circumstance, male legislators would most certainly have had to weigh the value of each woman's advice.

In evaluating the worth of each woman's advice, a variety of personal characteristics would be considered. Some of these would involve personalities and other intangibles that transcend quantification, while other characteristics might be easily identified and quantified. For example, we might expect women with seniority to be more influential, inasmuch as continued electoral success and the political acumen that it represents is almost universally appreciated by legislators. A male might have surmised that a politically successful woman legislator based her ERA vote, at least in part, on political expediency as opposed to individual preference or ideology alone. A female legislator's social status might have influenced men's perceptions of her as a cue giver. Women from high status occupations that require more education might have been more influential as cue givers. Such women might have been seen as better evaluators of the legal and social issues involved or as more shrewd judges of other cues.

HYPOTHESES AND DATA

Our expectations about female legislators and their role in ERA roll call votes can be summarized in two simple hypotheses. First, female legislators served as one very influential cue in determining the voting behavior of their male collegues. Second, the influence of female legislators varied according to their seniority and status. In order to test these hypotheses we gathered roll call data for all ERA votes cast between March 22, 1972, and March 22, 1979, the original seven-year period in which ratification was considered.[6] Furthermore, biographical data on all women who participated in the roll call votes were collected.[7]

The following analysis is limited to votes taken in the state senates. There are two rationales for concentrating on senates. First, the small size and greater opportunities for informal communication between members of most senates provides greater assurance that women's vote intentions were known to other members before each roll call was taken. That women's views were publicly known is essential to the concept to their providing a cue for other members, something that would have been less certain in the larger and more formal lower houses. Second, the greater visibility of female state senators made it easier to compile biographical data on them. Biographical data on female house or assembly members, especially those who served only a single term, can be unusually difficult to obtain.

ANALYSIS

Between 1972 and 1979, state senates in forty-six states voted yes or no on ERA. Only the senates of Arkansas, Mississipi, South Carolina, and Utah failed to formally dispose of the legislation. In five additional states, Delaware, Massachusetts, Michigan, Rhode Island, and Texas, the senates approved ERA by voice vote, thus eliminating the possibility for roll call analysis. In the forty-one remaining states, there were no women in ten senates at the time the ERA votes were taken. This results in thirty-one states and forty different ERA roll call votes that included female senators. Women cast a total of seventy-nine votes, with some individuals voting on more than one occasion. Female senators voted in favor of ERA eighty-two percent of the time while men supported the amendment with only sixty-three percent of their 1,961 votes on the forty roll calls.

Results of the forty roll call votes are summarized in Table 8.1. The votes of women's delegations are broken into three categories: unanimous in favor (28); divided votes (9); and unanimous in opposition to the ERA (3). These three categories are then broken into two subcategories for male support and opposition to the amendment. For the thirty-one roll call votes on which women gave a unanimous cue, the male contingent (in the aggregate) voted similarly to women on twenty-five occasions. Only in Arizona (1976), Florida, Georgia, and North Carolina (1977) did men vote in a manner inconsistent with a unanimous female cue. While this sort of evidence does not conclusively confirm our hypothesis about the influence of women on these votes, the finding of correspondence between female and male voting does constitute a *necessary if not sufficient condition* for proving the hypothesis.

A similar pattern of evidence can be found in the votes on which women were divided. Where a majority of a split women's delegation favored the ERA, the male membership also supported the amendment. This occurred on four occasions (in Indiana, 1977; North Dakota, 1975; Ohio; and Vermont). In each instance two women favored the amendment while a single woman stood in opposition. And when the figures were reversed in two votes, that is, when one woman favored the ERA and two opposed it, the male membership's vote also tilted against the amendment. If these divided votes are added to the unanimous votes we find that men voted the same as a majority of women eighty-four percent of the time.

A careful examination of the data presented in Table 8.1 suggests further the possibility that the cue-giving influence of women may have waned over the years. Every instance on which the male vote did not parallel the female vote occurred after 1973. A very large percentage of the parallel votes occurred in 1972 or 1973, especially 1972 when men agreed with women on thirteen roll call votes, all in favor of ERA, disagreeing in not a single instance. The possibility that female legislators' infuence may have waned is consistent with the speculation of Harris and Hain (1983: 294) that the importance of subject-matter expertise varies across time, the salience of the topic, and extent of partisan differences. As ERA became more controversial and salient to other cue givers, starting sometime in 1973, women may have lost

TABLE 8.1   Matrix of Female and Male Support for the ERA by State
            (State Senates Only)

		Males			
	For			*Against*	

Category 1: Females Unanimously for the ERA

Alaska	1972	(1)	Arizona	1974	(5)
Arizona	1975	(5)	Florida	1974	(1)
Colorado	1972	(1)	Florida	1975	(1)
Connecticut	1973	(3)	Florida	1977	(2)
Hawaii	1972	(1)	Georgia	1975	(1)
Idaho	1972	(1)	North Carolina	1977	(4)
Illinois	1972	(1)			
Illinois	1974	(3)			
Illinois	1976	(2)			
Iowa	1972	(2)			
Kentucky	1972	(1)			
Maine	1974	(1)			
Maryland	1972	(3)			
Montana	1974	(2)			
New Hampshire	1972	(2)			
New Jersey	1972	(1)			
New Mexico	1977	(2)			
Oregon	1973	(2)			
Pennsylvania	1972	(1)			
South Dakota	1973	(1)			
West Virginia	1972	(1)			
Wyoming	1973	(1)			

Category 2: Females Divided

Indiana	1977	(2-1)	Indiana	1973	(1-2)
Nevada	1977	(1-1)	Missouri	1977	(1-1)
North Dakoga	1973	(1-1)	Nevada	1975	(1-2)
North Dakota	1975	(2-1)			
Ohio	1974	(2-1)			
Vermont	1973	(2-1)			

Category 3: Females Unanimously Against the ERA

			Missouri	1975	(1)
			Nevada	1973	(1)
			North Carolina	1973	(1)

NOTE: Each matrix entry includes the state name, year of vote, and number of
      female votes: Category 1 (yes), Category 2 (yes/no), Category 3 (no).

power over this issue to a plethora of other cues including partisanship, constituent opinion, and interest group pressures.

DEVIANT CASES: A MICRO-ANALYSIS

The occasions on which men's votes did not correspond with those of female senators may indicate something of the power of other cues, cues that outweighed women's influence in determining the outcome of ERA votes.

Arizona. The 1976 Arizona vote provides an excellent illustration of competing cues. Five female senators all voted for the ERA, yet they could not influence but ten colleagues to vote with them. Fifteen Arizona senators voted not to kill the proposal in a tie vote, despite the strong and very public campaign by their female colleagues for passage. An explanation for the impotency of the five women cue givers doubtless resides in the partisan composition of the Arizona Senate. All five women were Democrats and they were successful in securing the support of all but one of the male Democrats in the Senate. But fifteen Republican members (along with one Democrat defector) provided partisan votes to defeat the amendment. If one or more of the women supporting ERA had been members of the Republican party, women may have been victorious, garnering the vote of enough Republican men to break the tie. But because the women were on only one side of a partisan vote, the outcome was probably jeopardized. Constituent cues also played a role in the vote's outcome. The only male Democratic senator that defected from the party cue reversed his earlier position on the ERA and voted no at the last moment, citing constituent lobbying (Arizona Republic, March 2, 1976). A year earlier this same senator, Bill Swink, also changed to a no vote, citing pressures by his wife and daughter, opponents of the legislation, as well as other constituents (Arizona Republic, March 21, 1975).

Florida. The role of partisanship and partisan cue giving also might help explain the 1974, 1975, and 1976 votes in Florida. Three of the four female votes in those three roll calls were cast by an independent, Lori Wilson, who was in fact the only nonpartisan member of the Florida legislature during those sessions. While it is not evident that this senator, three times prime sponsor of the ERA, was a maverick in her behavior other than her nonpartisan stance, the fact that she was not involved in partisan activities of either party may have resulted in a diminution of her effectiveness with members of one or both parties.

The possibility of partisan female influence is undermined, however, by the apparent lack of influence of the one female partisan that entered the legislature one year before the 1977 vote. Democrat Elizabeth Castor's presence did not change the number of Democrats voting against the ERA. There were eleven male Democrat votes against the ERA in 1975 and again in 1977, while Castor's vote increased the positive votes from fifteen to sixteen. Meanwhile, Republican votes against the ERA remained stable to kill the amendment's chances. Other than partisanship, cues that worked against female legislators' influence appeared to be constituent-supported conservatism of north Florida senators, intense anti-ERA lobbying by Phyllis Schlafley and her Eagle Forum, and a backlash against pro-ERA lobbying by the state's governor and telephone calls to recalcitrant lawmakers by Vice-President Mondale and others (Florida Times Union, April 14, 1977; St. Petersburg Times, April 14, 1977).

Georgia. A cosponsor of the legislation and only female senator, Democrat Virginia Shapard, was unsuccessful in influencing her colleagues to vote for the ERA in a 1975 roll call. Even Shapard's own party was not persuaded to join her cause; only thirty-seven percent of the male Democrats supported the ERA compared to forty percent of Republicans. The ineffectiveness of Shapard may be explained in part by her inexperience and lack of seniority. She had been elected only a year earlier. Prior to election, however, she had been involved in party politics according to her biographical statements. Shapard's problems also doubtlessly stemmed from the conservative ideology that dominates the Georgia Senate. Newspaper accounts of the floor debate prior to the vote indicated that senators attacked the ERA as an infringement on state's rights, a long-time rallying issue for southern conservatives (Atlanta Journal, February 18, 1975). These same accounts suggested further that the ERA was the victim of a strong opposition lobby. The cues of black senators Julian Bond and Horace Tate, strong advocates of the ERA, also reportedly turned some white senators against the amendment.

North Carolina. In 1977 a bipartisan group of four female senators was unsuccessful in efforts to pass the ERA. Neither the three Democrats nor the one Republican convinced even their own party colleagues to support the amendment. In fact, Carolyn Mathis was the only Republican to vote for the ERA. An analysis of newspaper accounts (Raleigh News & Observer, March 2, 1977; Charlotte Observer, March 2, 1977) does not provide a clear reason for ERA's defeat on this occasion. Strong cues in support of the ERA were given by outsiders. President and Mrs. Carter, Governor Hunt, and Secretary of Commerce Juanita M. Kreps, a former Duke university official, made telephone calls to key legislators thought to be undecided. Unlike in Florida, this outside pressure did not appear to create resentment, yet the calls went unheeded. Only one legislator voiced resentment about pro-ERA lobbying. Senator Jim McDuffie stated that he decided to vote no after a female county commission chairperson from his district said he did not "have the guts" to vote for the ERA. Perhaps as in the state of Georgia, a strong conservative disposition of most senators precluded their supporting an amendment generally perceived as liberal.

Several conclusions may be drawn from these deviant cases. First, cues from whatever source may not have been important in several of these states. Instead of relying on cues, legislators may have looked inward, relying on personal ideology to cast their votes. Second, in many instances partisan cues were important determinants of ERA votes. Even when women were successful in influencing the paty cue, as in Arizona, this could lead to defeat when the other party became polarized against the women's position. And when women were unable to influence their own party, they were almost always defeated in the chamber as well. Third, there is some evidence that women's cues were sometimes ignored in favor of cues provided by sources outside of the legislature, such as opposition lobbyists and constituent opinion. In most instances outside forces such as these would be less influential than cues from within the legislature (Uslaner and Weber, 1977); but because the ERA became such a visible and controversial issue, outside cues may have played an abnormally important role in the outcome of these votes.

CUE INFLUENCE, SENIORITY, AND STATUS

We have hypothesized that women should have been more successful as cue givers when they had greater seniority and came from higher status social backgrounds. Aggregate data analysis largely supports the seniority hypothesis, but only weakly supports the status hypothesis. The average tenure for "successful" women (i.e., when men voted the same as a unanimous delegation of women; the uppermost-left and lowermost-right categories in Table 8.1) was 4.9 years per woman legislator. The average tenure for "unsuccessful" women (the uppermost-right category) was only 2.0 years. Thus, men may have not followed the cues of women on six occasions because the women were relatively junior senators.

The data on social status, however, did not correlate as well with women's success. A measure of occupational prestige was used as an indicator of status.[8] The average prestige score of successful women was 62 while the average for unsuccessful women was 60. Although this difference in scores is in the hypothesized direction, the difference is not statistically significant given the relatively small number of cases.[9]

A micro-level analysis of the comparative influence of members of the nine divided women's delegations (the middle categories of Table 8.1) provides inconclusive findings regarding the effects of tenure and social status. Based on our hypothesis, we anticipated that when the female cue was divided, female legislators with greater tenure and social status would prevail. As Table 8.2 illustrates, that expectation is not borne out conclusively by the data. Overall, the female senator with the longest tenure successfully influenced the outcome on four occasions. On two occasions, the senior senator was not successful. And in three of the nine instances there was no difference in the tenure of the most senior pro-ERA and anti-ERA senators. Thus, it once again appears that there is a weak but positive relationship between tenure and women's cue-giving influence. The data also indicate once again that the relationship between influence and social status is weak. On four of nine occasions a female senator with lesser occupational prestige was more successful in cue giving than was her more prestigious colleague. On three occasions occupational prestige proved to be influential. And on two occasions the occupational prestige of the women did not differ significantly.

Where the outcome of nine votes cannot be explained by the tenure and prestige hypotheses, other competing cues may be responsible. This is illustrated by the 1973 vote in Indiana. The female senator, a Democrat, with the longest tenure (nine years) and greatest occupational prestige (lawyer and judge) was able to convince only fifteen of forty-seven male colleagues to vote with her in favor of the ERA. She was less influential than the most ardent opponent of ERA, a female senator with only four years of tenure who was a homemaker prior to entering politics (Gary Post Tribune, April 3, 1973). Possibly the most important asset she possessed was her party affiliation. Being a Republican, a member of the majority party, gave her a substantial edge over her more senior, but Democratic, colleague. It is interesting that the senior Democrat did convince Democratic men to vote for

**TABLE 8.2   ERA Vote and Selected Characteristics of Female Senators
(Divided Women's Delegations Only)**

State/Occupation	Year	Vote	Party	Tenure (years)
Indiana				
Lawyer	1973	Yes	Democrat	9
Bookkeeper		No	Democrat	1
Not Ascertained		No	Republican	4
		Yes = 16,	No = 34	
Business Manager	1977	Yes	Democrat	1
Teacher		Yes	Democrat	1
Not Ascertained		No	Republican	8
		Yes = 26,	No = 24	
Missouri				
Film Maker	1977	Yes	Democrat	1
Not Ascertained		No	Democrat	5
		Yes = 12,	No = 22	
Nevada				
Business Manager	1975	Yes	Democrat	1
Real Estate Agent		No	Democrat	8
Retail Business Owner		No	Democrat	1
		Yes = 12,	No = 12	
Business Manager	1977	Yes	Democrat	3
Retail Business Owner		No	Democrat	3
		Yes = 11,	No = 10	
North Dakota				
Technician	1973	Yes	Republican	1
Not Ascertained		No	Republican	1
		Yes = 30,	No = 20	
Real Estate Agent	1975	Yes	Democrat	1
Technician		Yes	Republican	3
Not Ascertained		No	Republican	3
		Yes = 28,	No = 22	
Ohio				
Lawyer	1974	Yes	Democrat	3
Reporter		Yes	Democrat	7
Reporter		No	Republican	2
		Yes = 20,	No = 12	

(continued)

TABLE 8.2 Continued

State/Occupation	Year	Vote	Party	Tenure (years)
Vermont				
Not Ascertained	1973	Yes	Democrat	1
Clerical Worker		Yes	Republican	7
Registered Nurse		No	Republican	5
		Yes = 19,	No = 8	

ERA (eleven to seven) over the cue of the third women, a first-term
Democrat and bookkeeper who opposed the amendment. But an overwhelming rejection of the ERA by Republican men (four to twenty-
five) sealed the fate of the proposal in 1973. Another factor that may
have affected his vote, muting the influence of the senior Democrat,
could have been the influence of another woman from outside the
chamber. Prior to this vote an outspoken nationwide opponent of
ERA, Phyllis Schlafley, came to Indianapolis and lobbied against the
amendment in one of the first of her many forays into the nation's
state capitols (Indianapolis News, February 1, 1973).

CONCLUSIONS

Where women were present and voting on the ERA in state
legislatures, roll call data suggest that women may have been an important source of cues for their male colleagues. While the data
available do not allow us to establish an unquestionable causal link
between women's cues and men's votes, the data are certainly consistent with this possibility. We have also demonstrated that women's
seniority may have had some impact on their effectiveness as cue-
givers. Senior women were generally more effective than junior
women in influencing male colleagues. We found a less certain relationship between women's cue-giving power and their occupational
prestige.

We also found evidence that women had to share influence over
ERA votes with other sources of internal legislative cues, especially
political partisanship, and many external cues including lobbying by
chief executives, nonelected female political activists, and constituents. The longitudinal pattern of voting suggests that these com-

peting cues became stronger as the years passed. Where women shared the views of competing cue givers, their influence was naturally greatest. But on occasions when women were at odds with other cues, their influence dwindled rapidly, especially if they were very junior or members of a minority political party.

These findings raise the possibility that female senators, at least as much as their male colleagues, were responsible for the ultimate defeat of the ERA. Serious opposition to the ERA began to emerge in the first months of 1973, about the same time when the first female senators began to vote against the ERA in the states of Indiana, Nevada, North Carolina, North Dakota, and Vermont. No female senators had voted against the ERA during 1972. Perhaps many male legislators began to perceive serious female opposition to ERA from 1973 on, causing them to waver in their support of the amendment and succumb to other opposition cues. This perception was no doubt reinforced by opposition cues from women in the Eagle Forum (a lobby group headed by Schlafley) and ardent constituent opponents. It is also plausible that the female opponents did not actually change the minds of men after 1972, but more likely, they merely used the token opposition by female senators after 1972 as an excuse or justification for their already firmly rooted opposition to the ERA.

Overall, this research suggests that women can often expect to be a useful source of cues for male colleagues confronted with roll call votes on women's issues. But the data also suggests that as such matters become more controversial, women must expect to form alliances with other sources of cues in order to be successful. In particular, women in state legislatures would be advised to work within the existing political party apparatus.[10] If we assume for a moment that most women's positions on most women's issues will be liberal ones, the task of working with party members should be easiest and most critical for female Democrats. As was observed in our analysis of ERA votes, when Democratic women could not influence their own partisan allies, women's efforts to influence the other political party were usually unsuccessful. Moderate to liberal Republican women generally confront a more formidable task in attempting to influence the votes of their typically more conservative male Republican colleagues. However, difficulties that women from either party encounter should become less problematic as more female legislators accrue more seniority and share the reins of political party and committee leadership along with their male counterparts.

NOTES

1. A discussion of cue giving and cue taking can be found in any number of legislative process textbooks. Two excellent and up-to-date books are by Harris and Hain (1983: 380-383) and Rosenthal (1981: 84-86).

2. Johnson and Carroll (1978: 40A) report that female legislators blame stereotyping of this sort for the difficulties they experience in establishing working friendships with male legislators.

3. Both of the Fords (Gerald and Betty) and the Carters (Jimmy and Rosalyn) were active in placing strategic telephone calls to recalcitrant ERA opponents. There is little evidence that these efforts were successful, however. It is even possible that the presidential efforts created a backlash among a few resentful legislators, as reported elsewhere in this chapter.

4. Hill (1981) found that the ERA was a popular topic among authors of letters to the editor. In an unpublished study of newspaper editorials, Hill found that a majority of major daily newspapers published pro or con editorials on the amendment just prior to the roll call vote in the state.

5. Numerous studies have pointed to the influence of legislative colleagues. The most recent, comprehensive analysis of this subject is by Uslaner and Weber (1977).

6. This tally includes only votes directly on ratification of the ERA. It does not include committee-of-the-whole votes, motions to table or other legislative maneuvers that produce roll call votes sometimes described by journalists as votes on the ERA.

7. Biographical data were collected from various sources including state "blue books," publications of the Center for the Study of American Woman and Politics at Rutgers University, and numerous "Who's Who" publications. State archivists and legislative clerks also provided the author with some data.

8. Occupational prestige scores were taken from Temme (1975).

9. I could identify the occupation of only forty women, seventy-seven percent of the applicable subsample discussed in this analysis.

10. Although desirable, it may prove to be a formidable task for some women to work with parties that often thwart female political careers. (Johnson and Carroll, 1978; Clarke and Kornberg, 1979; Kirkpatrick, 1974).

9

WOMEN ON THE STATE BENCH: CORRELATES OF ACCESS

Beverly B. Cook

The appointment of the first woman to the U.S. Supreme Court in 1981 symbolized for the nation the legitimacy of women's place in the judiciary. Beginning with the office of Justice of the Peace in 1870, women persevered for over one hundred years to reach the most powerful judicial position in the country. State and federal courts form a dual system, linked together by the movement of personnel and cases, but in terms of number of judges and cases the state segment is much the larger. With positions for 25,000 judges and combined annual caseloads in the millions, the fifty state and District of Columbia court systems provide more opportunities for women to become judges and to affect the development of law than the federal court system with its 1000 judges and 250,000 cases per year. The courts created by state government are important to women citizens as forums for the establishment of their state rights and for the resolution of disputes that affect the quality of their daily lives. Any understanding of women's struggle for equal participation in judicial decision making requires that our attention first be directed to the state and local level.

STATE AND LOCAL COURTS

The statement that "there is no such thing as a wholly local court in New York State" (Sayre and Kaufman, 1965: 522), is also true in every other state. However, the courts that operate under state authority can be categorized as "state" or "local" by two important attributes: (1) the qualifications for the judgeship and (2) the legal and administrative ties to state government. The location of the court in an urban or rural setting is not a good indicator of its type, since many limited jurisdiction trial courts are simply judicial districts within the state court system with the same jurisdiction and type of personnel regardless of population size or location. Some very large cities set the qualifications and the procedures for their own local courts. Appellate courts are clearly more state than local in their orientation. Those attributes that do provide distinctions between state and local courts have a relationship to women's share of judicial offices.

First, courts can be separated into two sets of the same size by the presence or absence of bar qualifications: attorney courts with approximately 12,000 judges and nonattorney courts with approximately 13,000 judges. The number of attorney judges and courts has steadily increased from a small proportion of the judiciary to parity with lay judges and courts. The categories are not entirely distinct since new attorney courts retain some "grandfathered" lay judges; and many nonattorney courts attract lawyers. The direction of the change toward more attorney judges reflects the increasing power of lawyers organized at the state level to control training, admission, and practice and to protect and extend professional interests.

The impact of the upgrading of qualifications is a smaller number of women in the judiciary. However, the proportion of women judges drawn from the female lawyer pool is larger than the proportion drawn from the female citizen pool. This difference in opportunity fits findings across the spectrum of political cultures and positions that women with more education and other resources are more successful than those with less in entering public institutions and taking powerful places.

The right to compete for judgeships was established in the states between 1870 and 1920. Until 1869, with the admission of the first woman to the bar in Iowa, women lacked the necessary credentials for holding office on the attorney courts. The denial of political rights also barred women from the lay courts until the same period when a few states and territories extended limited suffrage rights. Access to the bar and the polls are both privileges of state citizenship. So state and local officials have controlled women's opportunities for office on the state courts and also, since candidates must by custom belong to a state bar, on federal courts.

The second attribute defining a court as state or local is its relationship to the state court hierarchy and to state and local governments. At one extreme are state trial courts with minimal local government ties and exclusively judicial functions such as those within the unified state judiciaries of California, Illinois, and Kentucky. At the other extreme are local trial courts with no ties to state government except for their authorization under state law and with powers not exclusively judicial.[1] The type of local court created and financed by local government, whose judges handle no preliminary matters for and have no appellate ties to other courts and are not supervised or trained by state officials, have almost vanished.[2] A few states have entire systems that remain highly decentralized and disaggregated with many local courts, for example, Georgia and Tennessee.

Most trial courts operate in a netherland of mixed state and local control of their financing, administration, staffing, and reporting. The state or the local government may decide to establish the court or not, to set attorney or other qualifications, and to set higher or lower salaries and fees. The larger the number of local ties, the more parochial political and social attitudes would be expected to influence the sex identity of judge incumbents. Since the state cultures are increasingly sophisticated, one might predict some success for women in those courts closer to the state government; and in face more female judges are found on appellate courts and on trial courts in metropolitan areas with more state supervision and support.

Where both attributes—qualifications and government ties—define the court as local, one would expect fewer female judges. For example, the Philadelphia traffic and municipal courts, unlike most courts in metropolitan areas, do not require bar admission and have closer ties to the city than the state (Abraham, 1980). There are currently no female judges on these courts.

GAINING THE CREDENTIALS FOR STATE JUDGESHIPS

Women in every state became participants in the judicial process by winning their rights one at a time and not by a single act of "emancipation" into public roles. Admission to the bar was the first post-Civil War demand to which state governments responded after the U.S. Supreme Court insisted in 1873 (Bradwell versus Illinois, 16 Wall. 130) that the privilege of practicing law was within the power of state governments to bestow. Before 1900, thirty-four states had declared that sex was not a barrier to legal practice; and thus technically female lawyers in those states had the credentials for judicial office. However, in over half of the states women won the right to practice law before the right to vote. Apparently a small minority of educated women who wanted an elite occupation posed a lesser threat to male control than a female population that wanted an equal share of voting power. Moreover, in the states that denied suffrage, it was expected that female lawyers would not engage in judicial politics.

Judges themselves have tried to prevent women from becoming lawyers and judges (Cook, 1983a). In Massachusetts, after the state legislature authorized women to practice law (effectively reversing the highest state court's decision to the contrary), the justices ruled in 1882 that a woman could not be appointed as justice of the peace (Robinson, 1889). The state legislature then created a new office of special commissioner for women, with the same limited duties that seemed proper for female lawyers to perform as law clerks and reporters, while men handled the more important discretionary and adversarial work.

Inclusion of women on jury rolls, which made it possible for them to participate in the making of court decisions as laypersons, came even later. The barriers to taking a judgeship broke down for elite women before the barriers to the jury box for ordinary women. At least one woman reached the limited jurisdiction trial bench in each of twenty-six states before or in the same year that women as a class qualified for jury duty. The last continental state to admit women to the bar was Delaware in 1923; the last state to ratify the Nineteenth amendment was North Carolina in 1971; the last state to permit women to serve on juries was Mississipi in 1968. The rights of women to vote, to practice law, to perform jury duty, and to take public office are complementary to each other and based upon the same notions about female capacity. The interrelatedness of these rights was recognized by a male judge who voided a state law denying women the right to serve as jurors (Ex parte Mana, 172 P 987, 1918):

> [We] would then have a situation where a woman on trial for a crime might be brought to trial before a woman judge, prosecuted by a woman district attorney, defended by a woman lawyer, brought in court by a woman bailiff, and yet forced to a trial before a jury of men.

Private institutions shared in the preservation of barriers against female participation in court decision making. The law schools and organized bar produced few female candidates for attorney courts, and local business and political party organizations failed to socialize many female candidates for lay courts. While the requirement of law training for the attorney courts is explicit, the business experience expected of lay judges is not often specified. Exceptions exist in Arkansas where the county judge, who handles matters involving county taxes, roads, and property, should have a "good business education" and in Georgia, where the probate judge may substitute five years of service as court clerk for three years of law practice (Reincke, 1977).

TABLE 9.1 Timing of Sex Integration: the Polls, the Bar, and the Bench

State	Vote	Bar[a]	GJ[b]	Last Name	First Name	High Court	Last Name	First Name
Alabama	1953	1907	1979	Johnson	Inge	1975	Shores	Janie
Alaska	1913	1950	1982	Cutler*	Beverly			
Arizona	1887	1903	1950	Lockwood*	Lorna	1961	Lockwood*	Lorna
Arkansas	1917	1918	1947	Hale	Ruth	1975	Roy*	ElisiJane
California	1911	1878	1931	Bullock*	Georgia	1977	Bird	Rose
Colorado	1876	1891	1938	Ingham	Irene	1979	Dubofsky	Jean
Connecticut	1893	1882	1972	Kulawiz	Joanne	1978	Peters	Ellen
Delaware	(c)	1923	(d)			(e)		
Washington, D.C.	1920	1872	1968	Green	Joyce	1967	Kelly*	Catherine
Florida	1969	1898	1970	Grossman	Rhea			
Georgia	1970	1916	1977	Kravitch	Phyllis			
Hawaii		1888	1934	Buck	Carrick	1959	Lewis	Rhoda
Idaho	1897	1895						
Illinois	1913	1870	1923	Bartelme	Mary			
Indiana	1917	1875	1965	Shields	V. Sue			
Iowa	1894	1869	1977	Briles	Margaret			
Kansas	1861	1881	1976	McFarland	Kay	1977	McFarland*	Kay
Kentucky	1838	1912	1980	Peers	Olga			
Louisiana	1970	1898	1954	Burch	Fannie			
Maine	1920	1872				1983	Glassman	Caroline
Maryland		1902	1956	Lawlor	Kathryn	1979	Davidson*	Rita
Massachusetts	1879	1882	1959	Barron*	Jeannie	1977	Abrams*	Ruth
Michigan	1875	1881	1941	Neunfelt	Lila	1973	Coleman*	Mary

(continued)

TABLE 9.1 Continued

State	Vote	Bar[a]	GJ[b]	Last Name	First Name	High Court	Last Name	First Name
Minnesota	1875	1877	1974	Sedgwick	Susanne	1977	Wahl	Rosalie
Mississippi	1880	1914	1971	Prather	Lenore	1982	Prather*	Lenore
Missouri	1920	1870	1980	Forder	Anna			
Montana	1881	1890	1978	Barz	Diane			
Nebraska	1883	1881	1972	Sharp	Betty			
Nevada	1915	1902	1983	Shearing	Miriam			
New Hampshire	1878	1890	1982	Dalianas	Linda			
New Jersey	1887	1895	1972	Morgan	Sonia	1982	Garibaldi*	Marie
New Mexico	1910	1917	1971	Walters	Mary			
New York	1880	1886	1962	Mangan	M. Margaret	1983	Kaye	Judith
North Carolina	1971	1878	1949	Sharp	Susie	1962	Sharp*	Susie
North Dakota	1881	1905						
Ohio	1894	1873	1921	Allen	Florence	1923	Allen*	Florence
Oklahoma	1920	1898	1974	McCalister	Margaret	1982	Wilson*	Alma
Oregon	1878	1886	1954	Lewis	Jean	1982	Roberts*	Betty

State			GJ Court Judge[b]			SC Justice	
Pennsylvania	1920	1883	1941	Soffel*	Sara	1961	Alpern*	Anne
Rhode Island	1917	1920	1956	Murray	Florence	1979	Murray*	Florence
South Carolina	1969	1918	1974	Ramynke	Mildred			
South Dakota	1918	1893	1981	Gibbons	Julia			
Tennessee	1887	1907	1935	Hughes	Sarah			
Texas	1920	1910	1978	Durham	Christine	1982	Sondock*	Ruby
Utah	1919	1872				1981	Durham*	Christine
Vermont	1921	1914						
Virginia	1952	1894	1982	Keenan	Barbara			
Washington	1890	1885	1973	Niemi	Janice	1981	Dimmick*	Carolyn
West Virginia	1920	1896	1973	Tsapsis	Callie			
Wisconsin	1920	1875	1977	Krueger	Moria	1976	Abrahamson	Shirley
Wyoming	1900	1899	1982	Kail	Elizabeth			

a. Berkson (1982: Table 1).
b. General Jurisdiction Court.
c. Three states have not ratified the Nineteenth Amendment.
d. Seven states have never had a woman judge on GJ court.
e. Twenty-three states have never had a woman supreme court justice.
* Prior service on lower court.

The intrusion of women into the male monopoly over lawyering and judging proceeded in an incremental fashion. Women were over-qualified for the first judgeships available to them. They were lawyers serving on minor courts with limited or specialized jurisdictions that did not require legal training or in quasi-judicial administrative posts. For example, Ada Lee, admitted to the Michigan bar in 1883 after of-fice study, was nominated for the office of circuit court commissioner by three political parties and elected; she filled out her term despite suits brought to oust her on grounds of her sex (Robinson, 1889:20). Catherine McCulloch, who attended Union College of Law (later North-western) and passed the bar in 1886, won election as justice of the peace in Evanston and served from 1907 to 1913. Reah Whitehead, elected justice of the peace in Seattle in 1914, was on the same bench twenty-five years later. Marilla Ricker in the District of Columbia in 1883 and Carrie Kilgore in Pennsylvania in 1886 accepted quasi-judicial positions handling chancery matters, as did McCulloch in Il-linois in 1917.[3] All these women were members of their state bars and eligible for the better-paying and more interesting positions reserved for lawyers.

In the 1930s there were at least twenty-four female lawyers on lay courts in twelve states and only nine female lawyers on attorney courts in eight states (F. Cook, 1939). The justice courts in California, which have been more attractive than many other rural courts in terms of salary and recognition, included attorney judges before the state Supreme Court (525 P2d 72, 1974) and state legislature required bar admission for eligibility. Of the justice judges sitting between 1967 and 1974, 17 percent of the female judges (and 33 percent of the male judges) were lawyers. Of the lawyer judges 4 percent were women; of the nonlawyer judges 8.5 percent were women. (Arnold, 1967, 1973). In relation to the respective pools of eligibles, the California female lawyers were more successful than the laywomen in reaching the justice bench.

WOMEN ON THE NONATTORNEY COURTS

The distinction between attorney and nonattorney courts is not that one accepts only professional candidates for office and the other layper-sons, but that a single profession monopolizes the offices of the one type and that persons from a variety of occupational backgrounds, in-cluding lawyers, but especially persons in business, law enforcement, and other local government bureaus, share the offices available in the other type. The one-track career ladder to attorney courts, along with other considerations, seems to improve the access of women in comparison to the diverse and uncertain avenues to other courts.

Nonattorneys are eligible in forty-three states for minor court judgeships; their jurisdiction over civil disputes is limited to small dollar amounts in liability and fine. These judges work in small incorporated cities as well as in rural areas, often handling traffic offenses and minor matters such as disorderly conduct, petty larceny, and property damage (Silberman, 1979). The judges are not distributed through the states in the same pattern as those on attorney courts. Of the total known lay judges, 17.5 percent are in Georgia, 15 percent in New York, 12 percent in Texas; each of these three states has over 1000 lay judges. Eighteen other states have between 150 and 1000 judges on lay courts.[4] Thirteen states have from 50 to 150 lay judges; nine states have fewer than 50; and seven none.

The political power of the judge on a nonattorney court is often considerable. The JP in a rural community may be the only visible judicial figure. The powers to issue search and arrest warrants and to decide small claims are significant to local law enforcement officers and to local business owners. Those with investments in the rural political or economic community would have strong motivations to assure themselves of a cooperative incumbent on the court. The incentives for taking such offices, the small salary, erratic hours, and low prestige, appear unimportant only in comparison with the incentives of higher courts. Within the local community the judge's power to redistribute goods makes the judge a powerful official. Where these conditions occur, there is competition for the job and the likelihood of finding a woman on the bench relates to their presence in the linked occupations of law enforcement and business.

Judgeships on nonattorney courts are available to adult residents with high school education (or sometimes less). Women have the same qualifications as men but in proportion to the pool their success rate is low. Women first served on these courts before national suffrage but have never come near holding such offices in proportion to their share of high school graduates. Esther Morris, justice of the peace in Wyoming territory, was the first woman lay judge in 1870.

The disparity between female lawyers' expectations for the state attorney courts and their actual incumbency is about 50 percent, which is the ratio of the percentage of female lawyers to female judges. When 10 percent of the lawyers are women, about five percent are judges; when 12 percent are women, about 6 percent are judges. The disparity between women citizen's expectations for nonattorney courts and their success is worse. The prediction on the basis of a sex-neutral selection of judges from high school graduates is slightly over half female judges. The data available on these nonattorney courts are not as reliable or complete as on attorney courts, but women only hold 20 percent to 30 percent of the predicted seats across the nation. In a few courts, listed on Table 9.2A, laywomen do as well as female lawyers in winning judicial office.

Although the comparative disparity for laywomen is higher than for lawyers across the states, the number of women serving on non-attorney courts is greater. Table 9.2 shows that where nonattorneys control the largest share of the seats on nonattorney courts the pro-portion of women is much larger than when the nonattorney share declines to one-fourth or less. It is possible to compare the representa-tion of women in states that still support both kinds of courts. The in-filtration of the nonattorney courts by attorneys reduces the percen-tage of women toward their level in attorney courts. This erosion of the lay judiciary improves the situation of women, as well as men, with a law degree. As the percentage of women in the pool of legal professions moves toward parity, we do not yet know if female lawyers will share public offices equally or will instead be treated like the nonattorney women with the same preparation as men who (depending upon the state and the court) fell short of their share by 40 percent at the best to 100 percent at the worst.

Although all the candidates for attorney courts are necessarily career women, about sixty percent of the women on the nonattorney courts had full-time occupations before assuming the judgeship. The jobs of more than half these working women were law-related, such as court clerks and law secretaries who could move easily into judicial duties. One fourth were in traditional female occupations of teaching, welfare, and nursing; and one-fifth in small business as salespersons or accountants. A minority of the lay judges were previously housewives with considerable community service.

The following brief biographies are typical of many others (Lieb-man, 1955):

> Judge Miriam Oder Beaty, Probate Judge of Elk County, Kansas, took a short business course after high school and then worked as a secretary in a small plant for ten years. She married and stayed home with her two children for seventeen years and then found clerical employment with the county. After seven years in the social welfare bureau and the selec-tive service board, she was appointed judge in 1942 and won subsequent election through her 65th birthday.
>
> Judge Jessika Carswell, Probate Judge for Jefferson County, Georgia, attended college for a few years and then worked as city stenographer

TABLE 9.2 Percentage of Women Judges on Attorney and Nonattorney Courts

States	*Nonattorney Courts**		*Attorney Courts*	
	A. Nonattorney judges 50-100			
Georgia	Probate	29.5	Superior	1.7
Kansas	Probate[a]	26.3	District	2.1
Maryland	Orphan's	24.2	Circuit	3.9
North Dakota	County	22.5	District	0.0
Oregon	Justice	34.1	Circuit	2.4
South Carolina	Probate	31.1	Circuit	0.0
Vermont	Probate	31.6	Superior	0.0
Wyoming	Justice	24.0	District	5.9
	B. Nonattorney judges 5-25			
Arkansas	County	2.7	Circuit/Chancery	6.3
Colorado	County	10.4	District	5.6
Florida	County	11.0	Circuit	4.0
Idaho	Magistrate	9.6	District	0.0
Michigan	Probate	3.7	Circuit	3.6
Minnesota	Probate	1.8	District	2.8
Missouri	Probate[a]	7.0	Circuit	2.3
North Carolina	County	2.5	Superior	0.0
Oklahoma	Special	12.2	District	5.0

*Reincke (1977).
a. Prior to replacement of probate judges by magistrates.

and clerk to the local judge for ten years. She married after winning her judgeship.

Judge Lucy Viets, Probate Court of Hartford County, Connecticut, taught school and worked as a post office clerk until marriage. After eight years at home with two children she returned to her post office job for ten years and then served as secretary for a deputy sheriff for a period overlapping by five years her selection as a judge.

WOMEN ON ATTORNEY COURTS

In nineteeth-century America the qualifications and the selection procedures for judges on major courts better fit democratic norms. Bar admission was not required for many judgeships, and in any event admission followed a simple examination by the local judge. The raising of the standards for bar admission by requiring formal training transferred the gatekeeping power over the profession from the bench to the law school. To the extent that women could not gain admittance to law school they could not practice or aspire to judgeships.

The law schools erected high barriers against women, translating cultural views about women's place into explicit or hidden bans upon their entry as students (Epstein, 1981). Women and other outsiders, such as working men and naturalized citizens, found their opportunities in unaccredited night schools and programs for part-time students. The credentialing of law schools through a national association, and the setting of standards that only financially secure law schools could meet, effectively squeezed out these schools and students. Thus, improved standards for the bar and law schools severely depressed the number of women who could hope to become lawyers and judges on attorney courts. Note on Table 9.3 the reduction in the proportion of women law students from 1925 to 1955, which is partially associated with these professional reforms. Between the date of gaining suffrage when they first became fully eligible for judgeships, and the beginnings of contemporary feminism in the 1960s, women were pushed further away from law work by these national professional changes (Hummer, 1979).

Establishing her credentials as a successful trial practitioner posed the next barrier to the woman who had taken her law degree. A litigator by definition works in the public eye, subject to the criticism of her peers and of lay observers (Schafran, 1983). Few women prior to the 1970s would risk their reputations and psyches by representing clients in court, even if they could find clients who would trust them in an adversary role. They accepted the estate and family law work assigned to them by the social and legal mores and sometimes found congruent work on the specialized probate and family courts.

Appropriately, the earliest judgeships held by women on attorney courts were on the municipal courts, which handled primarily nonadversarial matters such as traffic and small claims, or on specialized courts dealing with marital disputes or child delinquency. The first municipal judge of a large city was Othilia Beals, who served in Seattle during the first world war and then "resigned in favor of a returned soldier" (Derry, 1949: 28). Besides the necessary bar credential, she had impressive mentors in her father, a trial judge, and her husband, a state supreme court justice. Mary O'Toole was appointed to the District of Columbia Municipal Court in 1921; Georgia Bullock to the Los Angeles Police Court in 1924; Lilian Westropp to the Cleveland Municipal Court in 1931; Anna Kross to the New York Magistrate's Court in 1933; Sadie Shulman to the Boston Municipal Court in 1937; and Dorothy Lee to the Portland (Oregon) Municipal Court in 1940.

TABLE 9.3 Women in the State Bar and Bench Over Time

	1925	*Percentage of Women* *1955*	*1983*
Law School	5.5	3.5	37.5
Practice	1.5	3.5	13.0
LJ Court	1.0	2.0	8.0
GJ Court	1.0	1.0	4.5
Appellate	1.0	1.0	5.5

SOURCES: Hummer (1979: Table 3); Coles (1974: Table II-1); and Cook (1983b: Table 1).

The presence of the first women on attorney courts seemed more palatable when they went to courts handling matters that belonged to women in their domestic roles. Florence Allen, the first woman on a state general jurisdiction court, refused the opportunity to take a segregated docket of divorce cases. But other women gained their seats on special courts or divisions because of their credibility as candidates. Mary Margaret Bartelme, admitted to the Illinois bar in 1894, worked with other social reformers for the creation of a juvenile court in Chicago in 1899. The male judge assigned to that court chose her as his assistant to hear cases involving delinquent girls in 1913. After national suffrage the Republican party nominated her for circuit court in 1923; she won the election and continued her work in the juvenile division until retirement ten years later (Freedman, 1980). The first woman reached this type of court by presidential appointment in 1918, when Kathryn Sellers went on the District of Columbia Juvenile Court. In 1921 Camille Kelley took over the juvenile court in Memphis; and in 1923 Virginia Mayfield was appointed to the Alabama Domestic Relations Court. Edith Atkinson, whose husband was also a judge, became juvenile judge in Miami in 1925; and Aldona Appleton joined the New Jersey Juvenile and Domestic Relations court in 1926. Both Rosalie Whitney and Justine Wise Polier went on family court in New York City in 1935; and Jennie Barron took the juvenile and domestic relations caseload in Boston from 1937 to 1959. In 1941 Anna Veters Levy was elected to the juvenile court in New Orleans.

Female lawyers, then, established their claims to the bench in the large metropolitan areas on the courts with the cases of least political and economic importance. They dealt with the problems of the ordinary person with traffic tickets, debts, difficult spouses, and unruly children. Female judges were not welcome to the same degree in different cities and states. The fairness of their consideration for judgeships can be estimated by the relationship between the percentage of available female lawyers and the percentage of judges. Female lawyers have been concentrated in urban areas; so their entry to judicial offices in major cities is not surprising. But as their numbers slowly increased, they did not automatically win a larger share of judge seats without effort and organization.

Of the fifteen states with the largest number of female lawyers in the age cohorts of candidates (35 to 55), California had the best record in 1950 and in 1980 for a fair proportion of women on the bench. Other states with good records at both points in time were the District of Columbia, Ohio, Pennsylvania, Florida, Michigan, New Jersey, and Missouri. States where the relationship between the female lawyer pool and judges showed less equity over time included New York, Illinois, Massachusetts, Maryland, and Virginia. The next section concentrates entirely on the attorney judges and examines the institutional features that support or undermine women's success in the judiciary.

GETTING THERE AND MOVING UP

Entering public life through the courts is different in a variety of ways from engaging in legislative or executive politics. Some of these differences allow women easier access to the major courts, while others serve to control their numbers and reduce their opportunities to use their authority for the beneift of other women. As newcomers to public life, women and other outsiders can participate with a lesser financial and psychic investment when the rules of access are fixed and known. But while the virtues of law as an institution—its certainty and logic—may infuse the organization of law schools and courts, they do not structure the political process of getting there. Women with ambition for judgeships cannot share their experiences across state lines, while women who try their fortunes on the electoral road to office in the other branches can learn from each other to mutual advantage. On the other hand, female lawyers who attain their first judicial offices then have a clear perspective on where and how to move up in the courts; while women in legislative or executive offices face more diffuse and implicit opportunity structures (Schlesinger, 1966).

Two major features which distinguish the judicial from the other branches are its hierarchical structure and its variety of selection procedures.

HIERARCHICAL STRUCTURE

The hierarchy of the courts provides a well-delineated career ladder. The court reform movement that began at the turn of the century has moved state court systems toward centralization of authority and simplication of structure. Within a court system the judges on the higher courts have considerable power to discipline lower court judges directly and through the reversal of their decisions. The hierarchical nature of courts means that a lower court attorney judge learns in the course of her daily work how to do the job and how to get the job at the next level. A lower position linked in this fashion to a higher position has been termed a "manifest" office. For a judge in such a manifest position there is little risk involved in setting one's sights upon the next court level. In contrast, a woman legislator or executive reaching for a higher office will move into a different organization at the price of time, money, and psychic energy. These expenses and the need for coalition building among constituent groups is atypical for winning higher office in the judiciary (Dubois, 1983). The reform of the courts to a bureaucratic and civil service pattern opens the way for outsiders to succeed once they gain their first position. Going up is easier than getting there, although the number of available positions diminishes toward the top of the judicial hierarchy.

Appellate Careers. The progress of women who have served on the state appellate benches can be examined for all states from the date that the first woman took such an office in 1923. Figure 9.1 shows where the women prepared for elevation and where they moved after their appellate service. Half of those who reached the highest court moved directly from trial judgeships; while those women who won a seat on an intermediate appellate bench came in the same proportion from law practices and from trial courts. A large majority of all women at both appellate levels are now sitting as incumbents; only a few are retired or dead. This fact emphasizes how recently women appeared on these courts.

Appellate women judges have made the judiciary their life careers. Very few have returned to private firms or corporate legal departments. One justice after defeat in a partisan election returned to the trial level. Of the state appellate judges, 7 percent have gone onto the federal bench, including Sandra D. O'Connor from the Arizona Court of Appeals to the U.S. Supreme Court. At the beginning of their practices, female lawyers have a variety of options in law work and politics, but those who reach the appellate level usually remain

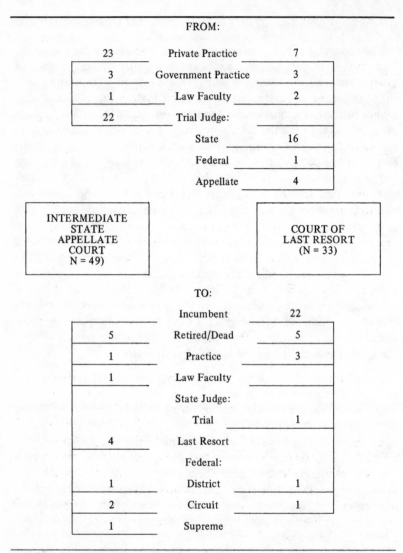

	FROM:	
23	Private Practice	7
3	Government Practice	3
1	Law Faculty	2
22	Trial Judge:	
	State	16
	Federal	1
	Appellate	4

INTERMEDIATE STATE APPELLATE COURT N = 49)		COURT OF LAST RESORT (N = 33)

	TO:	
	Incumbent	22
5	Retired/Dead	5
1	Practice	3
1	Law Faculty	
	State Judge:	
	Trial	1
4	Last Resort	
	Federal:	
1	District	1
2	Circuit	1
1	Supreme	

Figure 1:   Paths To and From State Appellate Benches, Female Judges, 1923-1983

short of a realistic chance for a more powerful executive office in the state or national capital.

Trial Careers. The situation of women on the trial court levels is less secure. The career decisions of women who entered the state courts during a five-year period, 1977 to 1983, show that almost half left during that period. Twenty percent of those returned to practice and almost the same proportion retired or died. The others stepped up the court hierachy. More women joined the limited jurisdiction bench during the five-year period than had been sitting there at the beginning. Most women on the general jurisdiction courts in 1977 remained on the same bench. Those elevated moved to the state appellate court or to the federal bench in about the same proportion. The turnover at this trial level was not as rapid as on the lower trial level; so that at the end of the period the increase in women incumbents was almost 100 percent.

VARIETY OF SELECTION PROCEDURES FOR STATE JUDGES

The statutory format for the selection of legislators and major executives in state and local government is popular election, whether partisan or nonpartisan. But structures for selecting judges vary among the states and include (1) the adoption of the same form of election for all officials; or (2) the retention of the historical form of legislative choice; or (3) the imitation of the federal system of executive nomination and senate confirmation; or (4) choice of inferior judges by superior judges; or (5) the innovation of a nominating commission, which constrains executive choice to a short list, combined with retention "on the record" (Berkson, 1980).

Female Judges and the Voters. Women find a place on the bench primarily through appointment; the suffrage has not directly improved their judicial opportunities. The advantage to women of non-electoral selection structures is that voter sex role prejudices do not prevent women's access to the bench (Hedlund et al., 1979). The female candidate for the bench is in a catch 22 situation. The characteristics considered appropriate for the lawyer—aggressive and confident—and for the judge—severe and firm—are stereotypically masculine. Candidates in competitive elections are expected to show these same qualities. But voters do not necessarily approve these qualities in female candidates. So the woman who proves her fitness for the public office violates the social expectations attached to her sex identity.

The name of the candidate on the ballot provides a cue to sex identity for voters. An analysis of nonpartisan election contests in California between 1976 and 1980 shows that female identity of non-incumbents had a strong negative impact upon the final election results (Dubois, 1983). But where the nominee is selected behind the doors of a governor's office, a party chief's headquarters, or a legislative committee room, the significant cue to the voter or the legislator who subsequently ratifies that choice will be party identity or leader approval rather than gender. It is not surprising, then, that women have been more successful in achieving judgeships where the public or their representatives in a legislature have a voice only in approving but not in choosing officials.

The prejudices of the voters, and particularly the women voters, toward women candidates for the bench may soon disappear if the 1983 polls of public attitudes toward women candidates for the most important national offices are good indicators. However, to date the political elite have been more responsive than the masses to the demands of women for a share of public offices. In general, the views of the educated elite on sex roles are more flexible and unconventional. They are also more conscious of the inconsistent values undergirding the political structure that provide rationales for elitist standards, for affirmative action, and for patronage in the choice of political authorities. Political leaders also understand the necessity of incorporating newly emerging groups into their coalitions. Even nominating commissions, originally created to reestablish professional standards for judgeships, appreciate the need to recognize and share power with nontraditional aspirants for office. Thus the chair of the judicial selection panel created by Mayor Koch of New York City to recommend criminal and family court judges apologized in 1983 for "a certain imbalance here in terms of minorities and women" at the swearing-in ceremony for six white male judges (Carroll, 1983).

Female Judges and the Governors. Women who must convince an electorate of their qualifications for a judgeship deal with ambivalent and risky events; in contrast, women whose appointment to the bench depends upon a single individual or small group are bound by unique attitudes and immediate political needs. A conservative attitude toward women's place on the part of the appointing authority is determinative, as is a radical viewpoint, which may produce dramatic gains in a short period. An example of the latter phenomenon is the change in percentage of women on the appellate bench in California across administrations. Governor Pat Brown between 1959 and 1966 selected women for two percent of the vacancies; Governor Ronald Reagan between 1967 and 1974 chose none. Governor Jerry Brown during his first term, 1974 to 1978, placed women in fourteen percent of the available judgeships at the appellate level (Culver, 1981: Table 1).

With a few exceptions, women reach the state appellate courts through appointment. The first woman on a state supreme court, Florence Allen, organized a statewide campaign to reach voters in Ohio in 1922 (Cook, 1981a). Forty years later the first woman on the Arizona Supreme Court profited from the name identity of her father, a former chief justice, in winning election. Women also reached the Michigan and Alabama high courts through electoral campaigns in the early 1970s. But the other women on appeals courts (eighty-eight percent) received their positions from governors, although some subsequently faced the voters to retain their seats. Only two lost their reelection bids against strong opponents. Two accepted seats on an interim basis knowing that the state party machines that controlled nominations were not sympathetic to their ambitions. Altogether, only five of the women justices were short-term tokens. Of the retired women justices, five served ten years or more; and of those now sitting, nine have had five years or more in office. However, most of the contemporary women justices are neophytes; half have been serving for less than two years.

Women on the intermediate appellate courts also gained their seats primarily by gubernatorial appointment (eighty-five percent). The electoral route has only been necessary in states with party competition, such as Ohio, Illinois, and Michigan, or at the point of the creation of new courts. When all new court positions are open at the same time, as occurred in Wisconsin and New Mexico, voters can be persuaded that the allotment of at least one position to a woman is fair. Appointed women who later faced the voters have been successful even in competitive and traditional states for two reasons: the less prestigious intermediate level does not generate strong challenges, and with little information or interest in this court level, the title of judge provides a ballot advantage regardless of sex identity.

Female Judges and Female Appointers. When a woman has the power of appointment, the chances of female candidates improve, simply because they are more likely to be found within the appointer's network. Male authorities habitually ask "where are the women?" and apologize that they would appoint them if they could find them. Women authorities know exactly how and where to find them. The opportunities of women for the bench improved with women governors in Connecticut and Washington. The more women on the nominating commissions reporting names to the governor, the more likely are women to appear on the lists.

Where judges choose other judges, then the presence of women on the higher courts helps to put women on the lower courts. In Illinois, the circuit judges vote on the candidates for associate circuit judges after considerable lobbying among themselves. The recent addition of a number of women at the associate level in Chicago reflects the activity of women on the circuit bench and their professional networks. One might expect more "assistant" judges and magistrates when there are more women among the judges who select them; but this form of selection happens to exist in a set of states with very poor representation of women, for example, Alabama, Alaska, Iowa, Nebraska, North Carolina, North Dakota, Oklahoma, South Dakota, and Virginia.

The path to the trial bench for women within any selection system is the same as for men. A recent comprehensive survey of general jurisdiction judges in all states found that about fifty-three percent win their seats from governors, forty-four percent from voters; two percent from legislators; and two percent from judges (Ryan et al., 1980: Table 6-2). A survey of the women sitting on state trial courts in 1977 and a matching sample of men judges found no significant difference in mode of accession by sex within states (Cook 1980a, 1983b). This similarity in the routes followed to the bench within a state does not mean that some structures of selection are not more advantageous for women than others.

There are three ways of distinguishing the selection structures that may have implications for female opportunities: (1) by their political or professional domination; (2) by the competitiveness and success of political control; and (3) by the degree of party and interest group strength.

Political or Professional Control. Any form of selection will provide an advantage to the sponsoring groups or to the individual candidates with special ties to the appointing authority. In partisan selection structures, party activists have earned credits applicable to judicial openings; and in reform structures, bar association activists have earned useful credits. Where the party club or the bar association screens judicial candidates, women must gain entry to the group in order to display the leadership and loyalty that would entitle them to consideration. The concept of institutional sexism covers such a linkage between social organizations, where access and recognition in one offers a necessary credential for the other.

For purposes of this analysis, there are two major types of selection structures, the political (N = 33), where voters, parties, legislatures, and governors dominate the process; and the professional or reform (N = 17), where nominating commissions run by lawyers screen candidates and restrict the options of the governor or mayor to short lists.

Women are slightly more successful in political forms, where fifty-five percent of the states have "fair" representation on the trial bench, than in the professional form, where forty-seven percent of the states do so. The definition of fair representation used throughout this analysis is a score of 1.0 or higher for the relationship between the number of trial judges expected from the number of available women in law practice and the actual number of women on the trial bench.[5] The direction of the advantage is the same for women on appellate courts. Forty percent of the states with a political process now have a woman on their Supreme Courts, and thirty-three percent of those with professional screening do so (see Table 9.4).

One might conclude that the legal profession, which resisted until very recently competitive admission policies for law schools, is continuing to treat women as second-class citizens in bar organizations and in influential law firms, where reputations are made to fit the standards of the reform screening process. Law groups, unlike political parties, have no selfish motivation for the integration of their leadership. However, in the long run, when the proportion of practicing women attorneys exceeds the token mark, bar associations will have to reward them with leadership positions just as parties recognize women in the electorate and among party members by providing representation of "their own kind."

Interparty Competition. Third parties, with no expectation of placing their candidates in office, have been more generous to women aspirants for the bench as well as for other offices. The Greenback Party in 1882 nominated Marion Todd, a Hastings law school graduate and lawyer in San Francisco, for California Attorney General. The Prohibition Party in 1887 at its state convention selected Ada M. Bittenbender as its nominee for district judge in Lincoln, Nebraska (Robinson, 1889: 25-27). Party control of judicial nominations means that women must persuade the party leadership of their capacity to win the election as well as handle the office. The more competitive the election, the less anxious is the party to take risks with candidates with liabilities. The Democratic party refused the nomination to Florence Allen in Ohio and to Hortense Sparks in Texas; Allen was able to transform her suffrage clubs into a personal campaign organization and won, but Sparks in a one-party state had to concede defeat.

A high level of partisan competition does not improve women's access to the bench. Competitive states, particularly those with reform structures of selection, have low representation. Only where the competition is controlled by interparty arrangements, as in New York

TABLE 9.4 Women on the Bench in Relation to Party Competition and Selection Structures

Party Control of State Politics	Interparty Competition Scores*	N =	Appellate		Trial	
			Political N = 35	Professional N = 15	Political N = 33	Professional N = 17
One-Party Democratic	.80–.99	11	.30 (3)	1.00 (1)	.22 (2)	.50 (1)
Strong Democratic	.68–.79	13	.55 (5)	.25 (1)	.75 (6)	.60 (3)
Democratic Advantage	.56–.67	9	.50 (4)	.00	.88 (7)	.00
Competitive	.55–.45	8	.50 (2)	.50 (2)	.50 (2)	.25 (1)
Republican Advantage	.44–.33	9	.00	.20 (1)	.25 (1)	.60 (3)
Total		50	.40 (14)	.33 (5)	.55 (18)	.47 (8)

*Bibby et al. (1983: Table 3.3).
a. The professional category includes states that have created by statute a nominating commission to prepare a short candidate list from which the appointing authority chooses. The political category includes selection by voter, party, legislature, or governor without nominating commission input.

City, do women win a reasonable share of nominations in exchange for their party work. One-party Democratic control of public office also depresses the size of the female contingent on the state courts. Such control exists in the states with traditional cultures and with electoral structures, where the party has neither stimulus nor need to reach out to new voters to maintain their monopoly over public offices. In one-party states women do better through the professional initiation of candidates. Where the Republican party candidates have a record of winning elections, women do somewhat better on the trial than the appellate courts, but through professional and not political processes. Women aspirants for the bench do best through political structures in the states which are strongly or usually Democratic. Twenty-two states are in this category.

Over the last twenty-five years the political complexion of the state bench has changed from a majority Republican to a majority Democratic. For the general jurisdiction bench across states about fifty-five percent of the judges report themselves as Democratic (Ryan et al., 1980: 126). The Democratic party controls political outcomes in thirty-one of the large state court systems with the most vacancies. Of the seventeen states which are competitive or tipped toward Republican success, nine have very small court systems with few available positions. The Republican states have generally adopted the professional method of screening judicial candidates; and the combination of factors reduces women's chances. Republican women in Republican states and Democratic women in Democratic states must plan their careers differently to reach their respective courts.

Interest Groups and Party Strength. Groups involved in politics want judges whom they consider safe in terms of their own interests. A female candidate will be recognized as safe on the basis of past dealings with the group that reveal her beliefs and commitments. In a competitive state, candidates who are acceptable to one group or party would be entirely unacceptable to others. The difficulty women face is that they have not been closely enough involved in the workings of associations, unions, or corporations to show that they do understand how things are done and who gets what in the state. As outsiders to the political and economic processes, women are unknowns and therefore backing them risks the status quo. One would expect, therefore, that women would not be found on the benches of those states where interest groups enjoy greater strength.

There is a reverse relationship between the strength of interest groups and the representation of women on the bench. Only a fourth of the states with strong or moderate lobbying groups have a woman now sitting on the state's highest court. But of states with weak interest groups, over ninety percent have women justices. The relationship between the power of interest groups and the proportion of women on trial courts is even more striking, as the representation of women improves in step with the decline of interest group influence.

On the other hand, outsider candidates need a strong party and clear rules of access in order to find and meet the standards for election. Since parties do not always have strong organizations where they are successful at the polls, a woman with the "right" party identity may not find a way of showing off her abilities. One would expect, then, that women would gain the bench in fair proportions where the majority party had a strong party organization. Table 9.5 also confirms this proposition. Where moderate or strong state level party organizations operate, states are more likely to have a woman justice than where a weak state level party organization exist. The relationship is even clearer for the trial bench, where the data base is stronger. There are significantly more women trial judges in states with strong local party organizations than in states with moderate or weak local party organizations.

Combination of Political Factors. The combination offering the best opportunity for women is a large state with a political structure of selection, strong party organizations and weak interest groups, under Democratic party hegemony. The least desirable combinations for women are small states with professional selection, strong interest groups and weak party organization, with a Republican advantage; or states under one-party Democratic control with strong interest groups. A particularly unfortunate combination exists for women in Iowa, Kansas, and Nebraska, where weak parties, high competition, and professional selection have depressed the size of the female contingent on their benches.

FEMALE JUDGES AND WOMEN'S INTERESTS

The same features of the legal profession and the judiciary that discourage the entry of women also decrease the likelihood that women who do become judges will act in the interest of women as a class. The standardization of law training, the professionalization of selection, and the bureaucratization of courts all mitigate against the emergence of female judges with feminist policy concerns.

TABLE 9.5 Party and Interest Group Strength in Relation to
Representation of Women on the State Bench

	Women Judges on State Bench			
	Highest Court Now		Trial Courts	
Political Environment	%	N	%	N
Interest Group Strength:[*]				
Strong	23	(22)	36	(22)
Moderate	28	(18)	56	(18)
Weak	90	(10)	80	(10)
Political Party Strength:[a]				
Strong	44	(9)	72	(18)
Moderate	41	(29)	45	(20)
Weak	25	(12)	33	(12)

[*] Morehouse (1981: Table 3-3).
a. Cotter et al. (1984). State and local party organizational strength of winning party.
b. Z-score of 1.0 or higher for number of judges predicted from size of female lawyer pool.

The training of women within law schools, which understand their social function as the molding of students to institutional traditions and not as the reform of the bar or the improvement of society, will produce women as well as men lawyers in a conventional mold. The price women pay for access is conformity to the system and its rules. Despite the variety in size and prestige of law schools, their inculcation of respect for the status quo based upon law is ubiquitous. For most white male students the values underlying the process and the substance of their learning are comfortable and utilitarian; but for outsider students, acceptance by the profession requires internalization of values that fit their new and not old status. Few can bear the psychological burden of following norms they morally reject; so staying in the profession means conversion to those values. As one critical theorist describes the experience of outsiders in law school (Kennedy, 1982: 56):

> Students who are women or black or working class find out something important about the professional universe from the first day of class: that it is not even nominally pluralist in cultural terms. The teacher sets the tone—a white, male, middle-class tone. Students adapt. They do so partly out of fear, partly out of hope of gain, partly out of genuine admiration for their role models.

When women get all the way to the bench, with its robe and power and salary, on the basis of their learning the virtues of logic and stability, one can hardly expect them to turn away from their good fortune. Helping other women would mean challenging the values that support the logic of the law and risking their own reputations for cooperativeness and common sense.

The hierarchical and bureaucratic nature of the modern court system improved the access of women, but these same features set constraints upon their decision making. The court administration and not the individual judge sets up the routines for case intake and processing. With the reform emphasis upon efficiency, the cooperative and not the creative judge receives reinforcement from peers, superiors, and legislators. Ironically, the same circumstances that brought women into the courts prevent them from acting with the degree of freedom that male judges enjoyed at an earlier time in smaller and more independent courts. Moreover, the female judges are located in the metropolitan courts, which are the most tightly supervised, and not in the remaining single-judge courts (Carbon et al., 1982). Even women who sustained their inclination to help other women throughout law school and practice may find few opportunities to bring other women into the system from the bench.

The consensual role requirements for judges, whether selected by political or professional procedures, are objectivity and impartiality. Women who survive the scrutiny of selection authorities have convinced them that they do not see themselves as the special representatives of women. Candidates sometimes admit to a special knowledge or sensitivity to women's problems, but the screening ritual requires solemn promises to follow *stare decisis* and to exercise restraint in using discretion. Judges of course do respond more favorably to some litigants than to others, whether conscious or not of their predispositions, with resulting disparities among decisions. The toleration of the proclivities of the traditional judge does not extend to the newcomer.

The judge with the common law "defect of sex" does not enjoy the presumptions of competency and objectivity that shield the establishment-type judge. Her behaviors are subject to a more intensive and critical oversight; and she must be prepared to rationalize decisions that would have been accepted without special notice if emanating from a less visible judge. Responsiveness to women's interests, then, may be more difficult for a female than a male judge; fortunately a few male judges (about eleven percent, Cook, 1981b) have feminist sensibilities. Just half of the female judges on the trial bench identify themselves as feminists; but expressed preferences and behaviors do not always match, particularly when the behavior does not stimulate system rewards. The percentage of female judges who will risk their own position to vindicate the rights of their own sex will necessarily be considerably fewer than the number of avowed feminists.

Whether or not women judges can afford to make creative feminist decisions depends very much upon their security within their state's structure of selection and tenure. The burden of making breakthroughs for women constituents will probably be taken up by those few feminists who are also risktakers and/or have life tenure. Having invested great effort in finding places for themselves in a law world that is still male-dominated, female judges have little energy, as they try to keep their own places, for those women left behind, except their natural allies, women in law school and the profession.

NOTES

1. The separation of powers among the three brances is quite weak in local government in some states. The mixture of functions comes about in several ways. In some states judges with important judicial duties are also given legislative authority; for example, the Arkansas county judges preside over the quorum court, which exercises local law-making power (Reincke 1977: 125). The justices of the peace in Tennessee have more legislative than judicial functions (Reincke, 1977: 1622). In other states the judicial and executive functions overlap. The mayor serves as judge in Arkansas on the city court: in South Carolina on the municipal court: in Delaware, Louisiana, and Ohio on the mayor's court; in Mississipi on some justice courts; and in Oklahoma on municipal courts not-of-record. The county commissioners serve as the county judges in some Oregon counties (Reincke, 1977: 1471). In North Carolina the clerk of the superior court is the probate judge. In Michigan the deputy clerk of the district court may be appointed as magistrate. The title of judge is a misnomer in some instances, since the responsibility is primarily bureaucratic. Judges with clerk functions are the justices in Maine and Mississipi, the surrogates in New Jersey, and the probate judges in New Mexico.

2. Two anachronisms survive in the municipal courts not-of-record in Missouri and Oklahoma.

3. *Notable American Women* is a contemporary directory that provides scholarly, short biographies of women judges. The first in the series includes women who lived between 1607 and 1950 and was published by Harvard University Press in 1971. The early women judges are Carrie Kilgore, Catherine McCullough, Marilla Ricker, and judge candidate Hortense Ward. The next volume in the series, entitled *The Modern Period*, covers women who died between 1951 and 1975, and appeared in 1980. Women judges are Annette Adams, Florence Allen, Jennie Barron, Mary Bartelme, Genevieve Cline, and Dorothy Kenyon.

4. These states are Louisiana, South Carolina, North Carolina, Ohio, Pennsylvania, Kansas, Virginia, Mississippi, Missouri, Alabama, Oklahoma, Tennessee, Iowa, New Mexico, North Dakota, Utah, West Virginia, and Wisconsin.

5. States with Z-scores of 1.0 or higher are categorized as fair in their proportion of women judges and states below as unfair. The Z-scores were calculated for 1982 from

the number of women judges predicted from the proportion of women attorneys in relation to the size of trial benches of at least fifty judges. Smaller states were categorized as fair on the basis of number of women judges. The states with Z-scores of 1.0 or higher in rank order from highest to lowest are California, New York, Florida, Michigan, Texas, Massachusetts, Missouri, Ohio, Minnesota, Colorado, Wisconsin, Pennsylvania, Arizona, Oklahoma, Maryland, Indiana, Arkansas, New Jersey, Illinois, Connecticut, Oregon, and Washington. The smaller states with a fair number of women judges are Alaska, Hawaii, Utah, and Wyoming. The total number of fair states is twenty-six and unfair states twenty-four. The fairness is only relative, since none of the states exceed ten percent women on their trial court level.

IV

WOMEN AND STATE AND LOCAL PUBLIC POLICIES

This section contains four articles that discuss women's influence on the making of policies of vital concern to them.

The first is a case study: Anne Wurr's "Community Responses to Violence Against Women: The Case of a Battered Women's Shelter." She describes how women in Santa Clara County, California, protested the lack of police protection for battered women; developed shelters and programs for survivors of domestic violence; improved the enforcement of laws preventing woman abuse; and induced local law enforcement agencies to institute new policies and training for police officers.

Martha A. Ackelsberg, in "Women's Collaborative Activities and City Life: Politics and Policy," argues that attention to the role of women in urban life helps overcome the workplace-community dichotomy characterizing most urban studies; expands our understanding of urban spatial structure; and offers a model of democracy based on relationships rather than on self-interest.

Emily Stoper, in "State and Local Policies on Motherhood," examines how state and local governments are embroiled in controversies in four policy areas: abortion, child care, child custody and support, and welfare. She considers barriers to, as well as possible bases for, constructive redefinitions of these policy areas.

Finally, Ellen Boneparth provides an overview assessment in her "Resources and Constraints on Women in the Policymaking Process: State and Local Arenas." Among the resources she discusses are such things as: access, accountability, number of female officials, such organizations as NOW, NWPC, and commissions on the status of women, techniques of direct democracy, and the gender gap among voters. Constraints include competition for resources, difficulty of budget reallocation, and zoning and planning obstacles to child care and single-parent housing. She concludes with suggested strategies for the 1980s.

10

COMMUNITY RESPONSES TO VIOLENCE AGAINST WOMEN: THE CASE OF A BATTERED WOMEN'S SHELTER

Anne Wurr

This chapter describes how women in Santa Clara County, California, protested the lack of police protection for battered women. After organizing shelters and developing programs for survivors of domestic violence, a grassroots effort was successful in improving enforcement of the laws that prevent woman abuse. As one result of community education, political pressure was applied to induce local law enforcement agencies to institute new policies and training for police officers. The process offers a model that could be replicated in other communities; it drew heavily on the experience of other shelters from throughout the United States.

Santa Clara County is situated at the south end of the San Francisco peninsula in a verdant valley that once produced most of the world's prunes and apricots. "Silicon Valley" has replaced the orchards, and the thriving computer industry attracts workers, putting pressure on the already overpriced housing market. While the southern part of the county has retained its rural character, the county seat, San Jose, is a densely populated metropolitan area, with Stanford University and surrounding cities to the north. It is more than an hour's drive from Palo Alto to the southern county boundary. Despite being known as the feminist capital of the world, because of its high proportion of female elected officials, battered women are also numerous and call the three shelters in ever-increasing numbers from fifteen different cities within twelve law enforcement jurisdictions.

The Mid-Peninsula Support Network for Battered Women was founded in 1978, after a needs assessment conducted by the Santa Clara County Commission on the Status of Women revealed an urgent need for battered women's services in the northern cities of the county. At that time, the Woman's Alliance (WOMA) in San Jose and La Isla Pacifica in rural Gilroy were already providing refuge and advocacy for battered women, many of whom were Spanish-speaking women who did not hold paid jobs outside the home. There is a myth that violence only occurs in the homes of disadvantaged people, but the battered women who called the commission from North County asking for assistance included women from all walks of life. The upper-middle-class Anglo enclaves of Palo Alto, Stanford, Los Altos, and Los Altos Hills included homes as violent as those in rural South County or urban San Jose. Nor was the abuse confined to conjugal relationships; these women were exwives, daughters, mothers, sisters, employees, and women and girls in dating relationships, as well as battered wives. Their abusers included physicians, university professors, ministers, and electronic engineers as well as unemployed men, blue-collar workers and alcoholics. Calls received by the Support Network crisis line around election time included some from women who would only give their first name, "Because my husband is running for public office."

Shelters for battered women in the United States are a phenomenon of the 1970s, although abuse of women has always existed (Brownmiller, 1975; Davidson, 1978; Dobash and Dobash, 1979). In Alabama and Massachussetts, wife beating was not declared illegal until 1871 (Steinberg, 1982). Even today, men act as though they have the right to dominate women, and some of them use physical force to enforce this authority (Schechter, 1982). A woman is more likely to be abused in her own home by a man she knows, and loves, than by a stranger on the street (Dobash and Dobash, 1979). Between 1900 and the 1920s, many major U.S. cities employed female police officers with social work training to help women and children find emergency housing where they would be protected from the continuing assault of brutal husbands and fathers (Roberts, 1976). By 1975, Haven House in Pasadena, California, had become a refuge for battered women married to alcoholics; it was one of the first battered women's shelters in the United States.

There were several catalysts for the recent realization that battered women's shelters were needed. The women's movement enabled women to speak out about the various aspects of their oppression. Charitable organizations were beginning to recognize that violence against women and children in their homes often led them to flee and join the transients, the jobless, and other homeless people in the search of a place to stay. Del Martin wrote *Battered Wives* at the suggestion of her publisher, who wondered whether England's domestic shame (depicted in *Scream Quietly or the Neighbours Will Hear* by Erin Pizzey) was also being enacted in U.S. homes.

The traditional institutions to which women turned for help had not been able to interrupt the endless spiral of violence against women; in many instances, they perpetuated the problem and left the battered woman and her children at risk (Martin, 1976; Roy, 1977; Fleming, 1979; Stark et al 1979; Straus et al, 1980; Pagelow, 1981; Schechter, 1982). These institutions included the law, medicine, including psychiatry, the church, and the family. Despite repeated attempts to escape male violence, many battered women gave up and silently endured the abuse. Others hid their injuries in shame and blamed themselves for their mates' behavior (Davidson, 1978; Fleming, 1979; Walker, 1979).

By the time Mid-Peninsula Support Network was founded, it had become apparent that residential shelters could not begin to address the overwhelming problem. Battered women were not necessarily looking for refuge; many had their own resources, but needed emotional support and practical assistance to stop the assaults. The community needed information about domestic violence so that preventive measures could be taken. In the Support Network's primary service area, there were no buildings immediately available that could be used as a shelter or money to buy one, so volunteers offered to provide emergency refuge in their own homes, and innovative programs were developed. Even after the residential shelter was opened, the safe homes, support groups, and legal programs enabled many more battered women to escape their abusers. The goal of the Support Network's Community Education program was to prevent domestic violence by improving institutional response to victims, as well as encouraging battered women to call the 24-hour crisis line or use the resources offered by peer counselors at the office.

The Support Network decided in 1980 that a high priority for its new community education program would be law enforcement. The goal was to persuade local police to respond more effectively to domestic disturbance calls in which there had been a violent assault. Each police department was urged to adopt specific policy concerning response to battered women, and then train its officers and ancillary personnel, such as dispatchers and receptionists. If an effective policy was developed, police injuries and callbacks would be reduced,[1] and battered women would be protected from further assault.

First, we distributed information about the Support Network to the police departments in our primary service area, northern Santa Clara

County. This included wallet-sized orange cards with the telephone number of the 24-hour crisis line, which could be handed out by officers to battered women. We made requests to meet with the police chiefs, but in most cases met with less-senior officers. A form letter was developed (see Appendix 10A) to give feedback to the chiefs about how a particular incident of domestic violence had been handled. At that time, the battered women who called us seldom reported the assault to police; in only about one out of every hundred actual beatings was police assistance requested. The following observations are taken from feedback letters:

> The police officer refused to write a report even though the suspect attempted to run down his ex-woman friend with his car in front of witnesses.

> The police officer said he could do nothing because it was just a family affair, even though the suspect had twisted Jessie's arm so badly he almost broke it; he also assaulted her 20-year-old daughter. The officer winked at the suspect on his way out.

> Officers refused to write a report or arrest the suspect because he is married to Evelyn. Even though she requested a citizen's arrest, they refused to let her do this. She offered to show them multiple bruises (on her torso) but they declined and left, after merely telling the suspect to leave.

> Sheila had a swollen face and had been pushed, hit, and chocked by her husband; yet the police did not write a report, much less arrest her husband.

By 1980, the lack of law enforcement for crimes of domestic violence was becoming a scandal. The Family Abuse Network began meeting monthly in 1981 to improve services to victims; it consisted of concerned individuals and representatives of agencies that provided counseling and assistance to families. A Domestic Violence Subcommittee of the Bar Association Family Law Executive Committee had also been meeting to discuss the problem and work on solutions; many of these attorneys knew that their client's restraining orders were not enforced by the police. Shelter representatives tried to meet with as many police chiefs as possible, but the results did not justify the time and effort it took to do this. A comprehensive approach was needed that would address the problem on a countywide basis. In 1978 and 1979, class action suits in New York City[2] and Oakland, California,[3] had been brought by battered women against the respective police departments. The consent decrees consisted of new policies to be followed by police officers responding to domestic disturbance calls. These rules imposed by the court were to replace the various informal methods of intervention that police officers had developed within their limits of individual discretion in the absence of departmental directives. Now the officers were to be trained in the new methods. By fall 1980, the San Francisco Police Department had also adopted similar policies as a result of highly organized community pressure by and on behalf of battered women.

The Santa Clara County Bar Association Family Law Executive Committee Domestic Violence Subcommittee noted that there were thirteen different law enforcement agencies in the county. A uniform policy throughout the country would facilitate officer training and enable effective responses for victims of domestic violence whose home, workplace, and children's schools might be located in more than one police jurisdiction. They developed a Proposed Uniform General Order on Domestic Violence that was based on general orders in effect in New York, Oakland, and San Francisco; the task took many months of work and involved shelter workers and family counselors as well as members of the Bar Association (see Appendix 10B).

At about this time, Assemblymember John Vasconcellos of San Jose introduced a bill that created the California Commission on Crime Control and Violence Prevention. Its charge was to try to determine the root causes of violence and identify preventative measures. One member of the commission was Del Martin, a San Francisco author and activist, whose presence ensured that domestic violence would be studied along with the more public and recognized forms of violence. As the commission was collecting research findings and holding public hearings throughout California, Santa Clara County addressed the problem at the local level: John Vasconcellos also spearheaded the formation of the Violence Prevention Task Force to work on local problems and proposed solutions. A Domestic Violence Working Committee was organized, composed of shelter representatives, counselors working with battered women, a professor in the Administration of Justice Department of San Jose State University, and a staff person from the County Executive's Office; it met monthly. This committee decided to work on obtaining endorsements from public agencies and community organizations for the Bar Association's Proposed Uniform General Order on Domestic Violence. The process was intended to be educational, as well as a means of developing the political clout needed to persuade county police chiefs to adopt the order.

Working in pairs, committee members contacted organizations and requested the opportunity to address them on the topic of domestic violence and the Proposed Uniform General Order. Some groups took several subsequent meetings to discuss the matter before endorsing the general order; others voted on it immediately. Letters of endorsement were collected from several organizations, including local NOW chapters, the Commission on the Status of Women, the county Child Abuse and Neglect Co-ordinating Committee, the Child Advocacy Council, and the North County Child Abuse Co-ordinating Council. The county Police Officer's Association was approached, but declined to endorse the order.

This process generated public discussion and drew media attention to the general problem of domestic violence, as well as to the Proposed Uniform General Order. Several of us found microphones thrust at us as we left meetings. Stories appeared in the local press and interviews were broadcast on the radio. A female reporter wrote two carefully researched, in-depth articles that appeared in the local newspaper.[4]

The next step was to present the Proposed Uniform General Order to the County Board of Supervisors and to the city councils with the request that they direct their respective law enforcement agencies to adopt the policies and train law enforcement officers.[5]

We contacted the supervisors and councilmembers who represented the district or city in which a shelter or know victims resided. These elected representatives were asked to present the general order as an item on the agenda of a regular public meeting. Once it was included on the agenda, we arranged for as many meetings with the remaining officials as time permitted. In one rural area, the police chief had already met with the shelter director and community groups; together they had developed a General Order on Domestic Violence that also included specific information on penal code sections and local community resources. The police officers had received training on the provisions of the order. At the end of the document the chief wrote this message of encouragement to his officers:

> It is hoped that this General Order will make it easier for officers to carry out their duties in this dangerous area of law enforcement. Your decisive action at the scene of an offense of domestic violence may set an example for victims to carry through by pressing charges and testifying. The patrol officer in these situations provides tremendous service to the community.[6]

Our lobbying of the five county supervisors was very successful. As the board moved quickly through its long agenda on September 15, 1981, we were rewarded with praise for our work. The Proposed

Uniform General Order was approved unanimously and the sheriff was instructed to adopt the policy and train his deputies.[7] The board was moving onto the next agenda item when someone remembered that a Law and Justice item should have been referred to the Justice System Advisory Board (JSAB)[8] before the supervisors voted on it. But this was an urgent matter that had become a hot political issue, and it could not wait. Their votes were on record, so the supervisors asked JSAB to study the document and recommend its adoption by all law enforcement agencies within the county.

The general order appeared on the agenda of JSAB's monthly meeting in due course. We had already identified friendly JSAB members and given them information about the general order so they could speak in its favor. They warned us that there was substantial opposition to it, and that, if a vote were taken, it would not pass. We made sure that our supporters were present at the meeting and prepared our speeches to JSAB; public input is encouraged for most of their agenda items. Since the Chair was a woman municipal court judge, we did not expect to be excluded. As it turned out, the discussion by JSAB members soon became heated, and the Chair tried to move on quickly by cutting out presentations from the floor. She relented in response to an uproar from the spectators, but allowed only short presentations from one or two speakers before hurriedly appointing a Domestic Violence Subcommittee, composed entirely of opponents to the general order. The appointed Chair of this subcommittee had been particularly obstructive, even though she served on the board of directors of one of the agencies that had been instrumental in developing the general order. An appointed community representative on JSAB, she had rapidly become coopted by the law enforcement contingent and was no longer speaking on behalf of her constituency.

We obtained a list of JSAB appointees and noted that the terms of several had expired, but they continued to serve because the supervisors had not appointed anyone else in their place. With the support of several women's organizations in the county, and the Commission on the Status of Women, we bombarded the supervisor who had appointed the Domestic Violence Subcommittee Chair with phone calls and suggested that his constituents would be more effectively served by someone other than her. He appointed someone else within a month. At the first meeting of the Domestic Violence Subcommittee, the Vice-Chair took over and maintained the job even when our foe returned to JSAB a few weeks later as the appointee of a different supervisor.

The new Chair of the JSAB Domestic Violence Subcommittee had political aspirations of his own. A former San Jose police officer, he taught Administration of Justice at a local community college and trained new police recruits from throughout the county at the police academy. A community activist, he had supported the development of community-based alternatives to incarceration and had developed a moderate base of personal support. He planned to challenge the incumbent sheriff and was at this time still testing the waters without actually declaring his candidacy. He had spoken out against the Proposed Uniform General Order at the JSAB meeting in spite of a lenghty previous meeting with two shelter representatives who had been his allies in an earlier, unrelated political struggle.

It so happened that his campaign managers were two women activists who had led the effort to channel county resources into alternatives to incarceration instead of building more jails. We knew them well and arranged to meet. We explained the history of the general order and noted that their candidate had not kept himself current on recent research concerning police intervention in domestic disturbances. He had shown us the training materials he had developed for the police academy, and they were based on research (Bard, 1969) since superseded by a Police Executive Research Forum Study (Loving, 1980). The campaign managers made copies of all the relevant information and suggested to their candidate that he study it carefully before returning to the campaign trail. They did not want to risk losing the support of individual women voters or the endorsement of influential women's organizations.

By the time the JSAB Domestic Violence Subcommittee met again, its new Chair had invited shelter representatives, patrol officers, attorneys who had developed the general order, and other interested people to join the JSAB members on the subcommittee. As a result of the chair's leadership, the general order's provisions were carefully studied, one by one. The main complaint from law enforcement officers was that the police might increase the likelihood of a suit against them for false arrest if officers encouraged battered women to make citizen's arrests. They were also concerned that officer discretion was being eroded by such a directive policy. These matters were discussed and some wording was changed, until a workable document was produced.

The Domestic Violence Subcommittee Chair presented it to JSAB with a strong recommendation, on behalf of the subcommittee, that it be adopted countywide. Still unwilling to take a stand, JSAB requested the sheriff to present the Proposed Uniform General Order to the police chiefs at their next meeting and ask for their opinion. We already knew the chiefs' opinion. That was why we had initiated the whole process in the first place. We were feeling discouraged at this obvious bureaucratic ploy; we were being given the runaround that is so effective in wearing down opposition to established practices.

However, the current Chair of the Santa Clara County Police Chiefs was the one chief who had written his own general order on Domestic Violence and trained his officers on its provisions. We knew that the sheriff would be unlikely to support a document identified with is political opponent, even though he himself had been instructed to adopt it by the board of supervisors. His deputies had not received training and he had not given much attention to it. His presentation to the chiefs would be perfunctory, at best. We decided to ask permission to attend the chiefs' meeting to explain the general order and its advantages to law enforcement agencies. We were invited to the March 4, 1982, meeting, which happened to be the day preceding a much-publicized community forum at which the California Commission on Crime Control and Violence Prevention would present its preliminary findings.

The police chiefs' meeting was not one that we will easily forget. We had walked into the lion's den! Every chief present vehemently opposed the general order, with the exception of the Chair, who remained silent. The speeches expressed indignation that we would presume to interfere, and several speakers said that they had already met with shelter representatives and they did not understand why we kept coming back and causing trouble. We tried to give objective reasons[9] for the provisions of the general order, but ended up by saying that we would keep coming back, too, if something wasn't done to improve the deplorable situation. Privately, we felt we had lost the battle, but later that day the Chair called to thank us for our presentation, and to say that the response was to be expected but he would undertake an educational process with his peers during his year of office as Chair. Rhetoric aside, there were no hard feelings and he was confident that the chiefs would see the advantage of the policy's provisions once they had had time to study it themselves.

The next day, at the California Commission Crime Control and Violence Prevention Community Seminar, we were greeted warmly by individual chiefs and we heard several of them speak in favor of arrest in domestic violence cases during the roundtable discussions held that day. It appeared that our efforts were beginning to reap results. One of the preliminary findings presented by the state commission concerned the role of the family in perpetuating intergenerational cycle of violence. It emphasized the fact that violence is learned behavior, and recommended that parents learn nonviolent methods of discipline for their children. The commission recommended that state law be amended to prohibit corporal punishment in schools. Concerning domestic violence, the recommendation was made that wife abuse should be treated as a criminal offense, and standardized criminal justice system responses should be encouraged, of which the Proposed Uniform General Order was an example.

In the aftermath of the community forum several positive steps were taken. In the Support Network service area, one police department has adopted as policy an updated version of the General Order on Domestic Violence. Three departments have received training based on its provisions, and the last has requested training in 1984. The topic of the California Peace Officers' Association March 1983 training bulletin was domestic violence investigation. It included many of the very same words that appear in the General Provisions of the Santa Clara County Law Enforcement Agency Uniform General Order on Domestic Violence and gave specific instructions to officers about their duties when called to a scene of domestic violence. It emphasized the importance of the officer's attitude toward the victim, especially in chronic battering situations:

> The danger here is that the victims may be left with the impression that they are being treated merely as a distraught spouse, or rebuffed lover, rather than an injured victim. They may also get the impression you feel they were somehow the cause of the assault. *A victim nvever causes a beating*, and you should not frame questions to imply such.[10] (Emphasis included in the original.)

During subsequent police training on domestic violence conducted by the Support Network, the refrain was often heard from police officers that the district attorney would not prosecute even when the police had brought a well-prepared case. The next stage of the criminal justice process, that of prosecution, is now being addressed and training has been given to the most recent group of new deputy D.A.s. This was achieved by a long process similar to that described for the police, and included political pressure applied to the front-runners in the race for district attorney in 1982. The incumbent district attorney was retiring after more than twenty-five years in office. Four attorneys, two from within the D.A.'s office, were competing for the election. We developed a questionnaire on domestic violence prosecution (see Appendix 10C) and asked each candidate to respond. Their replies became the basis for questions asked at candidates' meetings and were used by reporters writing about the various issues of the campaign. The eventual winner was reminded of his campaign promises and, although progress is slow, changes are being made in the way domestic violence cases are prosecuted in Santa Clara County.

The presiding judge of the superior court has been a knowledgeable leader in the effort to improve judicial remedies for domestic violence victims. In the family division, local rules were developed so that attorneys could represent their clients more effectively. Women seeking restraining orders have been directed to the few remaining agencies that can provide low-cost assistance. The Support Network has trained volunteers to prepare restraining orders and act as advocates for women representing themselves in court (*in pro per*).

The process of improving legal remedies for battered women continues in Santa Clara County. At the state level, legislation has been considered that would require police to recognize that domestic violence is a crime by making the general order apply throughout California. The state of Washington has such a law. Its passage would require women's advocates to form coalitions with law enforcement, and this may exceed our present lobbying resources. And this law, like all the others that would protect women, would still have to be enforced. There are at least thirty-six statutes in California that would protect women if they were enforced (Boylan and Taub, 1981). The political climate is changing towards more concern for victims of crimes, and it is possible that the law enforcement agencies themselves would preempt the need for such a law. Legislative efforts on behalf of battered women are more urgently needed to secure adequate funding for shelters.

At the national level, domestic violence prevention bills introduced into the past several congresses have not been successful. On June 23, 1983, the Select Education Subcommittee of the House Education and Labor Committee convened an oversight hearing in Washington, D.C., to confront the urgent need to help victims of domestic violence. Testimony was given by Susan Kelly-Dreis of the Pennsylvania Coalition Against Domestic Violence, who said that twenty-five battered women in the Pittsburgh area had been murdered after thay had been unable to find shelter; two of these spousal murder victims had been "protected" by restraining orders at the time of death.[11]

Nationwide, police response to battered women is still grossly inadequate. Most shelters are too overburdened to undertake extensive community education programs to reform institutional response to domestic violence survivors. Until we recognize that assaults that occur in the privacy of the home are crimes for which perpetrators should be held responsible, the intergenerational cycle of abuse will continue. Effective law enforcement would contribute to the effort to reduce domestic violence. Police in Santa Clara County have already taken the first step in that direction by being forced to recognize an urgent community problem. The process could be replicated in your community.

The specific lessons that can be leared from this case study include:

(1) The importance of community education as a means of eliciting reaction to a social problem. People cannot mobilize unless they know the problem exists.

(2) Existing women's formal and informal networks are readily available to assist oppressed or disadvantaged people organize to improve their situation.[12]

(3) Since domestic violence affects us all, directly or indirectly, it is possible to relate to a variety of constituencies for political and financial support.[13]

(4) Local politicians, as well as President Reagan, are concerned about the gender gap. Keep them informed about your goals for a violence-free community. Remind them that battered women come from all walks of life, and that shelter residents can be mobilized for political action along with NOW or the local women's service club.

(5) In this case, our personal connections as long-time residents in our community proved invaluable. We knew who to call for access to telephone trees, if quick phone calls to a city council or the board of supervisors were needed.

(6) We were able to pull strings and suggest women for appointment to boards (e.g., JSAB), or get unfriendly people removed by having access to local politicians. We had paid our dues by working to get them elected; now it was time to collect.

(7) The Commission on the Status of Women has provided on-going assistance, despite severe post-Proposition 13 budget cuts. Its presence as a recognized county commission helped us keep informed about what goes on in the county government center.

(8) The media, mainly through female professionals working at local TV and radio stations and as reporters for local newspapers, were sympathetic, but it was our responsibility to keep them informed by sending out press releases.

(9) Although women in positions of power were generally accessible to us, we were surprised when they were openly hostile or deprecating, such as

the female JSAB members. In retrospect, we should have spent more time and effort on education for them. At a crucial time, a female mayor was able to get us a meeting with a recalcitrant police chief, and a female police officer and deputy D.A. were articulate and persuasive at unexpected moments in public meetings. Allies also appeared when we were under fire in public; they often turned out to be formerly abused women or friends, employers, or relatives of battered women.

(10) We developed a mailing list of over 4000 names and mailed a quarterly newsletter that kept people informed of the problem and suggested ways in which they could help. We submitted articles and fact sheets to other organizations for inclusion in their newsletters.

(11) We found that the quickest way to get action was to go directly to the person at the top. It was too slow to work with police officers on a case-by-case basis; training was needed for everyone in the department, which meant reaching the chief first.

(12) Acknowledgment of work well done, help given, or for a well-written newspaper article, in the form of a phone call or short note of appreciation helped soften the more frequent occasions when we were complaining about the lack of effective response to the plight of battered women.

(13) By identifying potential allies, such as frustrated family law attorneys and family therapists, we broadened our base of support and gained access, through them, to other organizations. The Family Abuse Network, for example, included a Lutheran minister who later set up a workshop series for ministers and churches on domestic violence prevention. We also gained recognition by testifying and working for the Violence Prevention Task Force, and, by submitting written reports of our activities, disseminated information statewide as well as locally.

(14) The D.A. questionnaire was submitted by the coalition of groups working with domestic violence survivors, not by a single agency. Only one candidate complained that it insulted him; we mentioned this publicly.

(15) Knowledge of recent social science research was invaluable, and the most useful resource was *Response*, the publication of the Center for Women Policy Studies, 2000 P Street N.W., Suite 508, Washington, D.C. 20036-5997.

Domestic violence can be prevented at the local level by challenging established methods of dealing with the problem. Social science research has been helpful in exposing sexist attitudes, as well as for developing new models of intervention, but many law enforcement officials, and other professionals, are too overburdened to keep up with new findings. You can be a resource for them as well as for your local elected officials. By making use of your personal networks of friends, coworkers, church and club members, relatives, doctor, dentist, minister, and so on, you can rally support quickly and inexpensively. Because the problem is so pervasive, everyone knows of a victim, or may be survivor themself.

The battered women's movement is a grassroots effort that has been in existence for less than a decade, but already the public's attitude towards the problem of domestic violence has changed. Instead of accepting wife-beating as an inevitable and intractable problem, people are mobilizing to prevent it. The events described here occurred in conjunction with on-going countywide efforts to publicize the plight of survivors, as well as development of new programs and shelters. There is still work to be done and it is hoped that you will become a part of it. There is a wide variety of levels of involvement from direct services to writing legislation or influencing public policy.[14] You have already taken the first step by becoming aware of the problem and the possibilities for change.

APPENDIX A: MID-PENINSULA SUPPORT NETWORK FORM LETTER TO POLICE CHIEFS, 1980.

_____
                    Date

Dear Chief _____ of the _____ Police/Public Safety Department, our client, _____, was involved in an incident of domestic violence on _____ (date). Our client's evaluation of your department's services follows.

Officer _____

____Assisted the victim because her mate attacked or threatened her.

____Assisted the victim with a Civil Stand-by.

____Assisted the victim with the enforcement of a Restraining Order.
                              *****

____The officer was present when we arrived or came shortly after we did.

____It was necessary for us to make several calls before the officer arrived.

____Client went to the police station.
                              *****

____The officer was/was not understanding and sensitive to the woman's needs.

____The officer did/did not rush the woman unnecessarily during the Civil Stand-by.

____The officer did/did not give the woman a Support Network crisis card or phone number.

____The officer did/did not inform the victim of her right to make a citizen's arrest.

Even though there were obvious signs of injury to the victim, the officer said they were unable to make an arrest because:

____The couple were married or living together, and/or said this is a civil matter.

____There is no Restraining Order on file.

____Previous calls to the house have not resulted in any change in the situation.

____Alleged offender promised never to assault the victim again.

____The victim probably would not testify and/or the D.A. probably would not prosecute.

We understand that there may be misunderstandings or miscommunication in some cases. However, our client's perception of this situation is as follows:

You attention to this matter would be appreciated. Thank you.

Sincerely,

APPENDIX B:
SANTA CLARA COUNTY LAW ENFORCEMENT AGENCY PROPOSED UNIFORM
GENERAL ORDER ON DOMESTIC VIOLENCE

DEPARTMENT GENERAL ORDER   ORDER NO. X-X
CONTROL CODE (8-2-)   01/01/82

Index as: Domestic Violence
                   Temporary Restraining Orders

DOMESTIC VIOLENCE

The purpose of this order is to set forth new policies and procedures for domestic violence cases and temporary restraining orders therefor.

I. GENERAL PROVISIONS

A. *Definition*
Domestic violence is defined as any harmful physical contact between persons who are spouses, former spouses, parents, children, or any other persons who regularly reside in the household or who have regularly resided in the household within the last six months.

B. *Criminal Conduct*

Officers shall treat all alleged domestic violence as alleged criminal conduct. Officers shall treat requests for police assistance and criminal investigation from victims of domestic violence the same as all other requests for assistance in cases where there has been physical violence of the threat thereof.

C. *Dispute Mediation*

Dispute mediation shall not be used as a substitute for appropriate law enforcement actions in domestic violence cases where physical violence has occurred. Even though crisis intervention is highly valuable it should not be substituted for an appropriate criminal investigation.

D. *Case-Handling Requirements*

The existence of the elements of a crime shall be the primary factor that determines the proper method of handling the incident.

E. *Impermissible Considerations*

The following factors, for example, should not influence the officer's course of action in domestic violence incidents.

1. The marital status of the suspect and complaint;
2. Whether or not the suspect lives on the premises with the complainant;
3. The existence of lack of temporary restraining order;
4. The potential financial consequences of arrest;
5. The complainant's history of prior complaints;
6. Verbal assurance that violence will cease;
7. The complainant's emotional state;
8. Injuries are not visible;
9. The location of the incident (i.e., public or private place);
10. Speculation that the complainant may not follow through with the criminal justice process or that the arrest may not lead to a conviction.

F. *Felony Arrests*

In accordance with State law and standing department procedures on warrantless arrest, an arrest shall be made in a domestic violence incident when there is reasonable cause to believe that a felony has occurred.

G. *Misdemeanor Arrests*

Where an officer has reasonable cause to believe that a domestic violence related misdemeanor has occurred in his presence, the suspect may be cited or arrested.

In evaluating the likelihood of a "continuing offense" (one of the statutory conditions under which an arrest rather than a citation is required), officers shall consider the following factors.

1. Whether the suspect has prior history of arrests or citations involving domestic violence;

2. Whether the suspect has previously violated valid temporary restraining orders;

3. Whether the suspect has a prior history of other assaultive behavior (e.g., arrests/convictions for battery or aggravated assault);

4. Statements taken from the complainant that the suspect has a history of physical abuse;

5. Statements taken from the victim expressing fear of retaliation or further violence should the suspect be released.

H. *Citizen's Arrest*

When the elements of a lawful arrest are present, officers *shall* inform complainants of their right to make a Citizen's Arrest. Whenever possible such discussion shall be held out of the presence of the suspect;

Officers shall not dissuade complainants from making a Citizen's Arrest. The officer has the alternative of release under Penal Code 849 (b) (1) where the officer is satisfied there are insufficient grounds for making criminal complaint.

I. *Removal of Suspect*

When a complainant requests that an officer remove a person from the premises and it can be shown that the complainant is in lawful possession of the premises (for example, by showing a rental agreement, cancelled rent check, lease, grant deed, rent receipts or other documents, or verification from apartment manager), and the person desired to be removed is not in lawful possession of the premises, the responding officer shall:

1. Request that the person leave the premises and stand by until the person has removed his belongings and left the premises.

2. Should the trespasser refuse to leave upon request, the officer should arrest the suspect.

J. *Civil Stand-by*
When a complainant in a domestic violence incident requests police assistance in removing a reasonable amount of personal property (e.g., a suitcase) to another location, officers should stand-by a reasonable amount of time until the complainant has safely done so.

K. *Medical Assistance*

If a complainant claims injuries, whether visible or not, which require medical attention, officers shall administer first-aid as appropriate and offer to arrange for proper medical treatment.

L. *Documentation*

Officers shall document each account in appropriate reports and collect appropriate physical evidence in cases where domestic violence has occurred.

II. TEMPORARY RESTRAINING ORDER

A. *Verification of Order*

In domestic dispute incidents where a person advises an officer of the existence of a temporary restraining order pertaining to the dispute, the officer shall attempt to ascertain if such an order is on file with the department. The department should keep records in a readily accessible file.

B. *Arrest Criteria*

Officers shall make an arrest when there is reasonable cause to believe that the subject of the temporary restraining order has violated the order in the presence of the officer, and one of the following conditions has been met:

1. The existence of the order and proof of service to suspect has been verified by the member;

2. The complainant produces a copy of the order as the proof of service on the suspect;

3. The existence of the order has been verified by the member and no proof of service is required because the order reflects that the suspect was present in court when the order was made; or

4. The complainant produces a copy of the order and the order reflects that the suspect was present in court when the order was made to that no proof of service is required.

5. Violators shall be cited or booked on Penal Code Section 273.6 in addition to any other violations committed, such as aggravated assault, battery, or trespass.

C. *No Verification of Service*

When an officer verifies that a restraining order exists, but cannot verify either proof of service on the suspect or the fact that the suspect was present in court when the order was made so that no proof of service is required, the officer shall:

1. Inform the suspect of the terms of the order;

2. Admonish the subject of the order that he is now on notice and that continued violation of the order will result in his arrest; and

3. The officer shall immediately notify the Department that the suspect has been informed of the terms of the order. Appropriate documentation shall be noted in the restraining order on file at

the department. In addition, this information shall be included in the police report.

4. If the complainant has no copy of the order, so that the officer is unable to inform the subject of the terms of the order, then the officer shall inform the complainant of the necessity or recording proof of service with the Department.

5. If the complainant has a copy of the restraining order, the officer shall serve the subject of the order with the copy or the order and, upon request, sign a proof of service.

III. PROCEDURES

A. *Report Headings*

Officers making incident reports allegedly involving domestic disputes shall mark the reports with both the primary offense followed by a slash mark and the words "Domestic Violence" (e.g., Aggravated Assault/Domestic Violence).

B. *Coding*

Departments shall institute a method for retrieval of statistical information of domestic violence incidents.

This order cancels and supercedes General Order _____ of 19_____.

By order of:

_____

Chief of Police

APPENDIX C: QUESTIONNAIRE FOR DISCTICT ATTORNEY CANDIDATES, 1982

1. Do you regard domestic violence as a serious social problem in Santa Clara County?

2. Do you agree with the following statement? "The protections of the U.S. Constitution and the California Constitution and Penal Code do not stop at the threshold of a family residence; crimes of violence committed in the home should be prosecuted in Santa Clara County."

3. Are you familiar with Los Angeles City Attorney's Domestic Violence Program? If so, would you institute a similar program in Santa Clara County? If you're not familiar with this program, would you like information on it?

4. Do you think that attorneys in Santa Clara County District Attorney's office could benefit from training on domestic violence?

5. Would you set up a special unit in the District Attorney's office to handle all aspects of domestic violence cases (vertical prosecution model)?

6. Given the present structure of the District Attorney's office, would you assign three or four deputy District Attorneys to form a panel which would meet regularly to evaluate cases for prosecution?

7. Please indicate whether you have read any of the following:
   (a) *Prosecution of Spouse Abuse: Innovations in Criminal Justice,* by Lisa Lerman, Center for Women Policy Studies, Washington, D.C., 1981.
   (b) *Prosecutor's Responsibility in Spouse Abuse Cases,* U.S. Department of Justice, 1980.
   (c) *Los Angeles County Attorney Domestic Violence Program*, by Burt Pines, 200 North Main, #1800, Los Angeles, 90012, November 1978.

8. What are our criteria for prosecuting domestic violence cases?

9. Are you aware of other D.A.'s offices (e.g., Alameda County) which no longer require the victim to sign a complaint in domestic violence cases?

10. Can a spouse abuse case be won without the victim's testimony?

11. Are you aware that a situation exists at present in Santa Clara County whereby domestic violence referred by law enforcement officers to the District Attorney are not prosecuted, even when thorough police work has been done and the victim is willing to testify?

12. Are you aware that battered women have to go to the District Attorney's office in person and file a complaint at the Citizen's Complaint Desk, whereas a victim assaulted by a stranger on the street would not be expected to go to those lengths in order for the case to be prosecuted?

13. Would the jail over-crowding situation influence your decision as to whether a domestic violence case should be prosecuted?

14. Are you aware that Santa Clara County has a program for batterers diverted under provisions of P.C. 1000.6? Do you have any ideas for improving this program?

15. Are you aware of P.C. 273.5, the domestic violence statute? What would your criteria be for changing felonies or misdemeanors under this?

16. What kind of liaison would you provide with law enforcement agencies on domestic violence cases?

17. Further remarks:

NOTES

1. A study by the Police Foundation three years later confirmed that arrest of domestic violence suspects was the most effective method of preventing further violence (Sherman and Berk, 1983).

2. *Bruno v. Codd,* 40 N.Y. 2nd, 165 (App. Div. 1978)

3. *Scott v. Hart,* No. C-76-2395 (N.D. Cal. 10/28/79)

4. Opal MacLean (*San Jose Post Record,* October 22, 1981, January 22, 1982).

5. In Santa Clara County, the sheriff is elected and serves a four-year term. His budget must be approved by the board of supervisors; it is administered through the county executive's Law and Justice Division. The police chiefs are appointed by their respective city councils.

6. Chief Gregory Cowart, Gilroy Police Department (January 12, 1981).

7. The sheriff has responsibility for patroling unincorporated areas of the county; these are not as densely populated as the cities. His principal charge is supervision of the county jails and courtrooms and his deputies rotate through these services but spend more time in the jails and courts than out on patrol. The latter duty is preferred and more likely to be perceived by deputies as real police work. Battered women and domestic disturbances do not represent a significant case load for the sheriff, so being told to implement the general order was not a matter of great concern to him, other than the arrest provisions it contained that might have exacerbated the chronic jail over-crowding situation in the county.

8. The Justice System Advisory Board acts as advisor to the county board of supervisors. It was formed as a provision of AB90, a bill that rewards counties for not exceeding their allocation of state prisoners. Members of JSAB are predominately law enforcement officials and include the chief probation officer, the public defender, the presiding judge of the superior court and of the municipal court, the district attorney, a police chief from a large city and one from a small city, and so on; also, the county superintendant of schools and, as a result of community pressure, ten community representatives appointed by the supervisors.

9. Studies of domestic homicides in Kansas City (Meyer, 1977; Wilt et al., 1977) showed that police had been called previously to the homes of eighty-five percent of the homicide victims of suspects. In over fifty percent of these cases, they had been there five or more times. Familiy disturbance responses account for twenty-two percent of all police fatalities (Parnas, 1967).

10. *California Peace Officers Association Training Bulletin* (March 1983).

11. *Update: Congressional Caucus for Women's Issues,* Washington, D.C. (June 30, 1983: 7).

12. Many battered women became articulate, persuasive public speakers during the lobbying phase of this project. Some have chosen to go back to school or seek more challenging employment as a result of the experince.

13. Funding from corporations, and referrals of battered women from personnel offices, is more likely to occur if it is pointed out that unexplained absenteeism is one result of domestic violence. Police officers risk injury or death responding to domestic disturbance calls; it is in their own interest to prevent callbacks to the same household, and so on.

14. Contact your local battered women's shelter for information. Look in the telephone directory white pages under "Battered Women" or in the yellow pages under "Women's Services."

11

WOMEN'S COLLABORATIVE ACTIVITIES AND CITY LIFE: POLITICS AND POLICY

Martha A. Ackelsberg

What would it mean for women to be fully participatory citizens of a truly democratic urban political community? What changes in urban policy would follow from the integration of women's activities and behaviors into our understanding of the practice of urban politics?

A number of recent studies have explored the depoliticization of economic life in the United States over the past 200 years, and the development of a split between "economics" and "politics" in the American political consciousness (for example, Piven and Cloward, 1982; Wolin, 1981). Others have examined the implications of that split for urban politics and "the patterning of class" in particular (Katznelson, 1981; Kornblum, 1974; Bender, 1983). But despite the sensitivity of these works to issues of class, race, and ethnicity—and their implications for the potential of integrating work life and community life in a democratic polity—all are strangely silent about women, whose concerns have been largely absent from the American political agenda and whose actions have gone virtually unnoticed by students of urban political struggles.

Studies of women's lives and activities—especially those focusing on urban contexts—suggest that women experience their environment in ways that may differ significantly from the ways most men do. Much recent research, for example, has documented the prominent, if not predominant, role of women in urban struggles over what have been termed "quality of life" issues (i.e., housing, cost of living, and so on; see, for example, Levy and Applewhite, 1980; Kaplan, 1982; Lawson et al., 1980; Gilkes, 1980; Cockburn, 1977b; Ettorre, 1978;

Author's Note: This chapter builds on collaborative work with Myrna M. Breitbart (1982). I am grateful to Irene Diamond, Janet Flammang, and Philip Green for their comments on earlier drafts of this manuscript.

and Wilson, 1977). Similarly, both historians and analysts of the contemporary social scene have noted the significance of social networks, or webs of relationships, in the lives of (urban) women (see, for example, Cott, 1977; Saegert, 1980; Gilkes, 1980; Cockburn, 1977a; Ross, 1981; Ryan, 1979; Ulrich, 1980; Gilligan, 1982).

This chapter explores the implications of those differences both for our understanding of urban policy and, more broadly, for our notions of democratic citizenship. On the one hand, it examines what it might mean to integrate economics and politics, work and community, in a democratic polity which took into account the concerns and behaviors of women, as well as of men. On the other, and more generally, it begins to develop an analysis of the significance of relationships—not only in and for the lives of women, but also as a crucial (if as yet inadequately explored) aspect of democratic citizenship itself.

AVOIDING THE WORKPLACE-COMMUNITY SPLIT

Social historians and contemporary urbanologists alike have highlighted one significant characteristic of city spatial structure in the United States: the physical/geographical separation of workplace and residence. Some have focused on patterns of urban growth and their implications for urban political community (see especially Warner, 1962; 1968); others, on the consequences of the separation for the class and race segregation of metropolitan areas (e.g., Danielson, 1976; Downs, 1973). Some of the most provocative and suggestive recent work in this area, however, is that of Ira Katznelson, who explores in detail the connections between the separation of work and community and the development of industrial capitalism, and the specific implications of that separation for the structuring of urban political consciousness in the United States.

Katznelson's focus is on the specifically American response to that separation (characteristic of the development of industrial capitalism)—namely, a "split consciousness" among urban residents who see a "stark division . . . between the politics of work and the politics of community" (1981: 71). In his view, American workers look to unions, focused at the workplace, to resolve what they take to be economic issues; and they look to urban political parties, oriented around ethnicity and territoriality, rather than class, to resolve what they take to be political concerns—and never really join the two sets of issues. This perspective permeates all aspects of workers' lives—resulting in "a stark split between the ways workers in major industrial cities think, talk, and act when they are at work and when they are away from work in their communities" (p. 45). The political and strategic message of Katznelson's analysis is clear: "Community-based strategies for social change in the United States cannot succeed unless they pay attention to the country's special pattern of class formation; to the split in the practical consciousness of American workers between the language and practice of a politics of work and those of a politics of community" (Katznelson, 1981: 194). Only when urban activists succeed in *linking* what are perceived as two independent sets of concerns, making clear the dependence of communities on the context set by capitalist relations, can there be significant, transformative, change in urban areas.

While Katznelson's analysis hints at a new understanding of democratic citizenship, others have drawn the links somewhat more directly. Wolin (1981), Piven and Cloward (1982), and Bender (1983) all explore the development of the ideological split between economics and politics (or "private" and "public") in American consciousness, although they focus more directly on the consequences of the split for our understandings of democracy. Specifically, Wolin bemoans the shift from a participatory, democratic, and decentralist model of politics and citizenship (in which economic issues were thoroughly integrated) central to the structure and practice of U.S. democracy in the early years of the Republic, to a more passive, remote, inegalitarian, and representative notion of citizenship (which excluded the economy from democratic control), which has come to characterize U.S. politics since the early nineteenth century. His point is that it is not just that the economy has been depoliticized and removed from the realm of meaningful popular control, but that citizenship, as such, has been limited. People have come to develop passive and deferential dispositions toward politics.[1]

Along the same lines, Piven and Cloward (1982) argue that the insulation of property and economic policy from popular political control that structured late nineteenth-century politics in the United States "persuaded Americans that the most pressing issues of their daily lives had nothing to do with the democratic rights for which they had fought, and of which they were so proud" (p. 99). Yet Piven and Cloward are far from convinced that the battle has been lost: Welfare-state policies have undermined that division, even as they represented attempts to protect the context upholding it. In fact, Piven and Cloward have argued more recently, the welfare state has had a "transforming effect on popular understandings of what politics is about. It brought economic issues to the very center of democratic politics" (1983: 65). The separation between economics and politics has already been undermined in practice, and we are beginning to see the ideological implications: in American popular consciousness, they argue, there is an increasing recognition of the necessity for greater economic democracy if political democracy is to be a reality (1983: 59).[2] Clearly, in their view, the promise of overcoming the separation (in both ideology and in practice) is the promise of a more democratic political community.

Finally, a recent article by Thomas Bender argues in yet another vein for the necessity of integrating economic issues into the agenda of politics. He calls for us to reclaim, in a *democratic* context, the notion of a "moral economy"—to envision a city whose "moral, political, and economic universes of discourse [are] continuous" (1983: 20).

These analyses recognize the significance of class and race in structuring the dimensions of American political consciousness and action. And each make a powerful case for integrating economic and political issues, workplace and community concerns, and for the fundamental significance of such integration for the development of a truly democratic politics. Nevertheless, they read as if all workers—and virtually all urban citizens!—were male.

Since it is the most detailed—and the most suggestive—I shall focus, briefly, on Katznelson's analysis. Significantly, he devotes no attention at all to the specific experience of women, either as workers or as city dwellers. Thus, in his discussion of the relationship between suffrage and worker militancy in the nineteenth century, he states, "Modern industrial society in the United States, with its distinctive patterns of class interaction, was forged in the crucible of democracy. Workers as citizens did not feel they needed to battle the state, for they were included in its embrace" (p. 64). Surely, however, the workers he refers to were exclusively male (and white). In a more contemporary vein, he notes (in a passage cited above) that "workers in the major industrial cities think, talk, and act," differently, "when they are at work and when they are away from work in their communities" (p. 45; see also p. 71). Again, one has the sense that he is talking about *male* workers. As more than one feminist critic has pointed out,

> Men see a relatively clear divide between problems of home and problems of work, so this unwritten rule [that workplace issues are separate from "home" issues] seems to be adequate for them. Bills, household budgets, baby-sitters, and another baby on the way are all "invidivual problems." . . . But for women workers, especially for those with

children (whether single of married) that kind of separation is rarely possible. [Lawrence, 1977, cited in Ettorre, 1978: 510].[3]

His analysis, in short, gives no indication either that women workers exist, or that female workers' attitudes, approaches, or experience might differ from those of men.

Second, although he argues quite persuasively for the need to focus on the *social* relations of community ("people create a culture which in all its dimensions composes a set of resources for living in society and for affecting the contours of society," p. 1), Katznelson is apparently ignorant of the role women play in developing and maintaining such community. In the absence of any suggestion to the contrary, we are left with the presumption that (like the workers) the actors in the community movements, political machines, and neighborhood associations he describes are all male (see e.g., p. 210).

Finally, Katznelson and the others are remarkably oblivious to the growing feminist literature on urban spatial structure and on the significance of the split between workplace and residence for women's experience of the city. I shall argue that the assumptions about gender roles that apparently underly these analyses mask the interplay between workplace and community that already exists. Furthermore, they limit our understandings of community itself, and thus have important implications for *political* action. A new look at the relationship between workplace and community that fully integrates women will lead to a fundamental reconceptualization both of the split and of the nature and possibilities of democratic politics.

FEMINIST ANALYSES OF URBAN SPATIAL STRUCTURE

Feminist attention to the increased numbers of female-headed families, and to the feminization of poverty (i.e., the increased proportion of the poverty-level population composed of women and their dependent children) has made evident that women, and particularly poor women, are overrepresented in our older central cities (Pearce, 1979; Freeman, 1980: S6; Sims, 1983: 131). Feminist urbanologists have argued that such overrepresentation is both "cause and consequence" of the fiscal woes of those cities (Freeman, 1980: S13) and is directly related to the separation of workplace and residence that characterizes American urban areas. Marxist-feminist critics, in particular, have argued that the separation needs to be understood not just as a consequence of the demands of capitalist production relations but also as a "product of the patriarchal organization of household production" (Markusen, 1980: S23; also Gamarnikow, 1978: 395-97).

Specifically, the overwhelming predominance of single-family detached dwellings in American housing stock; the assumption that a single, nuclear, family will occupy any unit (even within apartment complexes); and the separation of residential areas from workplaces both reflect the social norms of the heterosexually constructed nuclear family and have significant consequences for women within central cities. Sex segregation of the labor market relegates women to relatively low-paid, low-status work, thus reinforcing their dependence on men and/or on the state (Burris and Wharton, 1982: 51-52; Walshok, 1979: 65-67; Freeman, 1980: S16; Markusen, 1980: S30). The scarcity of affordable housing in suburbs—increasingly where employment opportunities are to be found—assures that even many low-paying jobs will be largely inaccessible to poor women, especially single heads of households (Downs, 1973; Roncek et al., 1980: 167-168; Sims, 1983; Gamarnikow, 1978: 400-401). The greater availability of public transportation in central cities has resulted in a growing concentration of women—again, particularly those who are poor heads of households and dependent on public transport—in those cities (Lopata, 1980; Freeman, 1980: S12; Chabaud and Fongeyrollas, 1978: 429-31; Contras and Fagnani, 1978).

In short, the assumption that the "normal" family is one in which the husband/father is the breadwinner who "supports" a wife and children at home (a constellation that describes only approximately thirteen percent of "family" units in the United States at the present) has been central to the development of the spatial and socioeconomic differentiation of urban areas. Yet that same assumption—and its manifestation in social and economic polity—effectively and often severely penalizes those whose lives do not conform to the norm (Markusen, 1980: S37). Policies and practices deriving from this assumption are related to the feminization of poverty.[4] In addition, the operation of race- as well as sex-discrimination in the labor and housing markets assures that the situation of women of color, and, particularly, of those who are heads of households, is even more desperate (Bell, 1974; Barrett and Morgenstern, 1974; Erie and Rein, 1982: 74-75; Hartman, 1982; Sims, 1983: 130-134). In 1981, slightly more than one-third of all families headed by a single woman fell below official U.S. poverty levels; but 52.9 percent of families headed by a black women were poor, and the corresponding figure is slightly higher for families headed by Hispanic women (U.S. Bureau of the Census, 1982: Table 18).

In the view of these feminist critics, then, the patterning of urban space—in particular, the physical separation of workplace and home—is a product both of capitalist industrial development and of heterosexual social norms. Beyond that, they make clear that the *consequences* of spatial segregation fall differently on women than on men. To ignore those consequences is inadequately to understand urban dynamics and to be in danger of developing policies that will contribute to the continued subordination of women. On a theoretical level, for example, it is essential to see residence as workplaces and to recognize the connection between urban spatial structure (*including the separation of workplace and residence*), and women's exploitation both at home and at work. It means developing urban policies that will overcome women's economic dependence by truly opening up to women the opportunity for equal labor force participation. And the provision of such opportunity, in turn, will require formidable support structures—including child care, housing, and urban spatial arrangements that take children into account—allowing women *effective* access to those employment possibilities. More generally, it will mean exploding the assumption that everyone lives—or ought to live—in a male-headed nuclear family with a second adult present for suport, and then developing housing alternatives and child-care programs for people who do not live in such families (Sims, 1983; Diamond, 1982; Freeman, 1980; Markusen, 1980; Gamarnikow, 1978; Hayden, 1980).

These critics offer an important corrective to our understanding and analysis of the relationship between urban spatial patterns, intrafamily dynamics, and the treatment of women and men at the workplace. They insist that the spatial patterning of cities derives as much from patriarchal assumptions about household structures and relationships as from the requirements of capitalism. Nevertheless, it is important to note that neither the spatial separation of home and work nor the sexual division of labor are unique to, or definitive of, capitalist urban systems. "Socialist" systems are far from egalitarian with respect to the division of labor; and not all capitalist systems are characterized by the patterns of residential specialization and decentralization these critics deplore.[5]

Although feminist urbanologists offer us a much richer understanding of residence or community, and suggest that the home deserves recognition as a workplace, they still seem to accept, at least on a theoretical level, the distinction between workplace and community. Women are portrayed as disadvantaged in traditional workplaces; and as both exploited in, and also identified with, residential workplaces. The resolution these critics offer is to open up paid work to women on a more equal basis with men, and to recognize the dependence of the entire set of relationships on the exploited domestic labor of women.

It remained for a British analyst, Cynthia Cockburn (1977a), to go beyond this formulation and to explore the role of women as crucial links in the relationship between workplace and community, public and private, the state and the household. For, as she argues, women's roles in the household situate them uniquely to *experience* urban life in such a way as to challenge the very *assumption* of a dichotomy between workplace and community. Regardless of their status in the paid workforce, women in Western Europe and the United States bear primary responsibility for the nurturing of children (and of adult males!) within the household/family. It is they who are concerned with the care, education, and nurturance of those who will take their places as adult members of society.[6] But, as Cockburn points out, the responsiblity to maintain the household and its members means that women (even those who are not engaged in paid wage-labor) are active in the urban arena considerably *beyond* the limits of the so-called domestic sphere: for it is women who tend to be those who negotiate with landlords, markets, welfare officers, health-care providers, and the like. It is women who mediate the standards of living for their families, adjust budgets when wages (those paid to them, or to the others with whom they may be living) either increase or decrease, when rents fluctuate, when food prices increase, or when welfare services are cut (Cockburn, 1977a: especially chs. 2 and 6; see also Wilson, 1977: 4; Lawrence, 1977: 12).[7] Gilkes (1980) has even characterized the work of black women who struggle to maintain and improve their communities as an occupation in itself.

In other words, because of their place in the sexual division of labor, women experience, in their day-to-day lives, very specific relationships not only with the males to whom they may be related but also with shopkeepers and landlords, with employers (whether directly, as exploited workers; indirectly, through the men who may be the official support of their household; or, even more indirectly, through their own exclusion from the labor market), and with agencies of the state. The context of women's lives and daily activities belies the supposed distinction or separation between   public and private, workplace and community, state and household—for women's roles situate them to experience the interpenetration of these spheres. Thus, to understand women as living their lives solely within the realm of reproductive activity (or to treat a so-called sphere of reproduction as somehow distinct from a sphere of production, as many feminist-Marxist analysts do)—even for analytical purposes—is to miss both the complexity of women's lives and the implications of that complexity for the development of women's social and political consciousness (Cockburn, 1977b: 62-66).[8]

Specifically, Cockburn's analysis leads us to a number of important observations about political strategy that amplify and modify the analyses of Katznelson and others. First, it does not make sense to speak of struggles at work as separate from struggles in the community, or to describe struggles over community-based issues as somehow political, rather than economic. In Cockburn's words, "struggles around housing or benefits or schools are economic, as well as 'merely' political" (1977a: 163). Surely, looking at women's activism within black communities, for example, makes clear the interconnections (Gilkes: 220). Second, to recognize the relationship between workplace and household issues would change the nature of workplace struggles as well. In recent years, some workers have extended their efforts in negotiations and strikes to take account of the impact of work rules and policies on home life and on the conditions of work, as well as on wages and hours (Raboy, 1978; see also Cockburn's reports of her interviews with women activists, especially 1977b: 64). In addition, this analysis leads us to explore the specific reasons why women tend, disproportionately, to be in temporary jobs. We need to examine the effects of recent domestic cutbacks on the relative positions of women within and without the paid labor force (Cockburn, 1977a: 163; also Piven and Cloward, 1982: especially 136-142; Erie and Rein, 1982: 82-84).

To acknowledge these interconnections is to challenge the claim that only struggles at the workplace can result in fundamental social change. To focus only on workplace struggles is to ignore a significant proportion of people's own life experience (including the potentially consciousness-changing experiences of exploitation at the hands of landlords, shopkeepers, public employers, and so on) and to exclude all wageless people, and many women, from the possibilty of participating effectively in movements for social change (Cockburn, 1977a: 164-167; see also Ettorre, 1978: especially 507-510; Kaplan, 1981; Susser, 1982; and Ackelsberg, forthcoming). Finally, this perspective points up the particular role of women in urban social movements; for Cockburn claimed that women's involvement in struggle "sprang directly from their experience in the home" (1977a:

177; see also 1977b: 62; Ettorre, 1978: 507; Wilson, 1977: 4-5; Gilkes, 1980: 219, 228).

These observations, while exposing some of the limits of a public/private dichotomization, still fail to detail the nature of women's collaborative relationships that underly many urban social movements. Urban women live in a context of webs of relationships, informal and formal, which structure their patterns of interaction, give meaning and order to their lives, and may well be crucial factors affecting the development of their political consciousness.

Historians of popular protest movements have noted the prominent role of women in many urban movements (see, e.g., Levy and Apple-white, 1980; Kaplan, 1982; Lawson and Barton, 1980; Lawson, Barton, and Joselit, 1980).[9] Some have suggested that their prominence in these types of activities is a consequence of a specific female consciousness, which derives from women's particular place in the social-sexual division of labor. Temma Kaplan, for example, has argued that as primary caretakers of households and communities—regardless of their status in the paid work force—women have developed a special sensitivity to quality-of-life issues. Both historically and in our own time, that sensitivity has led them to demonstrate, riot, and demand from the state that it fulfill its proper role in providing adequate urban social services (see, in particular, Kaplan's discussion of bread riots in Barcelona, 1918-1919, 1982). Similarly, Lawson and associates (1980) note the prominence of women in tenant organizing for better housing, both in the early part of this century and in the contemporary period, in New York City. They suggest that women's "numerical predominance" in tenant organizing is attributable, in part, to "woman's role as homemaker and budget supervisor." In that role, she spends a great deal of time around the home, and is likely to feel, immediately and directly, any "increase in rent or deterioration in services" (1980: 256).

Yet Lawson and associates also emphasize the importance of friendship and other networks in contributing both to the development of women's political consciousness and to their availability for mobilization. In their words, "the common activities of women in their building and neighborhood . . . all tend to create social ties that can provide a basis for mobilization" (p. 257). Kaplan argues that women met regularly at various communal spots (e.g., markets, water taps, and the like), which became important loci not only for the exchange of gossip, but also for political organizing.[10] Gilkes points out that once black women "are 'out there' and have shown some skill in solving problems shared by other members of the community, people

seek them out" (1980: 221). Finally, the activities of such organizations as the National Welfare Rights Organization or the National
Congress of Neighborhood Women—particularly the success of the
latter in mobilizing large numbers of working-class women to action
on issues such as housing, schools, and social services—provide further evidence of the power of women's networks and their implications for women's participation in urban social movements (see, for
example, Brightman, 1978; Susser, 1982; and, though she discusses a
British context, Cockburn, 1977b: 65-69). If we ignore these specific
gender-related experiences of women in urban contexts, we will fail to
understand at least some of the sources of women's activity in the
community. And political movements which fail to acknowledge and
address these differences will also fail effectively to incorporate
women or to address issues which are crucial to their day-to-day lives.

As a number of analysts have argued with respect to other aspects
of women's lives, women's experience of the city is *relational*, importantly rooted in webs of association, collaboration, and mutual
support (Gilligan, 1982; Susser, 1982; Saegert, 1980). Historians have
demonstrated that, throughout U.S. history, women's networks have
been crucial, both in providing material support to individual women
and their families and in providing the context for broader political
activity (see, for example, Smith-Rosenberg, 1975; Cott, 1977; Ryan,
1979; Ackelsberg, 1983). Contemporary urban women who develop
collaborative relationships with their neighbors around child care,
transportation to and from welfare centers, shopping, or the like are
also able to call on those networks when their communal lives are
threatened (see Susser, 1982; Gilkes, 1980; Lawson, Barton, and
Joselit, 1980; Stack, 1975).

In addition, these very activities—even if undertaken in defense of
what might be seen as narrowly-domestic concerns—often challenge
both the supposed distinction between the public and the private
spheres and women's own understandings of their place in families
and communities. For example, Lois Gibbs and others at Love Canal
may have engaged, initially, in protesting the dumping of toxic wastes
out of their understanding of their place as protectors of the home.
But their experience in organizing changed them fundamentally,
broke down the supposed distinction between domestic and public
arenas, and challenged the bases of many of their marriages. One of
the women activists Cockburn interviewed reported that "when you
start getting involved, you find you're not a cabbage any more.
You've got a mind and can do things. . . . I think Tom's realized I'm a
human being since I did this [started a tenants' association]. He used

to think I had no ideas and opinions of my own. And you grow into it yourself, and believe those things about yourself, in the end" (1977b: 67, 69).[11]

COLLABORATIVE ACTIVITIES AND DEMOCRATIC POLITICS

What are the implications of these studies? What might it mean to incorporate these new perspectives and treat women's experience of the city as an important element of our conceptualizations of city life?

First, taking women's lives seriously requires that, in political analysis, strategy, and policy recommendations alike, we explore the links between state policy, workplace issues, and community/residential issues. One consequence here is to explode the presumed dichotomy between workplace and community, public and private; and, conversely, to explore the connections between familial structures, economic relations, and urban spatial structure—specifically, between employment and housing as they affect women. Some clues as to the potential policy implications of such a perspective might be taken from the experience of the Montreal Citizen's Movement, a contemporary urban movement that has explicitly attempted to link workplace and community issues (specifically housing costs and availability, and control over the quality of the urban environment) and in which women have been notably active (Roussopoulos, 1982; Raboy, 1978).

Aside from the obvious advantages to women—who have been the hardest hit by unresponsive urban policies—there would be fiscal advantages, as well, to the cities themselves. As it is now, low wages and lack of access to jobs make women more dependent on public resources—for example, transportation and housing—than are men of similar class and ethnic background. If women's employment options were improved, and if adequate housing were available, they would be able to make more, and more substantial, contributions to the urban tax base. "For these reasons alone urban finances would be improved by increasing women's employment opportunities and pay" (Freeman, 1980 S13).

Second, a rethinking of analytical categories to take account of women's experience would add new dimensions to the community side of the picture. It would mean expanding what Katznelson, Kornblum, and others have seen as the relatively limited potential of community-related issues (which, on their view must of necessity focus on ethnic-territorial claims and, therefore, founder on the rocks of particularism and divisiveness) to recognize the ways in which women's organization to improve the community's quality of life has grown out of existing networks, and united people *across* racial and ethnic lines. The transformative potential of a focus on quality-of-life issues is enormous—even if largely (to date) untapped by mainstream parties and social change movements.[12]

We would need to look, for example, at the ways in which urban spaces are structured. Do the patterns of housing and social services presuppose the universality of heterosexually constructed nuclear families? (For some examples of alternatives see Hayden, 1980; Stamp, 1980.) Do they take into account the needs of women with children, or of others who do not live in famlies so constructed? (Sims, 1983; Diamond, 1982). Are there places for children to play? Do policies and programs support, or do they undermine, existing urban networks? Can we devote resources and attention to programs which will support such networks and existing collaborative patterns, rather than ignore their existence and see only patterns of decay?[13] It is important to note that, although Katznelson and Kornblum are aware of the significance of community feeling among the people they studied, and acknowledge the importance of communal networks in sustaining a certain degree of class consciousness, neither examines the ways in which those networks operate. Yet, it is precisely such community-based networks, rooted largely in *women's* collaborative activities, which provide the context and basis for the *class* consciousness they so value in those communities. To put it another way, this analysis suggests that we must not only take seriously the *actions of women* in their communities, but also recognize that what goes on in urban communities, even within the confines of particular households, may have public, political import.

Finally, to integrate the activities and concerns that have traditionally been the province of women into the urban political-economic arena will have fundamental consequences for our understanding of urban democrary itself. Wolin (1982) has articulated a notion of democratic citizenship—one based in the citizen as active participant in collective decision making, rather than as a "bearer of rights"—which can provide a useful starting-point for this discussion:

> A political being is not to be defined as the citizen has been as an abstract, disconnected bearer of rights, privileges, and immunities, but as a person whose existence is located in a particular place and draws its sustenance from circumscribed relationships: family, friends, church, neighborhood, workplace, community, town, city. These relationships

are the sources from which political beings draw power . . . and that
enable them to act together . . . From a democratic perspective, power is
not simply force that is generated; it is experience, sensibility, wisdom,
even melancholy distilled from the diverse relations and circles we move
in (Wolin, 1982: 27; see also Evans and Boyte, 1982: 57; Pitkin and
Shumer, 1982: 46, 48; Walzer, 1970: especially chs. 10 and 11).

A number of aspects of this perspective merit attention. First, given
Wolin's sensitivity to issues of the origins of power, and the location
of power in community, it is particularly striking that he devotes little
or no attention to the specific position of women within American
political communities. Yet it is precisely such a concern with origins
that should alert us to the importance of taking women's specific experience into account when formulating a full understanding of
democratic participation and citizenship. Second, he emphasizes the
importance of recognizing *diversity* within a democratic political community. Finally, he suggests that democracies treat people not so
much as isolated individuals, but as members of communities. Each of
these elements of his definition has important implications for the effective integration of women into a democratic political community in
urban areas.

It seems clear that, both historically and in our own day, much of
women's political consciousness and activities in urban contexts
develop out of their participation in networks of friends and
neighbors on a daily basis. Such networks tend to be "spontaneously
organized"[14] (in the sense of lacking in formal leadership structures),
and nonhierarchical. Yet members can be readily mobilized, whether
for help on an individual basis or to respond to broader community
issues. Many women who become activists on the local (and then
supra-local) scene do so not because they have been called out by
unions, by political parties, or even by formally structured community
organizations. Instead, they respond to the issues which come before
them as members of households and, importantly, of the *communities*
(primarily, but not exclusively, of women) in which those households
are embedded.

Urban women, that is, do not come to politics as isolated, self-
interested individuals.[15] For them, the problem of politics is not—as
much traditional democratic theory would have us believe—that of
creating an allegiance to something *other* than the self,[16] but, rather,
finding ways to link the concerns, visions, and perspectives they share
with their neighbors to the political system that stands apart from
them and seems to control their lives. Studies of women in urban communities suggest that even participatory democratic theorists—those

who claim to be the most sensitive to the interconnections between political orientations (e.g., feelings of political efficacy) and social reality—may have put their emphasis on factors that miss the point of women's experience. Many urban women seem to have little or no difficulty acknowledging the connections between their concerns and those of others. They do not feel themselves to be in a competitive relationship with their fellow urban residents. Yet there is little theory of (urban) democracy which responds to the reality of their interconnected lives, or which can help them make sense—or political use—of those networks. Instead, we talk of the need to unite workplace and community. But women's lives have done that—and do it—on a daily basis, although perhaps without the consciousness that that is what they are about! (On this point, see also Diamond and Hartsock, 1981: 718-720). In Cockburn's words, "women bring a totality, an all-or-nothing feeling to action. It is something of which trade unions and political parties with their hierarchies and agenda know little, and to which they can give little. This totality is not just of the work day but of the whole day, not just of wages but of feelings, not just of economics but of relationships" (1977b: 69-70).

The perspective of networks and relationships provides us another angle of vision on the question of diversity, as well. Although much liberal democratic theorizing has been pluralistic (if not pluralist) in orientation, insisting that people can unite—e.g., across ethnic or racial lines—on the basis of common interests, or that their ethnic-racial interests can serve as the basis for political organization and pressure (so that conflicting interests can be resolved in the political arena), true diversity almost always appears as a threat to stability.[17] There is no guarantee, of course, that a politics that takes account of women's networks, or that focuses and builds on relationships between people, in general, will be open, nonracist, and nonexclusive. Yet, conceptualizing politics and political behavior around *relationships*, rather than around interests, provides at least the possibility of a more open, egalitarian perspective.

We return, finally, to the significance of community in a democratic politics. I have tried to suggest that much of the contemporary debate about workplace versus community organization, or about the limits of a community focus for social change, has been misplaced. For women, at least, the community—constituted of networks of friends and neighbors—*is* one locus of the development of whatever we might want to call political consciousness. It is in and through such networks, located at the interface of personal/household concerns and the impact of employer or public policy decisions, that many urban women engage in collaborative activity and begin to experience themselves, and others, as (potential) citizens of a democratic polity. It is precisely in the quintessential urban experience of diversity and difference—differences that rather than necessarily separating people, provide a context for the development of *relationships*—that women (and, presumably, men) can come to see themselves as competent social-political actors (see, e.g., Sennett, 1970—though he, too, ignores the specific situation of women).

This is not to suggest, of course, that employment discrimination is irrelevant to women, or that there is no need to address the separation of workplace from residence in American urban areas. On the contrary, these concerns are central to the lives of most urban women. But this examination of the situation of women in the city suggests that a simple focus either on employment issues, or on housing—even attending to the interconnections between these concerns—will not be sufficient to contribute, effectively, to integrating women fully into the context of urban political life. Instead, we must change the way we conceptualize that context, both to reflect the realities of women's lives and to make visible the networks and activities that underlie much of what we have taken to be democratic politics.

NOTES

1. Wolin's argument here, as well as those of Piven and Cloward and Bender, to be discussed below, is clearly indebted to the work of E. E. Schattschneider (1960), who firt drew connections between the restriction of the agenda of politics and its implications for democratic participation, as well as control. See also Burnham (1965).

2. Walzer (1978) and Green (1981) made similar arguments.

3. Compare, for example, Cockburn's report of her conversation with a woman activist:

> May Hobbs, a couple of years after the night cleaners' campaign in which she played a leading part, said to me: "People always wanted me to speak about cleaners, nothing but that. That was a small part of it for me. I'm a woman. It's one big struggle, a woman's struggle, it's not just organizing round our jobs, but it's to do with housing, health, everything that affects you" [1977b: 64].

4. See, for example, Pearce (1979); Currie, Dunn, and Fogarty (1980); Sidel (1982); Erie and Rein (1982); Erie, Rein, and Wiget (1983).

5. I am grateful to Irene Diamond for making clear to me the limitations of the apparent determinism of some of their analyses with respect to the relationship between capitalism and patriarchy.

6. Socialist-feminist critics have termed this process the "social reproduction of labor." I prefer to avoid that usage, primarily because of its economistic connotations. Clearly, the process of preparing people for full membership in society is a requisite of any ongoing social group.

7. For a discussion of a smaller phenomenon—the absorption by women of variations in standard of living—but which does not quite make this argument about the sexual division of labor see Oren (1973: 107-25).

8. Myrna Breitbart and I have been developing aspects of this argument—specifically with respect to the formation of urban women's political consciousness—in "Pathways to Social Change" (1982). I delivered an early version of the argument here about the implications of Cockburn's analysis to a Workshop on Feminist Policy Analysis at the 1982 annual meeting of the American Political Science Association in Denver, Colorado. Lawrence has noted that women's relationship to *home*, as well as to work, is fundamentally different from men's. "Thus, home," she notes, "is a radically different experience for male and female workers. For the former it is a compensation for the unpleasantness of work, for the latter it is more work—although both may also perceive the home as an escape from the workplace" (1977: 14-15).

9. Much of the analysis to follow was developed, originally, as part of "Pathways to Social Change" (1982).

10. My own work interviewing Spanish anarchist women who were active in some of those struggles confirms the importance of informal networks. Many women were unable, for example, to describe how plans for consumer strikes or bread riots were communicated to the people of the neighborhood: "One simply heard about it," they would report, or, "you would be on the street and you would hear that all should be at such-and-such place at such-and-such time."

11. See also Cockburn (1977a: 177-79). Ettorre discusses the shift from localized, reactive, struggles to more "sweeping campaigns" in various elements of the British Women's Liberation movement (1978: 507-512); and Gilkes describes the development of a broader consciousness among women in a black community in the United States (1980: 219-228). See also Hayden (1978: 404-419); 1981: chs. 4, 9, 11); Evans and Boyte (1982: 60-61); Cott (1977).

12. Harry Boyte (1980) has been one of the strongest proponents of a strategy that incorporates neighborhood/community-based activities. Yet, although he acknowledges the importance of the feminist movement in the United States, he, too, largely ignores the specific role of women in neighborhood organization.

13. The questions I raise here are meant to parallel those raised by Gans (1962), where he challenged the conventional wisdom that the West End of Boston was a "slum"; the work of Carol Stack (1975), who challenged the claim that urban black families are chaotic and unstructured; and the similar work of Ida Susser (1982) with respect to a white working-class community in Brooklyn.

14. "Spontaneous organization" is a term introduced by Colin Ward (1973) in his discussion of the theory and practice of anarchism in daily life.

15. Irene Diamond and Nancy Hartsock make a similar point in their claim that we need to develop categories of political analysis more encompassing than "interests" that "reduce the human community to an instrumental, arbitrary, and deeply unstable alliance" (1981: 719). Much of my thinking about relationships that underlies the remainder of this chapter was developed in ongoing conversations with Irene Diamond and also with T. Drorah Setel.

16. This problem is, of course, one classic formulation of the liberal dilemma of politics: how to maintain identity and self-interest in the context of a political community; or, conversely, how to form a political *community* out of a conglomerate of self-interested individuals. It is an issue that Hobbes, Locke, Rousseau, and Mill (among others) all addressed—and all seemed to think that some major transformation (either

of human personality or of social relationships) would be necessary if community were truly to be possible.

17. The list of those who fear diversity as a threat to stability—especially among American political scientists—is all too familiar. I mean to include in it, among others, S. P. Huntington, S. M. Lipset, H. McCloskey, R. Dahl, N. Polsby.

12

STATE AND LOCAL
POLICIES ON MOTHERHOOD

Emily Stoper

This chapter is based on the premise that it is women's unique role as mothers, more than any other factor, that limits their opportunities and colors their experience in virtually all aspects of their lives. This is true to a great extent even for the roughly twenty percent of women who never become mothers, because they have been socialized with the expectation that they will become mothers and others treat them as if they were or some day would be mothers.

The way in which motherhood shapes the experiences of women varies a great deal across cultures and is influenced by a wide variety of social institutions, including governments. Most previous research on American government policies about mothers and their children has focused on the national government in Washington (Kamerman, 1980; Steiner, 1976). This article will focus on the variety of ways in which state and local governments in the United States influence the institution of motherhood.

That institution is very much in flux in the United States today, because of a combination of the rising divorce rate of the 1960s and 1970s and the long-term trend of ever-greater numbers of married women and mothers in the workforce. These social and economic trends have made motherhood a controversial issue, about which social commentators from feminists to born-again Christians have had a great deal to say (see, for example, Blumenfeld, 1975; Chesler, 1979; Chodorow, 1978; Fraiberg, 1977; Lasch, 1977; Rich, 1976; Sebald, 1976). The relationship between mothers, their families, and society, once taken for granted, is now highly problematic.

At the same time, there is a national mood, affecting all levels of government, of disillusionment with government spending as a means of improving the quality of life. The "taxpayers' revolt" has become the primary constraint for those concerned about social services for families. After a substantial expansion of government spending on such services in the 1960s and early 1970s, the pendulum has swung the other way.

However, the retreat from public commitment to children may be more apparent than real. There has always been a recognition by mothers of every shade of opinion, from the most feminist to the most traditional, that children are not raised in a vacuum; rather, they are raised in the context of a community, from which their values and goals are derived. This recognition accounts for the long history of mothers' involvement in community work—through the PTA, their extended families (especially in the working class and minority groups), churches and synagogues, and neighborhood and civic associations. More recently, this community participation has been in the form of local elective and appointive officeholding.

Thus, it seems likely that a redefinition of the relationship between mothers, families, and society will come not from the national government (which is obsessed with simultaneously containing communism and the deficit) but rather from the communities, through daily practice and local government policies. Local government, of course, exists within the legal and fiscal framework of state government. State and local governments influence the institution of motherhood in myriad ways, four of which will be the focus of this article: abortion, child care, child custody and support, and welfare.

First, by regulating the availability of abortion, state and local governments influence how much freedom women have to decide whether and when to become mothers. Second, through licensing policies for private child care and other standards for public child care, they influence both the quality and availability of child care outside the home, thus affecting the degree to which mothers of young children can be employed or can engage in other pursuits. Through their tax policies they ease or fail to ease the financial burden of child care. Third, through their policies about child custody and the level of child support payments after divorce, they strongly affect the lives of the 16.6 percent of all American families that are headed by women (U.S. Department of Labor, cited in "Women's Political Times," March/April 1983: 1). And fourth, by setting the level of welfare payments and determining eligibility requirements, they profoundly influence the lives of poor parents, most of whom are women.

Fathers, of course, are also affected by any policies that are designed to help in raising children. But, at least in the four major policy areas under discussion here, it is mothers' role that is problematic. It is mothers, after all, who get pregnant and sometimes have abortions. It is mothers whose entry into the labor force in unprecedented numbers has created a huge new demand for child care. It is mothers who are all too often left in poverty or near-poverty after a divorce. And it is mothers who are over ninety percent of the adults on welfare.

State and local governments are deeply embroiled in controversy in all four of these policy areas. This situation results in serious hardships for mothers and their children and in widespread violations of the law. Yet in the absence of clear goals based on a new social contract between mothers, families, and society, satisfactory policies are not likely to be developed. Let us now examine the four policy areas in order to determine both the barriers to, and the possible bases for, a constructive redefinition.

ABORTION

Surely the most controversial area of motherhood policy is abortion. State and local governments no longer have the power to decide whether it is legal. The U.S. Supreme Court has ruled in Roe v. Wade (1973) that abortion is legal during the first six months of pregnancy. In June 1983, the court also struck down a whole series of state and local regulations, known as the "Akron laws" after the Ohio city that first passed them, that made it more difficult to obtain an abortion. These regulations included requirements that all abortions of women over three months pregnant be performed in hospitals rather than abortion clinics, that doctors read a statement mentioning the risks of abortion but not those of childbirth and stating that the fetus is "a human life," and that all minor, unwed girls must obtain their parents' consent, no matter how mature they are (Oakland Tribune, June 16, 1983: 1).

In other respects, though, the court has given the states freedom to act as they see fit regarding abortion. For example, in 1977 it ruled that the U.S. Constitution does not require states to fund abortions for indigent women. Today thirty-five of the fifty states do not fund abortions for women on Medicaid (Jennings, 1983). Medicaid abortions were funded by the federal government until 1977, when Congress first passed the Hyde Amendment (to the annual Labor/HHS appropriations bill) banning such funding. In those states that do not fund abortions, up to a third of the poor women denied funding will give birth and a large percentage of their babies will become welfare dependents (Scheier, 1980: 5; Trussell et al., 1980: 127). State policy on whether to fund abortions for poor women has had a significant impact on abortion rates, which vary from 6.9 (per one thousand women aged 15-44) in West Virginia to 45.8 in New York. Those states that fund abortion have an average rate of 30.8. States that do not fund abortions have an average rate of 20.9.

Of the fifteen states plus the District of Columbia that do fund abortions, seven do so by court order, not by vote of the legislature, thus sidestepping the controversy.[1] Whether a state funds abortion voluntarily or by court order makes almost no difference in its abortion rate (U.S. Bureau of the Census, 1982-1983: 70). This indicates that it is not state-by-state differences in citizens' underlying attitudes but rather the policy differences themselves that cause the variations in state abortion rates.

Local government policies affect the abortion rate in another way that may be even more significant: through the nonuse of the police power to prevent harassment. Three-quarters of abortion are performed in clinics, and in many states, especially in counties outside metropolitan areas, harassment of the clinics by abortion opponents effectively prevents their operation (Barton, 1979: 27-28). This is doubtless one major reason why every one of the fifteen states with abortion rates under twenty per thousand women is predominantly rural.[2] Having no abortion clinic within several hundred miles of where one lives is an even more effective deterrent to having an abortion than lack of government funding if one is poor, judging from these statistics.

Opponents' tactics include aggressive picketing, vandalism, harassment of clinic employees and their children, refusal to sell needed materials to a clinic, shootings, firebombings, and arson. Most of these actions could be prevented by the police, if they were so inclined. Similar tactics have been attempted in major metropolitan areas, but clinics there continue to exist, in spite of periodic sabotage, in large part because police enforcement is more effective.

Such destruction—and the widespread tolerance of it by the police—could not exist without an atmosphere of bitterness and hatred between opponents of abortion and proponents of free choice. At the core of the dispute is a difference in attitude about the nature of childbearing: a gift from God to be unconditionally accepted or an arduous social responsibility to be undertaken only as a matter of completely free choice by the mother. Neither side seems to concede any validity to the arguments made by the other side. Pro-lifers imply that those who advocate choice are legitimizing murder and are like Nazis. Pro-choice advocates imply that alleged concern about the right to life is a hypocritical mask for a desire to keep women barefoot and pregnant.

Yet in their private lives almost all women acknowledge both the value of a woman's ability to control her own reproductive life and the experience that a fetus is far more than just a mass of cells to be disposed of at will without a second thought. They see childbearing as both a gift from God and an arduous responsibility. The two positions are not logically opposed; they are two aspects of the truth.

Probably the most effective strategy for ending the harassment of abortion clinics would be the establishment of a dialogue between pro-lifers and pro-choicers within each local community, a dialogue based on an acknowledgment of the validity in the other side's position and the sincerity of its concern. The dialogue could focus on a common concern of both pro-life and pro-choice women: developing means to reduce the demand for abortion (and thus the abortion rate) by reducing the number of unwanted pregnancies. In communities where such a dialogue existed, there still might be a few fanatics who wished to engage in harassment tactics. But it would be very difficult for a public agency such as the police to continue to have a policy of implicity condoning such behavior.

The women's movement's support for the right to choose abortion is sometimes interpreted as reflecting a negative attitude about motherhood, since every abortion is of course a choice not to have a child. It is therefore important that in each community where the movement is vocal in its support for the right to choose abortion, it should be active in efforts to seek community support, through a variety of programs, for raising children. These could include child health programs, support for the schools, improvements in foster care, and many others. Three of the most significant child-related programs—child care, child custody and support, and welfare—will be discussed in the remainder of this article.

CHILD CARE

Mothers are entering the labor force in increasing numbers. It is estimated that in 1983, forty-two percent of mothers with children under age 3 and fifty-four percent of mothers with children aged 3 to 5 work outside the home (Children's Defense Fund, 1983: 133). The pressure for community involvement in assuring that these children are well cared for is bound to increase.

Support for child care is most logically a local government function, since child care, like public education, should reflect the values and customs of local communities. But as of 1978 all state and local governments combined were estimated to spend only $1.5 billion a year, out of total budgets of over $200 billion, on child care and related services (Auerbach, 1979: 33-43). This compares with $2.3 billion spent by the federal government, including tax expenditures (Norgren, 1981: 19-20), and some $6.4 billion spent by families (Woolsey, 1978: 133).

Much of the state money is for matching funds or supplemental funds for federal programs. Other state money goes for coordination of various child-related community services, information exchange, technical assistance, training programs, licensing, and information and referral services. The states themselves have not generally funded child care directly, except as supplements to federal programs, a requirement that was dropped in fiscal year 1982. Most of the federal money is given as grants-in-aid to community groups (and a very small number of government agencies and schools) to run child-care centers for welfare or potential welfare (very low-income) children. These programs have suffered heavily under the Reagan cuts, but little of the slack has been taken up by state or local governments.

The other major form of federal subsidy for child care is the income tax credit of a percentage (twenty to thirty percent, depending on income) of actual expenses, up to an expense ceiling of $2400 for one child and $4800 for two or more children. The states are far less generous. California allows a tax credit of only three percent, with the same expense ceilings as the federal government, but only if adjusted gross income is under $20,000 per year. Of the forty-two states plus the District of Columbia that levy a personal income tax, fifteen states have no tax credit or deduction for child care at all (*All States Tax Guide*, 1982: 177). Tax credits and deductions are really the major form of subsidy for child care in this country, since only 3.7 percent of 3-to-6-year-old children of mothers in the labor force are in formal day care centers, subsidized or otherwise.

A much larger number, 26.2 percent (Boles, 1980: 349), are in unsubsidized family or home day care, run by women in their own homes, usually for five to seven children, sometimes including one or two of their own children. Parents spend some $1.8 million a year on home day care by nonrelatives and only $547 thousand on day care centers (Bane et al., 1978: 24). The horror stories of small children being beaten, grossly neglected, and sometimes even killed all come from day care homes; on the other hand, some of the best day care in the country appears to be offered in such homes. Parents usually prefer their informality and homelike environment over child care centers. They often feel that the care given in these day care homes is more like what the children would receive in their own homes, especially since home day care is usually run by a neighbor of the same ethnic group and social class as the children.

The problem with home day care is that since parents are away at work all day, it is very difficult for them to evaluate the quality of care, and there are no organizational or professional assurances of quality or checks on the behavior of the caregiver. Small children are notoriously unreliable informants. A system of inspection and licensing by local governments might at least offer protection against the worst abuses.

Almost all states do require that all child-care facilities with more than a handful of children (the exact mininum varies) must be licensed. But in practice these licensing requirements often harass and discourage would-be providers of child care while failing to set meaningful standards. As a consequence, an estimated ninety percent of family day care is unlicensed (U.S. Department of Labor, 1979: 9). Providers just do not want to be bothered with the confusion created by overlapping jurisdictions of health, sanitation, zoning, building, and fire departments. In some places, a license cannot be obtained without a substantial bribe—and those who pay the bribe get the license without meeting the requirements.

In any case, the requirements rarely bear any relationship to those factors that make for quality in child care, namely, the quality of the personnel and equipment. Only five states (Georgia, Massachusetts, New York, Ohio, and Vermont) require providers to have any training or demonstrated ability to work with children as a condition for receiving a license. Another six states require them to be able to read and write (U.S. Department of Health, Education and Welfare, 1978: 42). Most states require only a building inspection (with standards varying greatly in reasonableness and toughness), health tests for providers, fingerprinting of providers (to ensure that they do not have a history of child abuse), and an orientation meeting for providers.

The license sometimes also specifies the maximum number of children and the minimum number of staff permitted. This last is potentially the most meaningful of the licensing requirements but is difficult for parents to monitor. Local governments could perform a real service by increasing the number of unannounced inspections to prevent overcrowding or understaffing.

Beyond this, it would probably be counterproductive to add to the list of licensing requirements, since parents are doubtless the best judges of what are the important qualities in a child-care provider or facility. Lengthening the list of requirements might simply increase the percentage of unlicensed facilities. To make the present requirements more enforceable, though, it would be helpful if local governments cracked down on corruption and cut through red tape, so that most providers are not deterred from even seeking a license.

In areas other than licensing, there is much more that states and local governments could do in the area of child care. They could introduce or expand tax credits or deductions, thus effectively providing subsidies for child care without in any way limiting parents' freedom. They could provide seed money for new facilities, especially in underserved areas, poverty areas, and for underserved groups, such as infants, handicapped children, and children with minor illnesses. They could pass laws requiring open access for parents to all child-care centers during operating hours without a requirement that the parents warn the center of their impending visit.

They could provide parents with more information by funding information and referral services in all local areas, perhaps generously enough so that these services could include in their files solicited and unsolicited comments from past users of particular child-care facilities. Some of these services could be funded to provide technical assistance, training, and support groups for providers.

Everyone but the poor will no doubt continue to be expected to pay for their own children's care while they are at work. The social consensus required for large-scale government financing of child care for the nonpoor is simply not present in this country. But state and local governments (mostly through locally administered state programs) could do far more to upgrade the standards of child care, especially family day care, and to ease the financial burden of middle-income parents through the tax system, while assuring that the poor (who do not benefit significantly from tax breaks because they pay little or no income tax) receive enough subsidies so that the cost of child care does not become a barrier to their employment or education. Smaller and more numerous subsidized day care centers would also give the poor more choice of centers and perhaps more voice in influencing the child care their children receive.

Why do state and local governments do far less than they could to improve child care and make it more affordable? Why do over one-third of the states with a personal income tax offer no tax deduction or credit at all? The answer to both these questions is that child care is controversial. To a large degree, it is a benefit for employed parents of small children in families where both parents are employed or only one parent is present. And maternal employment when small children are present, at least when it is not absolutely necessary to ward off destitution, is one of the issues dividing feminists and traditionalists.

It is true that a flood of recent research has found that children of employed mothers are very similar in every major respect to children of nonemployed mothers in their own social class (Hoffman and Nye, 1974). Nevertheless, research is not infallible and the deep-rooted cultural belief that it is best for small children to stay home with their mothers dies hard.

President Nixon vetoed the 1971 Comprehensive Child Care Act in large measure because he received an enormous number of letters that apparently persuaded him that child care was a threat to the family (see Auerbach, 1979: 91-94, for full text of veto message). At the same time, he was supporting an increase in child care subsidies for welfare mothers in order to encourage them to find jobs—so obviously he did not see child care as a threat to the poor family. Perhaps the perceived threat in government-subsidized child care is not so much to the children's well-being as to the breadwinning role of the father, who is usually not present in welfare families.

AFTER DIVORCE

Unfortunately, today increasing numbers of young children are living in poor or near-poor households with no father present. The rising divorce rate, combined with the continuing segregated, low-paid labor market for women, has resulted in the feminization of poverty. An overwhelming 31.4 percent of all families with a female head are poor, compared to 5.3 percent of all families with a male head (Bates, 1983: 2). This situation is largely caused by the low earnings of women—still only 59 percent of those of men. "Half of all full time female workers are not now able to support two children without additional income" (Bates, 1983: 6). For the majority of women, divorce or separation means a precipitous drop in standard of living—a drop averaging 73 percent, according to a recent California study (Weitzman, 1981: 1251)—although other studies show smaller drops.

Increasing numbers of women and children are facing such a plight. By the 1990s, it is estimated, only fifty-six percent of American children will spend their entire childhood with both biological parents (Weitzman, 1981: 1183). And in spite of all the talk about joint or "shared" custody or custody for fathers, over ninety percent of children after divorce are in the sole custody of their mothers—in the vast majority of cases, because both parents prefer it that way or assume that it must be that way. So we almost always have the paradoxical situation that the parent who is least able to support the children is the one who is given responsibility for them after a divorce.

It is true that some divorced fathers must make child support payments, but far less true than is popularly believed. According to a major study commissioned for International Women's Year, only forty-four percent of divorced or separated mothers in the United States reported that they had been awarded child support. The figure drops to twenty-five percent among black mothers (Jones et al., 1976: 19). And less than twenty percent of all divorced women are awarded any alimony (Weitzman, 1981: 1221).

Even when child support is awarded, the amounts are almost always far less than half the actual cost of raising a child—in part because there is usually no provision for adjusting the award for inflation (Weitzman, 1981: 1240). In Los Angeles in 1977, the average monthly amount was $126 per child (Weitzman, 1981: 1233), a fairly typical sum. Moreover, many fathers just do not pay even these inadequate amounts, which are set on the basis of their ability to pay. A 1978 Census Bureau study found that only about half the women awarded child support received it as ordered (Weitzman, 1981: 1253). And only about 20 percent of all divorced or separated mothers receive child support regularly, with an additional seven percent receiving it sometimes (Jones et al., 1976: 29). In short, the vast majority of the 16.6 percent of American children under 18 who live with their single-parent mothers (U.S. Department of Labor, cited in "Women's Political Times," March/April 1983:1) are being supported solely by their mothers.

Studies have shown that where states and counties adopt effective methods of collecting child support payments, there can be spectacular improvements in the amounts collected (Jones et al., 32-42). This is even true for the fathers of children on welfare (Leman, 1980: 210-212). A bill introduced in Congress in 1983 by Marge Roukema (Republican, New Jersey) would automatically withhold child support payments from fathers' paychecks; this would doubtless be extremely effective. And California recently passed a law permitting attaching part of a father's paycheck after a single month of delinquency in child support payments.

Why, the reader may ask, do the courts not increase the amount of child support payments and award child support in more cases? And why do state legislatures and the U.S. Congress not pass tougher laws for the collection of delinquent child support payments?

Fundamentally, the same answer can be given to both these questions. Fathers often do not think it is fair that they should be forced to pay for half the expenses of children with whom they no longer live and therefore with whom they probably no longer have the tight emotional bonds that are associated with family. And since most judges and legislators are fathers, they are perhaps more easily able to empathize with the position of divorcing fathers than with that of divorcing mothers. It is also interesting to note that public resentment against nonpaying fathers and therefore public support for enforcement focuses almost entirely on fathers of children on welfare, who usually have the least ability to pay.

Fathers rebel against what they see as unfair child support payments not only by falling into arrears but also by organizing politically for "fathers' rights." This often takes the form of lobbying to have state laws changed so that there is a presumption of joint or shared custody, as is now the case in at least two states (Science News, 1982: 73). In the remaining states, the law is written to favor giving custody to whichever parent is in "the best interests of the child"—which in practice is nearly always interpreted by judges to be the mother, since she is usually the emotionally "primary" parent.

Mothers are far less enthusiastic than fathers about the move to change the law toward favoring shared custody. Obviously, it removes from them an advantage that they feel they have earned (by being the primary parent in almost every family)—and by doing so weakens their bargaining position in disputes over the division of marital property and the amount of child support and spousal support. A legal presumption of shared custody may also make it more difficult for them to avoid contact with an abusive or violent husband.

Moreover, shared custody does not necessarily make a mother's financial situation any easier. She loses the right to any child support and she still has to maintain housing with adequate space for her children. She may lose her tax exemption for children who no longer live with her full time. Their father then may or may not pay for significant amounts of food, clothing, and so on. Some fathers may ask for joint custody just so that they do not lose control of their children—but may never provide anywhere close to half the care of the children, especially if this was not their pattern during the marriage. Shared custody, when it works, is in many ways more civilized and humane, because it allows the children to maintain a close relationship with both parents. It would also appear to be more consistent with feminist goals. Some feminist writers have seen equal sharing of parenting as the key to the liberation of women (Chodorow, 1978; Dinnerstein, 1977). Yet feminists have joined with more traditional women in opposing a legal presumption of shared custody, largely because they fear this would worsen the problem of postdivorce impoverishment.

Thus we see that men and women who are divorcing often have radically opposed views about what is fair. Each party to a divorce tends to see himself or herself as victimized. Fathers' sense of grievance about paying for children with whom they no longer live (and in some cases rarely or never see) has led them to engage in violation of the law on a large scale—in the form of stealing or snatching their own children, spiriting them away to another state, and obtaining legal custody of them there, often before the custody decision has even been made by the court in the children's home state. (Less frequently, mothers may steal their own children, too.) This is done either as a means of gaining permanent custody or in order to coerce the wife into relinquishing her right to child support or in some other way accepting an unfavorable divorce settlement. The government estimates there are some 25,000 child stealings a year; private groups say at least 100,000 (Gill, 1981: 15).

The government's handling of child stealing seems to reflect the view that this is a family quarrel that it had best stay out of. Most police and public officials have a hands-off attitude. The U.S. Congress has repeatedly declined to pass legislation making stealing one's own child a federal crime. Of the states, California has the strongest law: It will actually arrest a child snatcher if there is a custody decree and if the victimized parent finds the snatcher. Most states will not arrest a child snatcher but will permit civil remedies. In either case, the victimized parent must actually find the child.

Since 1981, there has been a federal Uniform Child Custody Jurisdiction Act, which states that if custody has been awarded in one state, another state may not take jurisdiction over the case. This law has several gaping loopholes, including a provision for exception if the transfer of jurisdiction is in the "best interests of the child" and a failure to require that a state first determine if custody has been granted in another state. However, the biggest problem with all the laws against child snatching is that they take effect only after a custody decree, and most snatchings occur before such a decree is issued.

States could be much more helpful in assigning police to assist parents in finding their stolen children, before or after a custody decree, and in passing laws making child stealing an offense subject to arrest and heavy fines and imprisonment. They could also press the federal government to set up a computerized system, which states could be required to check before hearing any custody case, to see whether custody has been granted in another state.

These changes would prevent thousands of tragic situations in which children are lost to one of their parents, sometimes permanently, often for long periods. The changes would not, however, remedy the underlying cause of child snatching, which is the feeling on the part of fathers that the whole system of child custody and child support is unfair to them. Any efforts to change this system along the lines fathers prefer will run up against women's fears about the impoverishment of divorced mothers and their children.

There are only three ways out of this predicament, none of them attainable by tinkering with state and local (or, for that matter, federal) laws. One way is for the community to take substantial responsibility for the expenses of raising all children, including support of the mother while she is out of the workforce caring for small children. Another way is for fathers and mothers to redefine their roles so that they are much more similar to each other, thus eliminating much of the economic disadvantage of mothers. The third way is the restoration of the old norm that divorce is socially unacceptable, at least for couples with children. None of these changes is likely to occur in the near future.

MOTHERS, THE STATE, AND POVERTY

Even if these changes did occur, they would not completely solve the problem of poverty. Some families would still have to resort to Aid to Families with Dependent Children (AFDC), commonly known as welfare, in order to care for their children.

Although the national government pays for fifty-four percent of the costs of welfare (San Francisco Chronicle, September 4, 1981: 20), policies on such vital matters as the level of funding and eligibility rules are set by the states and administered by local governments. As a consequence the level of welfare payments varies enormously, from an average monthly payment of $88 in Mississippi to $399 in California (1980 figures from U.S. Bureau of the Census, 1982-1983: 342). Even the highest of these is well below the poverty line.

Most of the people on welfare are single mothers and their children; only one in nine welfare families has an unemployed father present and half of these are disabled (Levitan, 1980: 33). In many states families with fathers present are not eligible to be on AFDC, no matter how poor they are.

From the point of view of state and local governments, the welfare system is not in crisis. The welfare rolls are not expanding. In 1981 public aid recipients (AFDC plus Supplemental Security Income) were 6.7 percent of the population, down from 7.1 percent in 1975 (U.S. Bureau of the Census, 1982-1983: 341). About sixty percent of welfare families are off the rolls in three years or less, though some of these go back on again (Lyon, 1978: 240). Only 7.1 percent of welfare families remain on the rolls for over ten years (1979 figure from U.S. Bureau of Census, 1982-1983: 343). Most of the adults on welfare are poorly educated and have little or no job experience. For such women, if they have two or more small children who would have to be placed in child care, it is economically irrational to seek employment (Steiner, 1971: 51, 70). Yet at any given time, some 18 percent of welfare mothers are employed (Lyon, 1978: 240). The average number of children per welfare family is only 2.3 (Levitan, 1980: 32).

In view of all this, why is welfare so frequently regarded by both the general public and policy makers as in crisis? The whole welfare system has a sour taste, experienced as anger and resentment by much of the public and shame and bitterness by many of the recipients. To welfare recipients, the system seems ungenerous and stigmatizing; to the general public, the existence of a large number (some 10.8 million) people on welfare seems an affront to the American dream, a statement that for many people both the free market economy and the traditional family cannot be made to work. In our individualistic culture, there is a strong temptation to blame welfare mothers for being on welfare. Many welfare mothers have responded in kind by angrily blaming the system for their plight, for example, through the welfare rights movement of the late 1960s and early 1970s. This pattern of mutual blame is an obstacle to attaining the goals of both welfare recipients and the government. In this state of mind, neither is likely to take effective action to improve the situation; any action that is taken tends to be geared instead toward harming the other, for example, cheating and griping by recipients, petty harassment and arbitrary benefit cuts by the government.

Although welfare is not in crisis, certain improvements are in order. For example, more assistance could be given to welfare mothers who wish to seek employment. That assistance could take the form of more access to training and educational programs (not necessarily specifically geared to the poor), more effective enforcement of laws against sex and race discrimination in employment (some 44 percent of welfare recipients are black, according to the U.S. Bureau of Census, 1982-1983: 343), more and better subsidized child care, better public transportation, and so on. For those welfare mothers for whom it is appropriate not to work, at least for a few years, benefits could be more generous and less stigmatized.

What would it take to create public support for these improvements? Public recognition of a simple fact: Welfare mothers are homemakers. As such, they are performing the socially valuable (if not valued) task of raising children. For this, they are being supported far less generously by the government than are most non-AFDC homemakers by their husbands. The public generally feels that homemakers should have the right to choose whether or not to be employed. There is no reason not to give welfare mothers this choice as well. Welfare mothers are as likely to enter the labor force as other women when there are jobs available with adequate wages. In the six major guaranteed income experiments conducted in the 1970s, it was found that even the presence of a guaranteed income reduced the amount of employment of female heads of households by only fourteen percent (Anderson, 1978: 105-117).

The whole atmosphere of mutual recrimination surrounding welfare is caused by the failure to acknowledge the benefit to society created by all mothers, even those who do not live in standard families (see Stoper, 1983). Welfare could be accepted by its recipients with dignity and proffered by society in a spirit of generosity if the contribution of all mothers were simply acknowledged.

CONCLUSION

This article has examined four state and local government policy areas relating to motherhood: abortion, child care, child custody and support after divorce, and welfare. All four of these policy areas are marred by an uneven and ill-defined commitment by society both to the protection and nurturance of children and to assistance for parents, especially mothers, in raising the next generation. Focus at the national level is unlikely to create this commitment since family policy is so marginal to the central concerns of the federal government. The best hope for the emergence of a new covenant between mothers and society lies in the thousands of local communities in which women are active.

The absence of such a covenant has led to large-scale violations of the law in all four areas. The abortion area is so riven with bitter conflict between pro-choice and pro-life advocates that the system is not even providing police protection in many areas for women exercising their constitutional right to abortion, with the result of widespread violence and intimidation. In the area of child custody and support, conflict between mothers and fathers, both individually and collectively, is so intense that it frequently leads to child stealing. In the area of welfare, a niggardly and begrudging system results in a great deal of petty cheating, documented by participant observer studies (Sheehan, 1976; Stack, 1974). Even in the area of child care, the inadequacy of licensing practices has resulted in widespread illegal operation of unlicensed child care facilities, as well as enormous numbers of violations in the operation of licensed facilities. Such violations of law, in addition to their direct harm, undermine the task of motherhood by presenting to children a model of adult lawlessness and irresponsibility.

The opposing groups in these conflicts are not likely to see eye to eye, but in each case the bitterness of the debate could be greatly reduced by a recognition on each side of the other side's genuine, although different, commitment to the quality of child-rearing. In many communities this would be the essential first step toward a partnership between families and communities in raising children.

Little leadership can be expected at the national level, especially in building a partnership between the government and mothers as the basis for full citizenship for women. Betty Friedan, in her latest book, *The Second Stage* (1981), calls for a new emphasis by the women's movement on changing the conditions of motherhood. But the book was greeted with resounding indifference or hostility by that movement, which is currently preoccupied with removing legal inequities (the Equal Rights Amendment, insurance discrimination) and with ending heterosexual violence against women (rape, battered wives, pornography, sexual harassment). Although important, these issues do not address the key structural obstacle to women's full participation in American society, which is the institution of motherhood as currently established. (While the movement does work to preserve the right to abortion, in most cases its style serves to maintain the bitter gulf between itself and pro-life women, thus making impossible any common work to improve conditions for mothers and children.)

It is in local communities, much of whose budgets are funded by state governments, that a movement could be formed to create a nation-wide commitment to assist families in raising children whenever such assistance is needed. That movement could be built around meeting parents' needs for fuller information about and more choices of child care in their communities, for more assistance in paying for child care, and for better enforcement of childcare licensing rules. It could be built around a community commitment to assuring that when mothers raise children alone, this does not result in the impoverishment or stigmatization of both, and that such families need not live in fear that the children will be stolen by their fathers. And it could be built around a commitment to assure that women's constitutional right to choose whether and when to have children will not be denied by violence or threats of violence—while at the same time the number of abortions is minimized by reducing the number of unwanted pregnancies. Finally, it could be built around a sense that welfare mothers are also serving the community by raising children and deserve assistance in obtaining employment or, when appropriate, in sustaining their families without employment.

All of these are worthy goals for state and local governments, consistent with their traditional concern for the education of children. The development of such goals could give state and local governments, now in the midst of a taxpayers' rebellion, a new sense that the tax money they spend made a real contribution to meeting the needs of their people.

NOTES

1. The states that voluntarily fund abortions are Alaska, Colorado, the District of Columbia, Hawaii, Maryland, Michigan, New York, North Carolina, Washington, and West Virginia. The states that fund abortion under court order are California, Connecticut, Massachusetts, New Jersey, Oregon, and Pennsylvania (Jennings, 1983).

2. Those states with abortion rates under 20 per thousand women aged 15-44 are Arkansas, Idaho, Indiana, Kentucky, Louisiana, Maine, Mississippi, Missouri, Nebraska, Oklahoma, South Carolina, South Dakota, Utah, West Virginia, and Wyoming (U.S. Bureau of the Census, 1982-1983: 70).

13

RESOURCES AND CONSTRAINTS ON WOMEN IN THE POLICYMAKING PROCESS: STATE AND LOCAL ARENAS

Ellen Boneparth

In theory at least, one of the strengths of political systems in which power is decentralized is that social movements have a variety of arenas in which to seek change, thus making the system more open and responsive. Historically, social movements in the United States have, indeed, pressed their demands in different political arenas depending on the character of their followings and the nature of their goals. The suffragists, for example, struggled for decades with a state-by-state strategy in seeking the vote for women, only to turn in the twentieth century, as their numbers grew and their cause gained legitimacy, to a national strategy of constitutional amendment (Flexner, 1959). Likewise, the Progressive Movement first gained strength in state and local governments before turning its efforts, ultimately less successfully, to national politics.

In the second half of the twentieth century, social movements have tended to focus on the federal government, in part because of the expanding power of the federal government vis-a-vis the states and in part because the goals of the movements could not be realized at the state level. The civil rights movement of the 1950s and 1960s, for example, pursued a national strategy as the only way to overcome the intransigence of the South. The antiwar movement of the 1960s and 1970s had no choice but to work in the national arena where decision making on foreign and military policy occurs.

With the rebirth of feminism in the 1960s, the women's movement channeled most of its energy into seeking change at the national level, modeling many of its goals on the antidiscrimination effort of the black movement while, at the same time, borrowing protest tactics and grassroots lobbying techniques from the antiwar movement. While feminists did not restrict their activities exclusively to the national scene, their early success in Congress and the Supreme Court reinforced the belief that the federal government was the most appropriate arena in which to fight for change (Freeman, 1982).

In the 1980s several factors have converged to cause feminists to begin rethinking their political strategies. The depressing defeat of the Equal Rights Amendment has awakened feminist activists to the reality that regional opposition to the women's movement is powerful enough to block change that depends on a broad national consensus. The changing political climate in the United States, reflected in the election of conservative presidents and congresses in the late 1970s and 1980s, highlights the difficulty not only of achieving new national policy on behalf of women but also, even more problematically, of maintaining past policy accomplishments (Schafran, 1982). Finally, the electoral defeats of many promising women candidates at the national level have been hard-learned lessons regarding the obstacles to achieving greater representation in the highest male bastions of decision making (Ridgeway, 1983).[1]

The recognition of these present realities is meant neither to detract from the past accomplishments of the women's movement nor to suggest that the movement abandon continuing attempts to work at the federal level. On the contrary, the ability of the women's movement in the 1970s to raise issues, to formulate policy proposals, and to place many of these proposals on the national agenda reflects the impressive evolution of feminism from a grassroots movement to a national lobbying effort manifesting considerable sophistication and expertise (Costain, 1982; Gelb and Palley, 1982). Moreover, any diminution of activity at the national level presents the immediate threat of policy reversals (Ehrenreich and Piven, 1983), or worse, of policy successes by the anti-feminists of the New Right seeking to return women to narrowly defined traditional roles (Schafran, 1982).

The new realities do, however, compel activists to explore additional avenues of policy change at the state and local levels of government. An examination of the prospects for effecting public policy in these arenas makes clear that women both benefit from certain resources and face certain constraints which may require some modification of political strategy, but which may also offer new opportunities to improve the status of women.

Before discussing new approaches for women to influence public policy at the state and local levels, it is necessary to point out some problems in generalizing about state and local government. Most obviously, despite trends in the twentieth century toward the development of a more homogeneous national political culture and the standardization of state policy as a result of the intervention of the federal government, the United States remains a nation of regional differences. In the study of state and local government, the economic base, the extent of urbanization, the character of the party system and political structures, the population mix, and the regional culture all affect the nature of the policymaking process and policy outcome.

Women's concerns have traditionally met more positive responses in states and localities characterized by a progressive tradition—generally urban areas with a diversified economic base, a heterogeneous population, a governmental and party system that has undergone political reform, and a cosmopolitan, secular political culture. It is not coincidence, for example, that of the fifteen states that failed to ratify the ERA, thirteen are located in or border on the South or Southwest where traditional values concerning women's roles are still firmly implanted and where public policy has consistently reflected economic and political conservatism (Boles, 1979). Thus, while strategies for change in more progressive regions may involve promoting women's issues in more effective ways, the first stage in more traditional regions may, of necessity, involve making the political system more accessible and responsive.

A second difficulty in generalizing about policy making in state and local government lies in the changing nature of the federal system. While the 1960s were characterized by the expansion of public programs at the national level, the orientation of the last three presidential administrations has been toward injecting new life, at least at a rhetorical level, into the relationship between the federal, state, and local governments.

The new thrust, whether carrying the labels of dual federalism, creative federalism or the new federalism may be intended to revitalize state and local roles in policy making or may simply be a smokescreen for phasing out federal commitments and responsibility for social programs (Gittell, 1982: 1). In either case, groups seeking to affect public policy must assess the potential for achieving their goals in one arena or another, according to where they are likely to find both the receptivity and resources to meet their demands. One pattern seems clear, however. Many groups, including women, active at the federal level in the 1960s and early 1970s have been unprepared to expand sufficiently their struggles to the state and local level, either because they saw their best hope as trying to maintain federal programs or because they lacked the organizational bases to switch arenas (Boyte, 1982: 116; Gelb and Palley, 1982: 179). Thus, if the real intent of the new federalism is to allow social programs to slip through the cracks of the federal system, this intent may be unintentionally aided by groups that have put most of their eggs in the federal basket.

RESOURCES: ACCESS AND ACCOUNTABILITY

Given the difficulties of generalizing across regions and over time, it is still possible to highlight some of the resources available to women seeking to influence public policy at the state and local level. The most obvious resource for women, as with other special interest groups, is access to the decision-making process. This access comes, first and foremost, from sheer physical proximity to the centers of power. Because women labor under the dual burdens of home and work, their ability to leave home responsibilities in order to function on the national scene is far more circumscribed than that of men. Whether they are seeking influence as community activists, lobbyists, political party or governmental officials, their capacity to combine family, work, and political roles is greatly enhanced by the ease of working in their own communities or in the state capital.

A second obvious resource for women lies in the fact that women are far better represented in state and local government than at the national level. This pattern is explained by many factors not the least of which is, again, the dual burden. Although many younger women today are assuming political roles, it nevertheless remains true that most women enter politics after their childbearing and childrearing years are over (Diamond, 1977). Because for a large proportion of national officials the recruitment process involves climbing the ladder from local and state politics to national positions and because for women this climb starts at a later age, the likelihood of significantly expanding the ranks of women politicians at the state and local level remains far greater than at the national level (Lee, 1976).

Merely increasing the number of women in the political elite does not, of course, guarantee that women's public policy concerns will receive greater or more favorable attention. Representation by women of women's interests is not a given, nor can feminist activists be assured that female policy makers interested in women as a constituency will align themselves with the feminist cause.

Three factors do suggest, however, that increasing female representation has benefits for women. First while not *all* newly emerging political women are oriented toward women's rights, surveys suggest that the majority are (Mezey, 1978b). Second, except in cases of ardent anti-feminists, many women officials, if not initially women's rights supporters, reveal a tendency to be educable and to become more closely identified with women's issues.[2] Finally, regardless of her political predispositions, any woman in the political elite serves not only as a role model for other women, but also often as a pathbreaker for public acceptance of women in new political roles (MacManus, 1981).

The increase in the number of women officeholders in state and local government has important ramifications. First, it often puts women officeholders in the role of selecting personnel for bureaucratic and/or leadership positions, thereby enabling them to open the doors for other women. For example, a county board of supervisors in California with a female majority selected the county's first female county executive; and the board of trustees of the state university system, on which several strongly feminist women serve, selected the system's first woman chancellor as well as two female university presidents.

Beyond recruiting women for new positions, established women officials also have the potential to serve as mentors to newcomers to politics. Political mentors have been critical in the making of the careers of many politicians, male and female. The dearth of women at the top has meant, however, that junior women have had little choice but to turn to men for sponsorship and guidance. While there is nothing inherently wrong with male mentors prompting female proteges, the relationship is nevertheless restricted by social norms, as well as subjected to outside scrutiny that make the interactions between mentor and protege less fully developed (Boneparth and Dowdall, 1979). While a male mentor and his female protege may not usually share a weekend of golf, women mentors and women proteges are free to develop their relationships both in and outside the office.

Access for women to state and local government through proximity and through increasing female representation is aided by certain systematic variables. Because of the deeply ingrained sexism of the American political parties, female candidates and women's groups at any level have often needed or chosen to work outside the party structures (Ridgeway, 1983; Tolchin and Tolchin, 1976). Since many local governments are nonpartisan and since in many states the party systems are notoriously weak, women often have the opportunity to break into political activity without seeking party support.

Clearly, organizational support of some kind is necessary to mount political campaigns or influence public policy. In the absence of strong parties, interest groups play a major role; and the amount of support women can generate within interest groups varies considerably with the goals and structure of the group. On the one hand, the major economic interest groups—business, labor, and professional associations—have been no more enthusiastic, in fact often less so, about bringing women into leadership positions and rallying behind women's issues than the political parties. On the other hand, noneconomic groups—social welfare, consumer, antinuclear, environmental, political reform, civil rights, and community action organizations—have been more open to promoting women to leadership positions and, occasionally, to endorsing women's issues.

While women have channeled some energy into working through existing interest groups, their primary thrust in state and local government has been to create their own organizations, ranging across the political spectrum from electoral and issue groups, such as the National Organization for Women and the National Women's Political Caucus with their vast numbers of state and local chapters, to community groups involved in providing services to women in the fields of health and welfare, child care, education, counseling and employment, to independent women's rights organizations involved in research, lobbying and litigation. As varied as the goals of these groups are their organizational forms, which include traditionally structured, hierarchical organizations, antihierarchical collectives, and loosely structured networks. While the traditionally structured groups have an easier time gaining access to political decision makers because of the familiarity and acceptability of their work styles, the autonomous, less traditionally structured groups have the advantage of innovation, developing work styles especially suited to their goals such as collective decisionmaking and engaging in protest activities without risking hard-earned political legitimacy. Thus, the weakness of the political parties and the openness of the political system at the state and local levels to newly established interest groups make state and local government accessible to women not only as officeholders but also as lobbyists.

The success or failure of women's lobbying efforts in state and local politics depends on many different factors, including the resources of the particular group, the number of officeholders willing to champion women's issues, and the institutional backing the groups can muster. In this regard, one very important potential resource for women in state and local government has been commissions on the status of women. While national commissions have never done much more than study and make recommendations on women's issues, these quasi-governmental bodies at the state and local levels have played a variety of educational, administrative and advocacy roles (Stewart, 1980d). Needless to say, the more political the commissions have become, the more they have encountered political opposition, especially from the Right, which has used a variety of tactics to put them out of existence (Rosenberg, 1982). Nevertheless where state and local commissions continue to function they serve as an important link between grassroots feminists, women's organizations, and the elected and bureaucratic elites.

A last source of access women have in dealing with state and local government derives from the nature of the issues within their purview. Many of these issues—social welfare, health, education—fall into the category of women's issues because they are "people" issues, involving traditionally female values of caring, nurturance, and charity. In these areas, women officeholders and activists have often been acknowledged as having special expertise because of their records of professional involvement and community service in these fields or because of the stereotypical association of women with the home, family, children, the sick, aged, and needy.

Stereotyping these issues as women's issues does not necessarily always serve women's interests. Female elected officials are often channeled into these areas of specialization when, in fact, their political careers would be better served by assignments in traditionally male spheres of influence such as budgeting and taxation, economic development, or criminal justice. Moreover, while the acceptance of women's expertise on social issues opens up access to some political roles such as legislator or lobbyist, it often continues to restrict women to these roles in the minds of voters and male officeholders, barring them from high-level executive and judicial positions. The initial access women gain, however, from their association with social issues can, and often has been used, as a springboard to other positions in the power structure.

A final resource for women seeking to influence public policy lies in the various mechanisms of political accountability found in many state and local governmental systems. The techniques of direct democracy—the initiative, referendum, and recall—introduced by the Progressives in the early twentieth century have enjoyed a tremendous revival in the last decade with the spread of single issue politics, the application of computer technology for fundraising, and the targeting of voters for special interest campaigns (Quinn, 1983: 94-95; Fitzgerald, 1983: 96-101).

Women have not made adequate use of the techniques of direct democracy—the initiative, referendum, and recall—introduced by the necessary to mount such campaigns are enormous and in part because many of the successful measures have been conservative proposals to lower taxes or to prevent government intervention in such fields as the environment or gun control (Fitzgerald, 1983: 96-101). Moreover, the accelerated use of recall elections to express dissatisfaction with elected officials often appears to have a somewhat antifeminist thrust, as many of these recall attempts, fortunately unsuccessful, have been directed at highly placed women officeholders.[3]

Nevertheless, women have the potential to use these measures in behalf of their causes, whether the issue is the passage of a state ERA, the restoration of public funding for abortion, or the removal of an antifeminist elected official. A resource women do have in many states and localities is a large number of grassroots activists available to circulate petitions to qualify measures for the ballot and to get out the vote. The recent success of the nuclear freeze initiative makes clear that grassroots activists with limited funding can be as effective as wealthy special interests in going to the voters. Morever, often the mere threat of an initiative campaign can move a state legislature or city council to take action on an issue that would otherwise lie dormant.

Accountability in state and local government is also often achieved through requirements that fiscal policies be taken to the voters through special bond issues or taxing measures. This, too, is an area where women might channel their energies in order to raise funds for special needs such as low-income housing for single parents, child care centers, or battered women's shelters. Again, the conservative tide among voters, swept along by taxpayers' revolts, makes such a strategy somewhat precarious at present; however, state and local governments have shown a great reluctance in their normal budgeting processes to making women's needs a priority and the mere threat of a campaign by women to compel funding through the electoral process may result in the allocation of additional resources to women's concerns.

What is being suggested here is basically that women build electoral coalitions not only around candidates, but also around issues. The recent discovery that a gender gap exists in political opinion at the national level opens the door to using women's voting power on behalf of candidates and issues in state and local government as well.[4] While the gender gap may have originated in fears of interventionist foreign and military policy, the domestic consequences of such policies in terms of cutting funding for social services and programs are becoming significant issues as well for women voters. It seems reasonable to expect that using the ballot box to pit social needs at the state and local level against the subsidies awarded to special interests may be as effective a way to go as lobbying elected officials.

CONSTRAINTS:
COMPETITION FOR RESOURCES

Although state and local governments present significant opportunities for women seeking to affect public policy, there are also some rather serious constraints on women working in these arenas. First, although access to political positions may be facilitated in many areas by weak political parties, women's electoral groups do not operate in a vacuum. Independent campaign organizations abound which have extensive resources for influencing the electoral and appointment processes. Women's groups, constituting only one of these many interests on the state and local political scene, are generally less well-heeled and less well-connected than their opponents. Winning is not simply a matter of being there.

Lobbying on issues also requires resources—money, expertise, organization, contacts—which well-established groups have in much greater supply than newer groups. Added to this is the obvious constraint that women's groups are generally change-oriented and lobbying for public change is considerably more difficult than lobbying to maintain the status quo.

The competition for political resources in order to elect supportive public officials is a critical first step for women in areas where traditional elites continue to dominate the policymaking process. This lesson was learned the hard way in the ERA ratification struggle when handfuls of reactionary state legislators buried the amendment in committees or when moderate legislators made verbal commitments of support only to renege on their commitments in the voting. While national women's groups and women from more progressive areas gave considerable energy and financial support to political campaigns in these areas,[5] outside resources were not sufficient to challenge the traditional power structure. Until women are better organized politically in conservative regions (which will probably require ongoing support from national organizations in the initial stages), the effort to affect public policy will continue to suffer from a dearth of political leaders willing to address women's issues.

Even with supportive leaders in place, the competition for resources remains the critical issue. Given the nature of state and local issues, the kinds of policy benefits women seek typically involve generating support for social programs. While at the national level, many of women's policy successes have involved the passage of antidiscrimination measures (which are less costly to implement than social programs), at the state and local level, the emphasis is very much on finding funds for transfer payments and social services.

It is this very problem—declining public resources and relatively fixed budget priorities—that puts the greatest constraint on women seeking support for state and local programs. Without debating the wisdom of the approach, the federal government maintains levels of spending through techniques such as deficit financing and new forms of taxation, as well as cuts in social programs. These techniques are often unavailable to state and local governments, either because of constitutional prohibitions of deficit financing or requirements of voter approval for new taxing measures. Thus, it is easier for women's groups to argue for a reallocation of resources at the federal level when such a large proportion of the budget goes to military expenditures, than at the state and local levels where the largest proportion of the budget is already going toward health, education, and social welfare.

The strain on state and local government budgets in recent years, given a stagnant economy in some regions and taxpayers revolts in others, has nullified progress women's groups have made on many issues. To illustrate, child-care centers and centers for displaced homemakers which originated at the state and local levels and expanded as a result of federal funding have often collapsed when federal funding was withdrawn and state and local governments were unable to continue to foot the bill (Sidel, 1982: 61). Likewise, while several states and local governments have accepted the principle of equal pay for work of comparable value in compensating government employees, most have been unable to find the funds to remedy acknowledged inequities in salary scales (Cook, 1983: 502-504).

What is needed is a creative and innovative approach to funding for social programs. Numerous states, for example, use part of the marriage license fee to support shelters for battered women. Expanding on such an approach, there is no reason, for example, why taxes on the sale of pornography should not be levied to support programs seeking to end violence against women. Or, just as developers are often required by controlled-growth advocates to conserve energy, protect the environment, and provide alternative transportation systems, so might developers be required, through planning, zoning, and building permit procedures to provide child care or housing for single parents.

Equally important is the sustained effort by women to maintain a share of dwindling federal and state aid for women's programs. Influencing the politics of the budgetary process requires much more than voting on the budget. It is not enough that women are better represented numerically in state and local government; they must be located on the budget and revenue committees, in the departments of finance and in the administrative agencies where guidelines for allocating funds from federal block grants or state aid packages are developed. Since, however, the growth in the numbers of women in state and local government is fairly recent, women are constrained by the lack of seniority necessary to secure the more powerful behind-the-scenes committee assignments and bureaucratic positions. Thus, the real competition for resources often occurs in settings where women's voices are yet to be heard.

STRATEGIES FOR THE EIGHTIES:
LOBBYING AND INSTITUTIONALIZING
WOMEN'S CONCERNS

While in some states and localities women have greatly increased their access to government either through the electoral, appointment or lobbying processes, there is clearly room for activist women to enlarge on their accomplishments of the last decade. The expansion of the number of women officeholders should be aided in the 1980s by an increase in the available pool of candidates. The legal profession has always provided a major recruiting ground for legislators; with the tremendous increase in the number of women lawyers,[6] especially in public sector positions, the movement of women from law to politics should be greatly enhanced. Another route to officeholding in recent years has been from the ranks of political staffers who include many women in their midst and who, having served apprenticeships working for officeholders, legislative committees, and administrative agencies, have the political and substantive expertise to move into elected office. The crucial link between being prepared and actually running is motivation. Since women are less likely than men to be self-motivated to enter electoral contests, an important role for women's organizations and women officeholders alike is to recruit viable candidates (Kirkpatrick, 1974).

Similarly, women must organize around the appointment process to expand the number of women serving on key legislative committees, in the judiciary, and on boards and commissions. The tremendous boost given women and minorities by ex-Governor Jerry Brown in California (Salzman, 1983: 19-20) is not likely to be replicated in most areas without a concerted effort by women's groups. In many areas, women's groups have established talent banks of women eligible to serve in appointive office but such activity must be carried further to include monitoring vacancies and coalescing around specific candidates for these vacancies.

Women have made great strides in lobbying through the creation of women's interest groups with lobbying arms in state capitals; however, additional pressure on the policymaking process is necessary. While going alone has the advantage of allowing women's groups to develop their own issues and set their own priorities, women's groups acting alone often lack the resources to have a major impact.

Two strategies lend themselves to increasing women's influence in the lobbying process. First, as more and more women move into the professions, business, and the labor force, they gain the potential to lobby for women's concerns by infiltrating their own working organizations. While women will undoubtedly encounter overt and covert sexism in these organizations which makes them far less congenial settings for political work, the added clout and financial backing of organizations such as the state and local Bar Association, Medical Association, Chamber of Commerce, or AFL-CIO will ultimately outweigh the disadvantages of working in a traditionally male environment. And, increasing numbers of female members may ultimately change the organizational environment.

A related strategy involved forming coalitions of women's groups with other special interest groups (Rosen, 1982: 208). Issue coalitions do have certain inherent disadvantages—namely, the need to educate other groups on women's issues, as well as the need to bargain and find compromise positions among coalition partners. The advantage of coalitions, however, is that the resources of numerous groups become available for the cause, without having to commit enormous time and energy to infiltrating these groups. The coalition strategy, when attempted on the federal scene, has often been quite effective (Gelb and Palley, 1982: 170). However, other than in several ERA battles, coalitions of women's groups with other change-oriented groups have been insufficiently developed in state and local government.

Women's lobbies can become even more effective if women's concerns are institutionalized in state and local government. Using as a model the Congressional Caucus for Women's Issues, which has over 100 male and female members, women can expand their influence within state legislatures by forming caucuses committed to working on women's issues.[7] In light of the fact that women's issues often suffer from being labeled as such, with the result that the direct and indirect benefits of policy change for men and children are less apparent, creative labeling of such caucuses to suggest a more inclusive context, around the themes of equal rights or family issues for example, might make these caucuses more attractive to a large number of officeholders.

Institutionalization of women's concerns can also occur in the executive branch through the creation of gubernatorial and mayoral advisors on women's affairs. Ideally, such advisors would not substitute for autonomous commissions on the status of women. Commissions, in their educational role, have been particularly effective raising issues (Cook, 1983: 499-500) but quite vulnerable to political backlash when they have taken on advocacy roles, and relatively ineffective, because of lack of access and expertise, in administrative watchdog roles (Rosenberg, 1982: 42-45). The benefit of institutionalizing women's concerns within the executive is that experts on the inside can undertake the regular monitoring of the impact of policy in *all* areas on women and the sharing of this information with outsiders.

In essence, what is being argued here is that women must use their increasing access to state and local government to pursue a combined insider-outsider strategy in influencing public policy. Too often women have been successful as outside pressure groups while failing to develop a growing presence within government, as was seen in the 1970s when legislative victories in Congress were unaccompanied by successes in the electoral arena and when gains in federal appointments during the Carter years were erased by the Reagan administration. The opposite pattern has also been evident: women achieving considerable success in state and local elections but failing to maintain pressure on newly elected women officials, as well as on male politicians who have received the endorsements of women's groups, to deliver on women's issues. While the constraints on influencing public policy are many, women do have growing resources that can be used to make the recent revival of federalism an opportunity for change, but only if the voices of women are strengthened both outside and within state and local government.

NOTES

1. Efforts to elect women to national or statewide office appear to be stymied with twenty-two women serving in the U.S. House of Representatives, two women in the U.S. Senate, and no women governors, as compared to female state legislators who hold thirteen percent of the seats (see Flammang, forthcoming).

2. While no longitudinal studies are available for female state and local officeholders, observation of California elected women, particularly those serving on city councils and boards of supervisors with more than token female representation, suggests that women who are not identified with women's issues when elected, often become women's rights advocates once in office.

3. In California, for example, recalls have been threatened or attempted against numerous women officeholders including the chief justice of the state supreme court, the mayor of San Francisco, and numerous city and county officials. While these recall attempts have not been initiated over feminist issues, it appears that opponents of these officials have been encouraged by the seeming vulnerability of female officeholders.

4. In fact, Kathleen Frankovic, Director of Surveys for CBS News, has concluded that the women's vote decided the outcome of the most recent gubernatorial elections of New York, Texas, and Connecticut (Congressional Caucus for Women's Issues, *Update*, April 29, 1983: 5).

5. The National Organization for Women, for example, raised $15 million for the ERA drive in six targeted states.

6. It is estimated that by 1990 one-fourth of the legal profession will be female.

7. A few states have established women's legislative caucuses and supporting research organizations such as the California Elected Women for Education and Research; however, these efforts could be expanded significantly to other states.

REFERENCES

ABRAHAM, HENRY J. (1980) The Judicial Process. New York: Oxford University Press.

ACKELSBERG, MARTHA A. (1983) "Sisters or comrades? The politics of friends and families," pp. 339-356 in Irene Diamond (ed.) Families, Politics, and Public Policies. New York: Longman.

—— (forthcoming) " 'Separate and Equal'? Mujeres libres and anarchist strategy for women's emancipation." Feminist Studies.

—— and MYRNA M. BREITBART (1982) "Pathways to social change: women, social space, and the development of political consciousness in urban struggles." Presented at the first annual meeting of the Anarchos Institute, Montreal, June 5.

ADAMS, WILLIAM C. (1975) "Candidate characteristics, office of election and voter response." Experimental Study of Politics (July): 76-91.

All States Tax Guide (1982) Englewood Cliffs, NJ: Prentice-Hall.

ALMOND, GABRIEL L. and SIDNEY VERBA (1965) The Civic Culture: Political Attitudes and Democracy in Five Nations. Boston, MA: Little, Brown.

AMUNDSEN, KIRSTEN (1971) The Silenced Majority. Englewood Cliffs, NJ: Prentice-Hall.

—— (1977) A New Look at the Silenced Majority: Women and American Democracy, Englewood Cliffs, NJ: Prentice-Hall.

ANDERSON, MARTIN (1978) Welfare: The Political Economy of Welfare Reform in the United States, Stanford, CA: Hoover Institution Press.

ARISTOPHANES (1967) The Congresswomen (Ecclesiazusae) (Douglass Parker, trans.) Ann Arbor: University of Michigan Press.

ARNOLD, KENNETH J. [ed.] (1967 and 1973) California Courts and Judges Handbook, first and second editions. San Francisco: California Law Company.

AUERBACH, STEVANNE (1979) Confronting the Child Care Crisis. Boston: Beacon.

BAER, DENISE (1978) "Theoretical issues in political socialization: The idenfication of a crucial stage using gender role as a paradigm case." Presented at the annual meeting of the Southern Political Science Association, Atlanta.

BANE, MARY JO, LAURA LEIN, LYDIA O'DONNELL, ANN STUEVE, and BARBARA WELLES (1978) "Child care in the United States." Wellesley, MA: Wellesly College Center for Research on Women.

BANFIELD, EDWARD C. (1965) Big City Politics. New York: Random House.

—— and JAMES Q. WILSON (1966) City Politics. New York: Vintage.

BARBER, JAMES D. (1965) The Lawmakers. New Haven, CT: Yale University Press.

BARD, MORTON (1969) "Family intervention police teams as a community mental health resource." Journal of Criminal Law, Criminology and Policy Science (2): 247-250.

BARKER, LUCIUS J. and JESSE J. McCORRY, Jr. (1976) Black Americans and the Political System. Cambridge, MA: Winthrop.

BARRETT, NANCY S. and RICHARD D. MORGENSTERN (1974) "Why do Blacks and women have high unemployment rates?" Journal of Human Resources (Fall): 452-464.

BARTOL, KATHRYN and MAX S. WORTMAN, Jr. (1979) "Sex of leader and subordinate role stress." Sex Roles (5): 513-518.

BARTON, JUDY (1979) "Abortion clinics under siege." Progressive (March): 27-29.

BATES, THOMAS H. (1983) "Feminization of poverty." Statement at hearings of California Assembly Human Services Committee, San Francisco, April 8.

BAXTER, SANDRA and MARJORIE LANSING (1980) Women and Politics: The Invisible Majority. Ann Arbor: University of Michigan Press.

BELL, DURAN (1974) "Why participation rates of black and white wives differ." Journal of Human Resources (Fall): 465-479.

BENDER, THOMAS (1983) "The end of the city?" Democracy (Winter): 8-20.

BERKSON, LARRY (1980) "Judicial selection in the United States: A special report." Judicature (October): 176-193.

——— (1982) "Women on the bench: A brief History." Judicature (January): 286-293.

BERNSTEIN, RICHARD J. (1978) The Restructuring of Social and Political Theory. Philadelphia: University of Pennsylvania Press.

BERNSTEIN, ROBERT A. (1982) "Why are there so few women in the House?" Presented at the annual meeting of the Southern Political Science Association, Atlanta.

BERS, TRUDY H. (1978) "Local political elites: Men and women on boards of education." Western Political Quarterly (September): 381-391.

BIBBY, JOHN F., CORNELIUS P. COTTER, JAMES L. GIBSON and ROBERT J. HUCKSHORN (1983) "Parties in state politics," pp. 59-96 in Virginia Gray, Herbert Jacob, and Kenneth N. Vines (eds.), Politics in the American States. Boston: Little Brown.

BLAIR, DIANE KINCAID and ANN R. HENRY (1981) "The family factor in state legislative turnover." Legislative Studies Quarterly (1): 55-68.

BLAY, EVA ALTERMAN (1979) "The political participation of women in Brazil: Female mayors," Signs (1): 42-59.

BLUMENFELD, SAMUEL L. (1975) The Retreat from Motherhood. New Rochelle, NY: Arlington House.

BLYDENBURG, JOHN and ROBERTA SIGEL (1983) "Key factors in the 1982 election day voter polls." Presented at the annual meeting of the American Political Science Association, Chicago.

BOALS, KAY (1975) "Review essay: Political science." Signs (Autumn): 161-174.

BOLES, JANET K. (1979) The Politics of the Equal Rights Amendment. New York: Longman.

———(1980) "The politics of child care." Social Science Review (September): 344-362.

BONEPARTH, ELLEN [ed] (1982) Women, Power and Policy. New York: Pergamon.

——— and JEAN DOWDALL (1979) "Mentors in academia: The perceptions of proteges." Presented at the annual meeting of the American Sociological Association, August.

BOURQUE, SUSAN C. and JEAN GROSSHOLTZ (1974) "Politics as unnatural practice: Political science looks at female participation." Politics and Society (Winter): 225-266.

BOVERMAN, K., S. R. VOGEL, D. M. BRAVERMAN, F.E. CLARKSON, and P.S. ROSEN KRANTZ (1972) "Sex-role stereotypes: A current appraisal." Journal of Social Issues (2): 59-78.

BOYLAN, ANN MARIA and NADINE TAUB (1981) Adult Domestic Violence: Constitutional, Legislative and Equitable Issues, Washington, DC: Legal Services Research Institute.

BOYTE, HARRY C. (1980) The Backyard Revolution. Philadelphia: Temple University Press.

———(1982) "Ronald Reagan and America's neighborhoods: Undermining community initiative," pp. 109-124 in Alan Gartner, Colin Greer, and Frank Riessman (eds.), What Reagan is Doing to Us. New York: Harper and Row.

BRIGHTMAN, CAROL (1978) "The women of Williamsburg." Working Papers (January/February): 50-57.

BROWNMILLER, SUSAN (1975) Against Our Will: Men, Women and Rape. New York: Simon and Schuster.

BRUCK, CONNIE (1983) "The case no one will win: Hishon v. King and Spalding." American Lawyer (November): 101-106.

BULLOCK, CHARLES S. and PATRICIA FINDLEY HEYS (1972) "Recruitment of women for Congress." Western Political Quarterly (September): 416-423.

BURNHAM, WALTER DEAN (1965) "The changing shape of the American political universe." American Political Science Review (March): 7-28.

——— (1969) "The end of American political parties." Transaction (December): 12-22.

BURRIS, VAL and AMY WHARTON (1982) "Sex segregation in the U.S. labor force." Review of Radical Political Economics (Fall): 43-56.

California Commission on Crime Control and Violence Prevention (1981, 1982) An Ounce of Prevention: Toward an Understanding of the Causes of Violence, Preliminary Report to the People of California and Final Report to the People of California. Sacramento: State of California.

CAMPBELL, ANGUS, PHILIP E. CONVERSE, WARREN E. MILLER, and DONALD E. STOKES (1960) The American Voter. New York: John Wiley.

CAMPBELL, ANGUS, GERALD GURIN, and WARREN E. MILLER (1954) The Voter Decides. Evanston, IL: Rolo Peterson.

CARBON, SUSAN, PAULINE HOULDEN, and LARRY BERKSON (1982) "Women on the state bench: Their characteristics and attitudes about judicial selection." Judicature (January): 294-305.

CARROLL, MAURICE (1983) "Head of panel on judges regrets an 'imbalance'." New York Times, February 8.

CARROLL, SUSAN (1977) "Women candidates and state legislative elections, 1976: Limitations in the political opportunity structure and their effects on electoral participation and success." Presented at the annual meeting of the American Political Science Association, Washington, DC.

——— (1979) "Women candidates and support for women's issues: Closet Feminists." Presented at the annual meeting of the Midwest Political Science Association, Chicago, IL.

CARVER, JOAN (1979) "The ERA in Florida." Presented at the annual meeting of the Southern Political Science Association, Gatlinburg, TN.

CAYER, N. JOSEPH and LEE SIGELMAN (1980) "Minorities and women in state and local government 1973-75." Public Administration Review (5): 443-450.

Center for the American Woman and Politics [CAWP] (1976) Women in Public Office: A Biographical Directory and Statistical Analysis. New York: R. R. Bowker.
—— (1978) Women in Public Office: A Bibliographical Directory and Statistical Analysis. Metuchen, NJ: Scarecrow Press.
—— (1981) "Women in elective office 1975-1980." Fact Sheet, CAWP. New Brunswick, NJ: Rutgers University.
CHABAUD, DANIELLE and DOMINIQUE FONGEYROLLAS (1978) "Travail domestique et espace-temps des femmes." International Journal of Urban and Regional Research (October): 421-431.
CHAMBERLIN, HOPE (1974) A Minority of Members: Women in the U.S. Congress. New York: New American Library.
CHESLER, PHYLLIS (1979) With Child: A Diary of Motherhood: An Intimate Account of Pregnancy, Childbirth and Mothering. New York: Thomas Y. Crowell.
Children's Defense Fund (1983) Children's Defense Budget. Washington, DC: Children's Defense Fund.
CHODOROW, NANCY (1978) The Reproduction of Mothering: Psychoanalysis and the Sociology of Gender. Berkeley: University of California Press.
CLARK, JANET (1979) "Party leaders and women's entry into the political elites." Presented at the annual meeting of the Southwestern Political Science Association, Forth Worth, TX.
—— and R. DARCY (1983) "Women candidates and political competition in the states." Presented at the annual meeting of the Western Social Science Association, Albuquerque, NM.
CLARK, PETER B. and JAMES Q. WILSON (1961) "Incentive systems: A theory of organizations." Administrative Science Quarterly (September): 129-166.
CLARKE, HAROLD D. and ALLAN KORNBERG (1979) "Moving up the political escalator: Women party officials in the United States and Canada." Journal of Politics (2): 442-477.
COCKBURN, CYNTHIA (1977a) The Local State. London: Pluto Press.
—— (1977b) "When women get involved in community action," pp. 61-70 in Marjorie Mayo (ed.), Women in the Community. London: Routledge and Kegan Paul.
COLEMAN, MARY and LESLIE BURL McLEMORE (1982) "Black independent politics in Mississippi: Constants and challenges," pp. 131-156 in Michael B. Preston, Lenneal J. Henderson, Jr., and Paul Puryear (eds.), The New Black Politics: The Search for Political Power, New York: Longman.
COLES, FRANCES SCOTT (1974) "Women in litigation practice: Success and the female lawyer," Dissertation, University of California, Berkeley.
CONTRAS, J. and J. FAGNANI (1978) "Femmes et transports en milieu urban." International Journal of Urban and Regional Research (October): 432-439.
COOK, ALICE H. (1983) "Comparable worth: Recent developments in selected states." Labor Law Journal (August): 494-504.
COOK, BEVERLY BLAIR (1980a) "Political culture and selection of women judges in trial courts," pp. 42-60 in Debra W. Stewart (ed.), Women in Local Politics. Metuchen, NJ: Scarecrow Press.
—— (1980b) "Women judges and public policy in sex integration," pp. 130-148 in Debra W. Stewart (ed.), Women in Local Politics. Metuchen, NJ: Scarecrow Press.
—— (1981a) "The first woman candidate for the Supreme Court—Florence E. Allen." Supreme Court Historical Society Yearbook: 19-35.

—— (1981b) "Will women judges make a difference in women's legal rights?" pp. 216-239 in Margherita Rendel (ed.), Women, Power and Political Systems. London: Croon Helm.

—— (1983a) "Lecturing on woman's place: 'Mrs. Jellyby' in Wisconsin, 1854-1874." Signs (Winter): 361-376.

—— (1983b) "The path to the bench: Ambitions and attitudes of women in the law." Trial (August): 48-55.

COOK, FIONA HALE (1939) Who's Who Among Women Lawyers. Boston: privately published.

COSTAIN, ANNE N. (1982) "Representing women: the transition from social movement to interest group," pp. 19-37 in Ellen Boneparth (ed.) Women, Power, and Policy. New York: Pergamon Press.

COSTANTINI, EDMOND and KENNETH H. CRAIK (1972) "Women as politicians: The social background, personality, and political careers of female party leaders." Journal of Social Issues (2): 217-236.

COSTANTINI, EDMOND and JOEL KING (1984) "The motives of political party activists: A factor-analytic exploration of the nexus between operational indicators and conceptual framework," Political Behavior, (forthcoming).

COTT, NANCY (1977) The Bonds of Womanhood. New Haven, CT: Yale University Press.

COTTER, CORNELIUS P., JAMES L. GIBSON, JOHN F. BIBBY, and ROBERT J. HUCKSHORN. (1984) Political Party Organization and American Politics. New York: Praeger.

COX, GARY W. (1983) "Electoral Choice in Double-Member Districts." Working Papers on Institutional Design and Public Policy, Department of Government. Austin, TX: University of Texas at Austin.

CULVER, JOHN H. (1981) "Governors and judicial appointments in California." State Government (Spring): 130-134.

CUMMINGS, BERNICE and VICTORIA SCHUCK [eds.] (1979) Women Organizing: An Anthology. Metuchen, NJ: Scarecrow Press.

CURREY, VIRGINIA (1977) "Campaign theory and practice—the gender variable," pp. 150-171 in Marianne Githens and Jewel Prestage (eds.), A Portrait of Marginality. New York: David McKay.

CURRIE, ELLIOTT, ROBERT DUNN, and DAVID FOGARTY (1980) "The new immiseration: Stagflation, inequality, and the working class." Socialistic Review (November-December): 7-31.

DANIELSON, MICHAEL N. (1976) The Politics of Exclusion. New York: Columbia University Press.

DARCY, ROBERT and SARAH SLAVIN SCHRAMM (1977) "When women run against men." Public Opinion Quarterly (Spring): 1-12.

DAVIDSON, TERRY (1978) Conjugal Crime. New York: Hawthorne Books.

DEAUX, KAY (1979) "Self-evaluations of male and female managers." Sex Roles (5): 571-580.

DEBER, RAISA (1982) "'The fault dear brutes': Women as candidates in Pennsylvania." Journal of Politics (May): 463-479.

DERRY, LAURA MILLER (1949) Digest of Women Lawyers and Judges. Louisville, KY: privately published.

DIAMOND, IRENE (1976) "Why aren't they there? Women in American state legislatures." Presented at the annual meeting of the American Political Science Association, Chicago.

——— (1977) Sex Roles in the State House. New Haven, CT: Yale University Press.
———(1982) "Women and housing: The limitations of liberal reform." pp. 109-117 in Ellen Boneparth (ed.), Women, Power, and Policy. New York: Pergamon Press.
——— [ed.] (1983) Families, Politics, and Public Policy: A Feminist Dialogue on Women and the State. New York: Longman.
——— and NANCY HARTSOCK (1981) "Beyond interests in politics: A comment on Virginia Sapiro's 'When are Interests Interesting'? The Problem of Political Representation of Women." American Political Science Review (September): 717-721.
DINNERSTEIN, DOROTHY (1977) The Mermaid and the Minotaur: Sexual Arrangements and the Human Malaise. New York: Harper Colophon.
DOBASH, R. EMERSON and RUSSELL DOBASH (1979) Violence Against Wives, A Case Against the Patriarchy. New York: Free Press.
DOWNS, ANTHONY (1973) Opening Up the Suburbs. New Haven, CT: Yale University Press.
DUBECK, PAULA J. (1976) "Women and access to political office: A comparison of female and male state legislators." Sociological Quarterly (Winter): 42-52.
DUBOIS, PHILIP L. (1983) "Judicial elections in California: A multivariate application of recent events." Presented at the annual meeting of the Law and Society Association, Denver, June 2-5.
DUVERGER, MAURICE (1955) The Political Role of Women. Paris: UNESCO.
DYE, THOMAS (1969, 1981) Politics in States and Communities, First and fourth editions. Englewood Cliffs, NJ: Prentice-Hall.
EASTON, DAVID and JACK DENNIS (1969) Children in the Political System. New York: McGraw-Hill.
EHRENRICH, BARBARA and FRANCES FOX PIVEN (1983) "The Left's best hope." Mother Jones, (September/October): 26-29.
EISENSTEIN, ZILLAH R. (1981) The Radical Future of Liberal Feminism. New York: Longman.
EKSTRAND, LAURIE E. and WILLIAM A. ECKERT (1981) "The impact of candidate's sex on voter choice." Western Political Quarterly (March): 78-87.
ELAZAR, DANIEL J. (1966) American Federalism: A View from the States. New York: Crowell.
ELDERSVELD, SAMUEL (1964) Political Parties. Chicago, IL: Rand McNally.
ELSHTAIN, JEAN BETHKE (1981) Public Man, Private Woman. Princeton, NJ: Princeton University Press.
EPSTEIN, CYNTHIA F. (1981) Women in Law. New York: Basic Books.
ERIE, STEVEN (1983a) "The organization of Irish-Americans into urban political institutions, 1840-1900." Presented at the annual meeting of the American Political Science Association, Chicago.
——— (1983b) "Women, Reagan and the new class war." Presented at the annual meeting of the American Political Science Association, Chicago.
——— and MARTIN REIN (1982) "Welfare: The new poor laws," pp. 71-86 in Alan Gartner, Colin Greer, and Frank Riessman (eds.), What Reagan Is Doing To Us. New York: Harper and Row.
———and BARBARA WIGET (1983) "Reagan revolution: Thermidor for the social welfare economy," pp. 94-119 in Irene Diamond (ed.), Families, Politics and Public Policies. New York: Longman.
ERIKSON, ROBERT (1971) "The advantage of incumbency." Polity (Spring): 395-405.
——— NORMAN LUTTBEG, and KENT TEDIN (1980) American Public Opinion: Origins, Contents, and Impact. New York: John Wiley.

ETTORE, E. M. (1978) "Women, urban social movements and the Lesbian Ghetto." International Journal of Urban and Regional Research (October): 499-520.

EVANS, SARA and HARRY BOYTE (1982) "Schools for action: Radical uses for social space." Democracy (Fall): 55-65.

FARAH, BARBARA G. (1976) "Climbing the political ladder: The aspirations and expectations of partisan elites," pp. 238-250 in Dorothy G. McGuigan (ed.), New Research on Women and Sex Roles, Ann Arbor, MI: Center for the Continuing Education of Women, University of Michigan.

FERREE, MYRA MARX (1974) "A woman for president? Changing respsonses 1958-1972." Public Opinion Quarterly (Fall): 390-399.

FESSLER, PAMELA (1982) "Women, minorities gain seats in Congress." Congressional Quarterly Weekly Report (November 6): 2805.

FITZGERALD, MAUREEN S. (1983) "Computer democracy," pp. 96-101 in Thomas R. Hoeber and Charles M. Price (eds.), California Government and Politics Annual 83/84, Sacramento, CA: California Journal Press.

FLAMMANG, JANET (1983) "Feminist theory: The question of power." Current Perspectives in Social Theory (Vol. 4), Greenwich, CT: JAI Press.

—— (forthcoming) "Female officials in the feminist capital: The case of Santa Clara county." Western Political Quarterly.

FLEMING, JENNIFER BAKER (1979) Stopping Wife Abuse: A Guide to the Emotional, Psychological, and Legal Implications for the Abused Woman and Those Helping Her. Garden City, NY: Anchor Books.

FLEXNER, ELEANOR (1959) Century of Struggle. Cambridge, MA: Harvard University Press.

FOWLKES, DIANE L. (1983) "Developing a theory of countersocialization: gender, race and politics in the lives of women activists." Micropolitics (Summer).

—— JERRY PERKINS and SUE TOLLESON RINEHART (1979) "Gender roles and party roles." American Political Science Review (September): 772-780.

FRAIBERG, SELMA (1977) Every Child's Birthright: In Defense of Mothering. New York: Basic Books.

FRANKOVIC, KATHLEEN (1982) "Sex and politics—New alignments, old issues." PS (Summer): 439-448.

FREEDMAN, ESTELLE B. (1980) "Mary Margaret Bartelme," pp. 60-61 in Barbara Sicherman and Carol Hurd Green (eds.), Notable American Women: The Modern Period. Cambridge, MA: Belknap Press.

FREEMAN, JO (1975) The Politics of Women's Liberation. New York: David McKay.

—— (1980) "Women and urban policy." Signs (Supplement, Spring): S4-S22.

—— (1982) "Women and public policy: An overview," pp. 47-67 in Ellen Boneparth (ed.), Women, Power and Policy. New York: Pergamon Press.

FRIEDAN, BETTY (1981) The Second Stage. New York: Summit Books.

GAMARNIKOW, EVA (1978) "Introduction." The Women and the City Issue, International Journal of Urban and Regional Research (October): 390-403.

GANS, HERBERT (1962) The Urban Villagers. New York: Free Press.

GEHLEN, FRIEDA L. (1969) "Women in Congress." Trans-Action (October): 36-40.

—— (1977a) "Women members of Congress: A distinctive role," pp. 304-319 in Marianne Githens and Jewel L. Prestage (eds.), A Portrait of Marginality. New York: David McKay.

—— (1977b) "Legislative role performance of female legislators." Sex Roles (1) 1-18.

GELB, JOYCE and MARIAN L. PALLEY (1977) "Women and interest group politics: A case study of the equal credit opportunity act." American Politics Quarterly (July): 331-352.

—— (1982) Women and Public Policies. Princeton, NJ: Princeton University Press.

GILKES, CHERYL TOWNSEND (1980) "'Holding back the ocean with a broom': Black women and community work," pp. 217-231 in La Frances Rogers-Rose (ed.), The Black Woman, Beverly Hills: Sage.

GILL, JOHN EDWARD (1981) Stolen Children: Why and How Parents Kidnap their Kids. New York: Seaview Books.

GILLIGAN, CAROL (1982) In a Different Voice. Cambridge, MA: Harvard University Press.

GITHENS, MARIANNE (1977) "Spectators, agitators or lawmakers: Women in state legislatures," pp. 196-209 in Marianne Githens and Jewel L. Prestage (eds.), A Portrait of Marginality. New York: David McKay.

—— (1983) "The elusive paradigm: Gender, politics and political behavior," in Ada W. Finifter (ed.), Political Science: The State of the Discipline. Washington, DC: American Political Science Association.

—— and JEWEL L. PRESTAGE [eds.] (1977) A Portrait of Marginality: The Political Behavior of the American Woman. New York: David McKay.

—— (1978) "Women state legislators: Styles and priorities." Policy Studies Journal (7): 264-270.

—— (1979) "Styles and priorities of marginality: Women state legislators," pp. 221-235 in Marian L. Palley and Michael Preston (eds.), Race, Sex and Policy Problems, Lexington, MA: Lexington Books.

—— (1980) "Education and marginality: Some observations on the behavior of women state legislators." (unpublished)

—— (1981) "Women state legislators: A reconsideration of characteristic values and attitudes." (unpublished)

—— (1982) "Who consults them? Women state legislators and pressure groups." (unpublished)

GITTELL, MARILYN (1982) "The 'new' federalism and old politics: Their impact on (urban) education," pp. 1-23 in Alan Gartner, Colin Greer, and Frank Riessman (eds.), What Reagan Is Doing to Us. New York: Harper and Row.

GLASER, BARNEY G. and ANSELM L. STRAUSS (1967) The Discovery of Grounded Theory: Strategies for Qualitative Research. New York: Aldine.

GOOT, MURRAY and ELIZABETH REID (1975) Women and Voting: Mindless Matrons or Sexist Scientists? London: Sage.

GORDON, LINDA (1975) "A socialist view of women's studies: A reply to the editorial, volume 1, number 1." Signs (Winter): 559-566.

GREEN, PHILIP (1981) The Pursuit of Inequality. New York: Pantheon.

GREENSTEIN, FRED (1965) Children and Politics. New Haven: Yale University Press.

GROSS, DONALD A. (1978) "Representative styles and legislative behavior." Western Political Quarterly (September): 359-371.

GRUBERG, MARTIN (1968) Women in American Politics: An Assessment and Sourcebook. Oshkosh, WI: Academia Press.

HARRIS, FRED R. and PAUL L. HAIN (1983) America's Legislative Process: Congress and the States. Glenview, IL: Scott, Foresman.

HARTMAN, Chester (1982) "Housing," pp. 141-161 in Alan Gartner, Colin Greer, and Frank Riessman (eds.), What Reagan Is Doing to Us. New York: Harper and Row.

HAYDEN, DOLORES (1978) "Melusina Fay Pierce and cooperative housekeeping." International Journal of Urban and Regional Research (October): 404-419.

—— (1980) "What would a non-sexist city be like?" Signs (Supplement, Spring): S170-187.

——(1981) The Grand Domestic Revolution. Cambridge: MIT Press.

HEDLUND, RONALD D., PATRICK K. FREEMAN, KEITH E. HAMM, and ROBERT M. STEIN (1979) "The electability of women candidates: The effects of sex-role stereotypes." Journal of Politics (May): 513-524.

HELLER, TRUDY (1982) Women and Men as Leaders. New York: Praeger.

HERSHEY, MARJORIE (1980) "Support for political woman: The effects of race, sex and sexual roles," pp. 179-197 in John C. Pierce and John L. Sullivan (eds.), The Electorate Reconsidered, Beverly Hill, CA: Sage.

HESS, ROBERT D. and JUDITH V. TORNEY (1967) The Development of Political Attitudes in Children. Chicago, IL: Aldine.

HILL, DAVID B. (1981) "Letter opinion on ERA: A test of the newspaper bias hypothesis," Public Opinion Quarterly (Fall): 384-392.

—— (1983) "Women state legislators and party voting on the ERA." Social Science Quarterly (June): 318-326.

HOFFMAN, LOIS WLADIS and F. IVAN NYE, with STEPHEN J. BAHR (1974) Working Mothers: An Evaluative Review of the Consequences for Wife, Husband and Child. San Francisco: Jossey Bass.

HOFSTADTER, RICHARD (1955) The Age of Reform. New York: Vintage.

HOFSTETTER, C. RICHARD (1971) "The amateur politician." Midwest Journal of Political Science (February): 34-50.

—— (1973) "Organizational activists," American Politics Quarterly (April): 244-276.

HULL, GLORIA T., PATRICIA BELL SCOTT, and BARBARA SMITH [eds.] (1982) All the Women Are White, All the Blacks Are Men, But Some of Us Are Brave. Old Westbury, NY: Feminist Press.

HUMMER, PATRICIA M. (1979) The Decade of Elusive Promise. Ann Arbor, MI: UMI Research Press.

HUNTER, FLOYD (1953) Community Power Structures. Chapel Hill, NC: University of North Carolina Press.

HYMAN, HERBERT (1959) Political Socialization: A Study in the Psychology of Political Behavior. New York: Free Press.

IGLITZIN, LYNNE (1974) "The making of the apolitical woman: Femininity and sex stereotyping in girls," pp. 25-36 in Jane Jaquette (ed.) Women in Politics. New York: John Wiley.

JACOBSON, GARY and SAMUEL KERNELL (1981) Strategy and Choice in Congressional Elections. New Haven, CT: Yale University Press.

JAQUETTE, JANE [ed.] (1974) Women in Politics. New York: John Wiley.

JENNINGS, M. KENT and BARBARA G. FARAH (1981) "Social roles and Political resources: An over-time study of men and women in party elites." American Journal of Political Science (August): 462-482.

JENNINGS, M. KENT and RICHARD G. NIEMI (1974) The Political Character of Adolescence. Princeton, NJ: Princeton University Press.

JENNINGS, M. KENT and NORMAN THOMAS (1968) "Men and women in party elites: Social roles and political resources." Midwest Journal of political science (November): 469-492.

JOHNSON, MARILYN and SUSAN CARROLL (1978) "Statistical report: Profile of women holding office: 1977," pp. 1A-68A in Women in Public Office: A Biographical Directory and Statistical Analysis. Metuchen, NJ: Scarecrow Press.

JOHNSON, MARILYN and KATHY STANWICK (1976) "Profile of women holding office." in Women in Public Office: A Biographical Directory and Statistical Analysis. New York: R.R. Bowker.

JOHNSON, ROBERTA ANN and EMILY STOPER (1977) "The weaker sex and the better half: The idea of women's moral superiority in the American feminist movement." Polity (Winter): 192-217.

JONES, CAROL ADAIRE, NANCY M. GORDON, and ISABEL V. SAWHILL (1976) Child Support Payments in the United States. Working paper #922-03. Washington, DC: Urban Institute.

JONES, WOODROW and ALBERT J. NELSON (1981) "Correlates of women's representation in lower state legislative chambers."Social Behavior and Personality (1): 9-15.

KAMERMAN, SHEILA B. (1980) Pareting in an Unresponsive Society: Managing Work and Family Life. New York: MacMillan.

KANTER, ROSABETH M. (1976) "Why bosses turn bitchy." Psychology Today (May 9): 56-89.

——— (1977a) Men and Women of the Corporation. New York: Basic Books.

——— (1977b) "Some effects of proportions on group life: Skewed sex ratios and response to token women." American Journal of Sociology (March): 965-990.

KAPLAN, TEMMA (1981) "Women and mass strikes." Presented to the summer workshop of the Smith College Project on Women and Social Change, Northampton, MA, June.

——— (1982) "Female consciousness and collective action: The case of Barcelona, 1910-1918." Signs (Spring): 545-566.

KARNIG, ALBERT and B. OLIVER WALTER (1976) "Election of women to city councils." Social Science Quarterly (March): 605-613.

KATZNELSON, IRA (1981) City Trenches. New York: Pantheon.

KAY, W.D. (1983) "Gender and policy disagreement: The case of nuclear power." Presented at the annual meeting of the Midwest Political Science Association, Chicago.

KELLER, EDMOND J. (1978) "The political socialization of adolescents in contemporary Africa." Comparative politics (10): 227-250.

KENNEDY, DUNCAN (1982) "Legal education as training for hierarchy," pp. 40-61 David Kairys (ed.), The Politics of Law, New York: Pantheon Books.

KIEWIET, RODERICK (1982) "The rationality of candidates who challenge incumbents in congressional elections." Social Science Working Paper 436, Division of Humanities and Social Sciences. Pasadena: California Institute of Technology.

KINCAID, DIANE D. (1978) "Over his dead body: A new perspective and some feminist notes on widows in the U.S. Congress." Western Political Quarterly (March): 96-104.

KING, ELIZABETH G. (1977) "Women in Iowa legislative politics," pp. 284-303 in Marianne Githens and Jewel L. Prestage (eds.), A Portrait of Marginality. New York: David McKay.

——— and JOAN McAULIFFE (1976) "Women county supervisors: Are they different?" Presented at the annual meeting of the American Political Science Association, Chicago, September 2-5.

KIRKPATRICK, JEANE J. (1974) Polical Woman. New York: Basic Books.

——— (1976) The New Presidential Elite: Men and Women in National Politics. New York: Russell Sage.

KORNBLUM, WILLIAM (1974) Blue Collar Community. Chicago: University of Chicago Press.

KRADITOR, AILEEN S. (1971) The Ideas of the Woman Suffrage Movement: 1890-1920. Garden City, NY: Anchor Press.

LAKE, CELINDA C. (1982) "Guns, butter and equality: The women's vote in 1980." Presented at the annual meeting of the Midwest Political Science Association, Chicago.

LAMSON, PEGGY (1968) Few Are Chosen: American Women in Political Life Today. Boston: Houghton Mifflin.

LANE, ROBERT E. (1959) Political Life: Why People Get Involved in Politics. Glencoe, IL: Free Press.

LASCH, CHRISTOPHER (1977) Haven in a Heartless World: The Family Besieged. New York: Basic Books.

LAWRENCE, ELIZABETH (1977) "The working women's charter campaign," pp. 12-24 in Marjorie Mayo (ed.), Women in the Community, London and Boston: Routledge and Kegan Paul.

LAWSON, RONALD and STEPHEN E. BARTON (1980) "Sex Roles in social movements: A case study of the tenant movement in New York City." Signs (Winter): 230-247.

—— and JENNA WEISSMAN JOSELIT (1980) "From kitchen to storefront: Women in the tenant movement," 255-271 in Gerda R. Wekerle, Rebecca Peterson, and David Morley (eds.), New Space for Women. Boulder, CO: Westview Press.

LEE, MARCIA M. (1973) "The participation of women in suburban politics: A study of the influence of women as compared to men in suburban governmental decision-making." Dissertation, Tufts University.

—— (1976) "Why few women hold public office: Democracy and Sexual Roles." Political Science Quarterly (Summer): 297-314.

—— (1977) "Toward understanding why few women hold public office: Factors affecting the participation of women in local politics," pp. 118-138 in Marianne Githens and Jewel L. Prestage (eds.), A Portrait of Marginality. New York: David McKay.

LEISERSON, AVERY (1983) "On defining politics and how to take it into account." News For Teachers of Political Science (Spring): 13.

LEMAN, CHRISTOPHER (1980) The Collapse of Welfare Reform: Political Institutions, Policy and the Poor in Canada and the United States. Cambridge: MIT Press.

LEPPER, MARY M. (1974) "A study of career structures of federal executives: A focus on women," pp. 109-130 in Jane Jaquette (ed.), Women in Politics. New York: John Wiley.

LEVITAN, SAR A. (1980) Programs in Aid of the Poor for the 1980s. Baltimore, MD: Johns Hopkins University Press.

LEVY, DARLENE GAY and HARRIET APPLEWHITE (1980) "Women of the popular classes in Revolutionary Paris, 1789-1795," pp. 9-35 in Carol R. Berkin and Clara M Lovett (eds.), Women, War and Revolution. New York: Holmes and Meier.

LIEBMAN, CHARLES [ed.] (1955) Directory of American Judges. Chicago, IL: American Directories.

LIPSET, SEYMOUR MARTIN (1960) Political Man. New York: Doubleday.

LOPATA, HELEN ZNANIECKI (1980) "The Chicago woman: A study of patterns of mobility and transportation." Signs (Supplement, Spring): S161-S169.

LOVING, NANCY (1980) Responding to Spouse Abuse and Wife Beating: A Guide for Police. Washington, DC: Police Executive Research Forum.

LYND, ROBERT S. and HELEN MERRELL LYND (1937) Middletown in Transition. New York: Harcourt, Brace and World.

LYNN, NAOMI (1975) "Women in American politics: An overview," pp. 364-385 in Jo Freeman (ed.), Women: A Feminist Perspective. Palo Alto, CA: Mayfield.

—— and CORNELIA BUTLER FLORA (1977) "Societal punishment and aspects of female political participation: 1972 national convention delegates," pp. 139-149 in Marianne Githens and Jewel L. Prestage (eds.), A Portrait of Marginality. New York: David McKay.

LYON, DAVID W. (1978) "The dynamics of welfare dependency," pp. 239-242 in Lester M. Salamon (ed.), Welfare: The Elusive Consensus. New York: Praeger.

MacMANUS, SUSAN (1976) "Determinants of the equitability of female representation on 243 City Councils." Presented at the annual meeting of the American Political Science Association, Chicago.

—— (1981) "A city's first female officeholder: 'Coattails' for the future female officeholders?" Western Political Quarterly (March): 88-99.

MAIN, ELEANOR C. and BETH SCHAPIRO (1979) "The recruitment of state legislators: A comparison of male and female life experiences." Presented at the annual meeting of the Southern Political Science Association, Gatlinburg, TN.

MANDEL, RUTH B. (1981) In the Running: The New Woman Candidate. New Haven, CT, and New York: Ticknor & Fields.

MARGOLIS, DIANE (1980) "The invisible hands: Sex roles and the division of labor in two local political parties," pp. 22-41 in Debra W. Stewart (ed.), Women in Local Politics, Metuchen, NJ: Scarecrow Press.

MARKUSEN, ANN R. (1980) "City spatial structure, women's household work, and national urban policy." Signs (Spring): S23-S44.

MARTIN, DEL (1976) Battered Wives. San Francisco: Glide Publications.

MARTIN, ELAINE (1982) "Women on the federal bench: A comparative profile." Judicature (January): 306-313.

McCLELLAND, DAVID (1975) Power: The Inner Experience. New York: Irvington.

McDONALD, JEAN GRAVES and VICKY HOWELL PIERSON (1984) "Female county party leaders and the perception of discrimination: A test of the male conspiracy theory." Social Science Journal (January).

McWILLIAMS, NANCY (1974) "Contemporary feminism, consciousness-raising, and changing views of the political," pp. 157-170 in Jane S. Jaquette (ed.), Women in Politics. New York: John Wiley.

MEEKER, B. J. and P. A. WEITZELL-O'NEILL (1977) "Sex roles and interpersonal behavior in task oriented groups." American Sociological Review (42): 91-105.

MERCHANT, CAROLYN (1980) "Earthcare: Women and the environment." Environment (June): 6-13, 38-40.

MERELMAN, RICHARD (1971) Political Socialization and Educational Climates: A Study of Two School Districts. New York: Holt, Rinehart and Winston.

MERRITT, SHARYNE (1977) "Winners and losers: Sex differences in municipal elections." American Journal of Political Science (November): 731-743.

—— (1980) "Sex differences in role behavior and policy orientations of suburban officeholders: The effect of women's employment," pp. 115-129 in Debra W. Stewart (ed.), Women in Local Politics. Metuchen, NJ: Scarecrow Press.

MEYER, KEENY JEAN (1977) Policy Intervention Data and Domestic Violence, Exploration and Validation of Prediction Models. Kansas City, MO: Police Department.

MEZEY, SUSAN GLUCK (1978a) "Does sex make a difference? A case study of women in politics." Western Political Quarterly (December): 492-501.

—— (1978b) "Support for women's rights policy: An analysis of local politicians," American Politics Quarterly (October): 485-497.

—— (1978c) "Women and representation: The case of Hawaii." Journal of Politics (May): 369-385.

—— (1980) "Perceptions of women's roles on local councils in Connecticut," pp. 177-197 in Debra W. Stewart (ed.), Women in Local Politics. Metuchen, NJ: Scarecrow Press.

MOREHOUSE, SARAH M. (1981) State Politics, Parties and Policy. New York: Holt, Rinehart and Winston.

National Women's Education Fund (1981) "Evaluation report: A survey of participants in training seminars conducted by the National Women's Education Fund, 1974-1980." Washington, DC: National Women's Education Fund.

National Women's Political Caucus [NWPC] (1983) National Directory of Women Elected Officials. Washington, DC: National Women's Political Caucus.

NELKIN, DOROTHY (1981) "Nuclear power as a feminist issue." Environment (January-February): 14-20, 38-40.

NEUSE, STEPHEN M. (1978) "Professionalism and authority: Women in public service." Public Administrative Review (September/October): 436-441.

NORGREN, JILL (1981) "In search of a national child care policy: Background and prospects." Western Political Quarterly (March): 127-142.

OREN, LAURA (1973) "The welfare of women in labouring families in England, 1860-1950." Feminist Studies (Winter-Spring): 107-125.

ORUM, ANTHONY M., ROBERTA S. COHEN, SHERRI S. GRASMUCK, and AMY W. ORUM (1977) "Sex Socialization and Politics," pp. 17-37 in Marianne Githens and Jewel J. Prestage (eds.), A Portrait of Marginality. New York: David McKay.

PAGELOW, MILDRED (1981) Woman-Battering Victims and their Experience. Beverly Hills, CA: Sage.

PARNAS, RAYMOND I. (1967) "The police response to domestic disturbances." Wisconsin Law Review (Fall): 60.

PEARCE, DIANA (1979) "Women, work and welfare: The feminization of poverty," pp. 103-124 in Karen Wolk Feinstein (ed.), Working Women and Families. Beverly Hills, CA: Sage.

PERKINS, JERRY and DIANE L. FOWLKES (1980) "Opinion representation vs. social representation: Or, why women can't run as women and win." American Political Science Review: (March): 92-103.

PIERSON, VICKY HOWELL (1983) "A visible difference: Women in the politics of the 1980's." Presented at the annual meeting of the Midwest Political Science Association, Chicago.

PITKIN, HANNA (1967) The Concept of Representation. Berkeley: University of California Press.

—— and SARA M. SHUMER (1982) "On participating." Democracy (Fall): 43-54.

PIVEN, FRANCES FOX and RICHARD A. CLOWARD (1982) The New Class War. New York: Pantheon.

—— (1983) "The American road to democratic socialism." Democracy (Summer): 58-69.

PIZZEY, ERIN (1974) Scream Quietly or the Neighbours Will Hear. Harmondsworth, UK: Penguin Books.

POLK, BARBARA B. (1974) "Male power and the women's movement." Journal of Applied Behavioral Science (10): 415-431.

PORTER, MARY CORNELIA and ANN B. MATASAR (1974) "The role and status of women in the Daley organization," pp. 85-108 in Jane Jaquette (ed.), Women in Politics. New York: John Wiley.

POWELL, LYNDA WATTS, CLIFFORD W. BROWN, JR., and ROMAN B. HEDGES (1981) "Male and female differences in elite political participation: An examination of the effects of socioeconomic and familial variables." Western Political Quarterly (March): 31-45.

PRESS, CHARLES and KENNETH VER BURG (1983) State and Community Governments in the Federal System. New York: John Wiley.

PRESTAGE, JEWEL L. (1977) "Black women state legislators: A profile," pp. 401-418 in Marianne Githens and Jewel L. Prestage (eds.), A Portrait of Marginality. New York: David McKay.

PREWITT, KENNETH (1970) "Political ambitions, volunteerism, and electoral accountability." American Political Science Review (March): 5-17.

Quest [ed.] (1981) Building Feminist Theory: Essays from Quest. New York: Longman.

QUINN, TONY (1983) "The proliferation of recalls in our single-issue society," pp. 95-95 in Thomas R. Hoeber and Charles M. Price (eds.), California Government and Politics Annual 83/84. Sacramento: California Journal Press.

RABOY, MARC (1978) "The future of Montreal and the MCM." Our Generation (4).

REINCKE, MARY [ed.] (1977) The American Bench. Minneapolis, MN: Reginald Bishop Forester.

RICH, ADRIENNE (1976) Of Women Born: Motherhood as Experience and Institution. New York: Norton.

RIDGEWAY, JAMES (1983) "No room on the ticket." Mother Jones (September/October): 23-52

RINEHART, SUE TOLLESON (1978) "Amateurism among women political party elites." Presented at the annual meeting of the Southern Political Science Association, Atlanta, GA.

ROBERTS, ALBERT R. (1976) "Police social workers: A history." Social Work (July): 294-299.

ROBINSON, LELIA J. (1899) "Women lawyers in the United States." Green Bag (November): 10-32.

RONCEK, DENNIS W., RALPH BELL, and HARVEY M. CHOLDIN (1980) "Female-headed families: An ecological model of residential concentration in a small city." Journal of Marriage and the Family (February): 157-170.

ROSEN, SUMMER N. (1982) "Labor—A movement at risk?" pp. 206-229 in Alan Bartner, Colin Greer and Frank Riessman (eds.), What Reagan Is Doing To Us. New York: Harper & Row.

ROSENBERG, MARIE BAROVIC (1972) "Political efficacy and sex role: Case study of Congresswomen Edith Green and Julia Butler Hansen." Presented at the annual meeting of the American Political Science Association, Washington, D.C.

ROSENBERG, RINA (1982) "Representing women at the state and local level: Commissions on the status of women," pp. 38-46 in Ellen Boneparth (ed.), Women, Power and Policy. New York: Pergamon Press.

ROSENTHAL, ALAN (1981) Legislative Life: People, Process and Performance in the United States. New York: Harper & Row.

ROSS, ELLEN (1981) "Survival networks and domestic sharing in an East London neighborhood, 1870-1914." Presented at the Berkshire Conference on the History of Women, Vassar College, Poughkeepsie, New York, June 18.

ROSSI, ALICE (1982) Feminists in Politics. New York: Academic Press.

ROUSSOPOULOS, DIMITRI (1982) Interview with Martha A. Ackelsberg, Montreal, August 1.

ROY, MARIA [ed.] (1977) Battered Woman: A Psychosociological Study of Domestic Violence. New York: Van Nostrand Reinhold.

RULE, WILMA (1981) "Why women don't run: The critical contextual factors in women's legislative recruitment." Western Political Quarterly (March): 60-77.

RYAN, JOHN PAUL, ALLAN ASHMAN, BRUCE D. SALES, and SANDRA SHANE-DOBUN (1980) American Trial Judges. New York: Free Press.

RYAN, MARY P. (1979) "The power of women's networks: A case study of female moral reform in antebellum America." Feminist Studies (Spring): 66-86.

SAEGERT, SUSAN (1980) "Masculine cities and feminine suburbs: Polarized ideas, contradictory realities." Signs (Supplement, Spring): S96-S111.

SALZMAN, ED. (1983) "Judging Jerry," pp. 19-22 in Thomas R. Hoeber and Charles M. Price (eds.), California Government and Politics Annual 83/84. Sacramento: California Journal Press.

San Jose Mercury News (1982) 1983 Answer Book for Santa Clara County. San Jose, CA: San Jose Mercury News.

SAPIRO, VIRGINIA (1981) "Research frontier essay: When are interests interesting? The problem of political representation of women." American Political Science Review (September): 701-716.

—— (1982) "Private costs of public commitments or public costs of private commitments? Family roles versus political ambition." American Journal of Political Science (May): 265-279.

—— (1983) The Political Integration of Women. Urbana: University of Illinois Press.

—— and BARBARA C. FARAH (1980) "New pride and old prejudice: Political ambition and role orientation among female partisan elites." Women and Politics (1): 13-35.

SAYRE, WALLACE S. and HERBERT KAUFMAN (1965) Governing New York City: Politics in the Metropolis. New York: W.W. Norton.

SCHAFRAN, LYNN HECHT (1982) "Women: Reversing a decade of progress," pp. 162-189 in Alan Gartner, Colin Greer and Frank Riessman (eds.), What Reagan Is Doing To Us. New York: Harper and Row.

—— (1983) "Women as litigators: Abilities vs. assumptions." Trial (August): 36-41.

SCHATTSCHNEIDER, E.E. (1960) The Semi-Sovereign People. New York: Holt, Rinehart and Winston.

SCHECHTER, SUSAN (1982) Women and Male Violence: The Visions and Struggles of the Battered Women's Movement. Boston: South End Press.

SCHEFTER, MARTIN (1983) "Political incorporation and exclusion of the Left: The organization of ethnic groups into urban political institutions." Presented at the annual meeting of the American Political Science Association, Chicago.

SCHEIER, RONNI (1980) "A cruel new tax on the poor." In These Times (November 5-11): 5.

SCHEIN, VIRGINIA ELLEN (1975) "Relationships between sex role stereotypes and requisite management characteristics among female managers." Journal of Applied Psychology (60): 340-344.

SCHLESINGER, JOSEPH A. (1966) Ambitions and Politics: Political Careers in the United States. Chicago: Rand McNally.

SCHRAMM, SARAH S. (1981) "Women and representation: Self government and role change." Western Political Quarterly (March): 46-59.

Science News (1982) "Kramer and Kramer." January 30: 73.

SEBALD, HANS (1976) Momism: The Silent Disease. Chicago: Nelson-Hall.

SENNETT, RICHARD (1970) The Use of Disorder. New York: Knopf.

SHABAD, GOLDIE and KRISTI ANDERSON (1979) "Candidate evaluations by men and women." Public Opinion Quarterly (Spring): 18-35.

SHANLEY, MARY L. and VICTORIA SCHUCK (1974) "In search of political woman." Social Science Quarterly (December): 632-644.

SHARPE, IVAN (1983) "Is the future female?" Working Woman (January): 73-77.

SHEEHAN, SUSAN (1976) A Welfare Mother. Boston: Houghton Mifflin.

SHERMAN, LAWRENCE W. and RICHARD A. BERK (1983) Police Responses to Domestic Assault: Preliminary Findings. Washington, DC: Police Foundation.

SIDEL, RUTH (1982) "The family: A dream deferred," pp. 54-70 in Alan Gartner, Colin Greer, and Frank Riesman (eds.), What Reagan Is Doing To Us. New York: Harper and Row.

Signs (1980) Special Issue on Women and the American City, (Supplement, Spring).

SILBERMAN, LINDA J. (1979) Non-Attorney Justice in the United States: An Empirical Study. New York: Institute of Judicial Administration.

SIMS, MARGARET (1983) "Women and housing: The impact of government housing policy," pp. 123-138 in Irene Diamond (ed.), Families, Politics and Public Policies. New York: Longman.

SMITH-ROSENBERG, CAROL (1975) "The female world of love and ritual." Signs (Autumn): 1-29.

SOULE, JOHN W. and JAMES W. CLARKE (1970) "Amateurs and professionals." American Political Science Review (September): 888-898.

SOULE, JOHN W. and WILMA E. McGRATH (1977) "A comparative study of male-female political attitudes at citizen and elite levels," pp. 178-195 in Marianne Githens and Jewel L. Prestage (eds.), A Portrait of Marginality. New York: David McKay.

STACK, CAROL (1975) All Our Kin. New York: Harper and Row.

STAINES, GRAHAM, TOBY E. JAYARTNE, and CAROL TAVRIS (1974) "The Queen Bee Syndrome." Psychology Today (January): 55-60.

STAMP, JUDY (1980) "Toward supportive neighborhoods: Women's role in changing the segregated city," pp. 189-198 in Gerda R. Wekerle, Rebecca Peterson, and David Morely (eds.), New Space for Women. Boulder, CO: Westview Press.

STARK, EVAN, ANN FLITCRAFT, and WILLIAM FRAZIER (1979) "Medicine and patriarchal violence: The social construction of a 'private event'." International Journal of Health Services (9): 461-491.

STEINBERG, ALAN (1982) "The criminal courts and the transportation of criminal justice in Philadelphia, 1815-1874." Dissertation, Columbia University.

STEINER, GILBERT Y. (1971) The State of Welfare. Washington, DC: Brookings Institute.

―――― (1976) The Children's Cause. Washington, DC: Brookings Institute.

STEWART, DEBRA W. (1980a) "Commission on the status of women and building a local policy agenda," in Debra W. Stewart (ed.), Women in Local Politics. Metuchen, NJ: Scarecrow Press, 198-214.

——— (1980b) "Organizational role orientations on female-dominant commissions: Focus on staff-commissioner interaction," pp. 149-176 in Debra W. Stewart (ed.), Women in Local Politics, Metuchen, NJ: Scarecrow Press.

——— [ed.] (1980c) Women in Local Politics. Metuchen, NJ: Scarecrow Press.

——— (1980d) The Women's Movement in Community Politics in the U.S.: The Role of Local Commissions on the Status of Women. New York: Pergamon Press.

STOKES, DONALD and WARREN E. MILLER (1966) "Party government and the saliency of Congress," pp. 194-211 in Angus Campbell, Philip Converse, Warren E. Miller, and Donald Stokes, Elections and the Political Order, New York: John Wiley.

STOPER, EMILY (1977) "Wife and politician: Role strain among women in public office," pp. 320-337 in Marianne Githens and Jewel L. Prestage (eds.), A Portrait of Marginality. New York: David McKay.

——— (1983) "Welfare as family policy." Presented at the annual meeting of the Western Political Science Association, Seattle.

STRAUSS, MURRAY, RICHARD GELLES, and SUZANNE STEINMETZ (1980) Behind Closed Doors: Violence in the American Family. New York: Anchor Books.

SUSSER, IDA (1982) Norman Street: Poverty and Politics in an Urban Neighborhood. New York: Oxford University Press.

TEMME, LLOYD V. (1975) Occupation: Meanings and Measures. Washington, DC: Bureau of Social Science Research.

TOLCHIN, SUSAN and MARTIN TOLCHIN (1976) Clout: Womanpower and Politics. New York: Capricorn.

TROUNSTINE, PHILIP J. and TERRY CHRISTENSEN (1982) Movers and Shakers: The Study of Community Power. New York: St. Martin's Press.

TRUSSELL, JAMES, JANE MENKEN, and BARBARA VAUGHN (1980) "The impact of restricting medicaid financing of abortions." Family Planning Perspectives (May/June): 120-130.

ULRICH, LAUREL THATCHER (1980) "A friendly neighbor: Social dimensions of daily work in northern colonial New England." Feminist Studies (Summer): 392-405.

U.S. Bureau of the Census (1982) Money Income and Poverty Status of Families and Persons in the United States: 1981. (Advance Data from the March 1982 Current Population Survey). Washington, DC: Government Printing Office. Current Population Reports, Series P-60, No. 134.

——— (1982-1983) Statistical Abstracts of the United States. Washington, DC: Department of Commerce.

U.S. Department of Health, Education and Welfare (1978) The Appropriateness of Federal Interagency Day Care Requirements. Report of Findings and Recommendations. Washington, DC: Office of the Assistant Secretary for Planning and Evaluation.

U.S. Department of Labor (1979) Community Solutions for Child Care, Washington, DC: Women's Bureau.

USLANER, ERIC M. and RONALD E. WEBER (1977) Patterns of Decision Making in State Legislatures. New York: Praeger.

VALIAN, VIRGINIA (1977) "Learning to work," pp. 162-178 in Sara Ruddick and Pamela Daniels (eds.), Working It Out. New York: Pantheon Books.

Van HIGHTOWER, NICKI R. (1977) "The recruitment of women for public office." American Politics Quarterly (July): 301-314.

Van WAGNER, KAREN and CHERYL SWANSON (1979) "From Machiavelli to Ms.: Differences in male-female power styles." Public Administration Review (January/February): 66-72.

VIDICH, ARTHUR J. and JOSEPH BENSMAN (1958) Small Town in Mass Society. Princeton, NJ: Princeton University Press.

WAHLKE, JOHN C., HEINZ EULAU, WILLIAM BUCHANAN, and LORNA C. FERGUSON (1962) The Legislative Process: Explorations in Legislative Behavior. New York: John Wiley.

WALKER, LENORE E. (1979) The Battered Woman. New York: Harper and Row.

WALSHOK, MARY LINDENSTEIN (1979) "Occupational values and family roles: Women in blue-collar and service occupations," pp. 63-68 in Karen Feinstein (ed.), Working Women and Families. Beverly Hills, CA: Sage.

WALZER, MICHAEL (1970) Obligations. Cambridge, MA: Harvard University Press.

——— (1978) "Town meetings and workers' control: A story of socialists." Dissent (Summer): 325-333.

WARD, COLIN (1973) Anarchy in Action. New York: Harper and Row.

WARNER, SAM BASS (1962) Streetcar Suburbs. Cambridge: MIT Press.

——— (1968) The Private City. Philadelphia: University of Pennsylvania Press.

WEITZMAN, LENORE J. (1981) "The economics of divorce: Social and economic consequences of property, alimony and child support awards." UCLA Law Review (August): 1181-1268.

WELCH, SUSAN (1977) "Women as political animals? A test of some explanations for male-female political participation differences." American Journal of Political Science (November): 711-730.

——— (1978) "Recruitment of women to public office: A discriminant analysis." Western Political Quarterly (September): 372-380.

———and MARGERY AMBROSIUS, JANET CLARK, and R. DARCY (1982) "The effect of candidate gender on election outcomes: A six-state analysis of state legislative candidates." Presented at the annual meeting of the American Political Science Association, Denver, CO.

——— and ALBERT KARNIG (1979) "Correlates of female office holding in city politics." Journal of Politics (May): 478-491.

WELLS, AUDREY SIESS and ELEANOR CUTRI SMEAL (1974) "Women's attitudes toware women in politics: A survey of urban registered voters and party committeewoman," pp. 54-72 in Jane Jaquette (ed.), Women in Politics. New York: John Wiley.

WERNER, EMMY E. (1966) "Women in Congress: 1917-1964." Western Political Quarterly (March): 16-30.

——— (1968) "Women in state legislatures." Western Political Quarterly (March): 40-50.

——— and LOUISE M. BACHTOLD (1974) "Personality characteristics of women in American politics," pp. 75-84 in Jane Jaquette (ed.), Women in Politics. New York: John Wiley.

WILSON, ELISABETH (1977) "Women in the community," pp. 1-11 in Marjorie Mayo (ed.), Women in the Community. London and Boston: Routledge and Kegan Paul.

WILSON, JAMES Q. (1973) Political Organization. New York: Basic Books.

WILT, G. MARIE, J. D. BANNON, R. K. BREEDLOVE, D. M. SANDKER, J. W. KENNISH, and R. K. SATWELL (1977) Domestic Violence and the Police. Washington, DC: Police Foundation.

WOLIN, SHELDON (1981) "The people's two bodies." Democracy (January): 9-24.
—— (1982) "What revolutionary action means today." Democracy (Fall): 17-28.
WOOLSEY, SUZANNE H. (1978) "Pied Piper politics and the child care debate,"
  pp. 127-145 in Alice S. Rossi, Jerome Kagan, and Tamara K. Hareven (eds.), The
  Familiy. New York: Norton.

INDEX

ABOUT THE CONTRIBUTORS

MARTHA A. ACKELSBERG is Associate Professor of Government and a principal investigator with the Project on Women and Social Change at Smith College, where she teaches courses on urban politics, political participation, and political theory. She has written about changes in the nature and structure of families, the sources of (urban) women's political consciousness, and on the Spanish anarchist movement, in particular, the consequences for women and men anarchist revolutionary activity during the Spanish Civil War. She spent the academic year 1983-1984 as a fellow of the Mary Ingraham Bunting Institute of Radcliffe College, writing about the social and political vision of the Spanish anarchist women's organization, *Mujeres Libres.*

MARGERY AMBROSIUS is a Ph.D. candidate in the Department of Political Science at the University of Nebraska—Lincoln. She has published two articles on state politics and is currently researching comparative state economic development policies.

DENISE ANTOLINI graduated from Princeton University in 1982. Her senior thesis, "The Impact of Women in the U.S. Congress: Ecclesiazusaen Statecraft?" examined the liberalizing influence of the past decade of women in the House of Representatives and won the Philo Sherman Bennett Prize in the Department of Politics. She is currently a student at the School of Law (Boalt Hall), University of California Berkeley and wishes to acknowledge the inspiration and guidance of Barbara J. Nelson.

JULIE DAVIS BELL is a Ph.D. student in the Department of Political Science at the University of California, Davis. She is currently conducting research in the areas of political leadership, interest group activity, and innovation in the public sector.

ELLEN BONEPARTH is a Professor of Political Science at San Jose State University and editor of *Women, Power and Policy* (Pergamon Press, 1982). She founded the International Women's Studies Institutes in Greece, Israel, and Egypt.

JANET CLARK is an Associate Professor of Political Science at the University of Wyoming. Her research interests include women in politics and state and local politics. She has published in such journals as the *Western Political Quarterly*, the *Journal of Political Science*, the *American Politics Quarterly*, and the *Social Science Journal.*

BEVERLY B. COOK is a professor of Political Science at the University of Wisconsin-Milwaukee, where she has been teaching courses on judicial behavior and on sex roles in the judicial process since 1967. Her book, *The Judicial Process in California* appeared in 1967 and her research on public opinion, judicial background and personality, judicial administration, and sentencing has been published in the *American Journal of Political Science*, the *International Political Science Review*, *Washington University Law Quarterly*, *Law and Society Review*, and other publications. The Social Science Research Council and Ford Foundation have supported her research. She has also been a member of the APSA Task Force on Women and American Government, 1981-1983.

EDMOND COSTANTINI is Professor of Political Science at the University of California, Davis. He is author or coauthor of articles appearing in *Western Political Quarterly*, *Journal of Social Issues*, *Journal of Personality and Social Psychology*, *Environment and Behavior*, *Law and Society Review*, *American Politics Quarterly*, *Judicature*, and *Political Behavior*, of *California Parties and Politics*, and a number of other publications in the public opinion and political leadership areas.

R. DARCY is Associate Professor of Political Science and Statistics at Oklahoma State University. He holds a Ph.D. from the University of Kentucky. His work in the areas of women in politics, public opinion, and statistical analysis has appeared in such journals as *Public Opinion Quarterly*, the *American Journal of Political Science*, the *American Political Science Review*, the *Journal of Marketing Research*, and *Women and Politics*. He spent the 1983-1984 academic year lecturing on these subjects at universities in this country, Europe, and the Far East. He is currently engaged in a study of women in Korean politics.

JANET A. FLAMMANG is Assistant Professor of Political Science at the University of Santa Clara, where she teaches courses in American politics and women and politics. She has published in the area of feminist theory and is currently working on a book on women and politics in Santa Clara County.

DIANE L. FOWLKES is Associate Professor of Political Science at Georgia State University. Her research interests center on gender politics in the United States. She is chairwoman of the American Political Science Association's Task Force on Women and American Government, which is writing course units for American government courses: *Citizenship and Change: Women and American Politics*. She is co-editor of *Feminist Visions: Toward a Transformation of the Liberal Arts Curriculum* (University of Alabama Press, 1984) and has published or forthcoming articles in the *American Political Science Review*, *Micropolitics*, *Social Science Journal*, and *Women and Politics*.

MARIANNE GITHENS, who is Professor of Politics and Public Policy at Goucher College and past president of the Women's Caucus for Political Science, co-edited *A Portrait of Marginality* with Jewel Prestage. She has recently published a critique of gender research in political science, "The

Elusive Paradigm,'' that was included in *Political Science: The State of the Discipline* edited by Ada Finifter. She is presently doing research on women's participation in the American peace movement.

DAVID B. HILL is Associate Professor of Political Science and Associate Director of the Public Policy Resources Laboratory at Texas A&M University. He is author of *Trends in American Electoral Behavior* (with Norman Luttbeg) and numerous scholarly articles in several sub-fields of political behavior. In the field of women and politics his research has focused on the recruitment and behavior of women legislators. He is currently engaged in a study of the role of women in the defeat of the ERA.

CAROL MUELLER is Research Scholar at both the Center for Research on Women, Wellesley College, and the Murray Research Center, Radcliffe College. She is a political sociologist who has researched the campaign for the ERA, the rise of women in public office, and public opinion on the status of women, focusing on the role of consciousness in social change. She is co-editor (with Mary Katzenstein) of a forthcoming book, *Changing Paradigms: New Theoretical Perspectives on the Women's Movements in the United States and Western Europe.*

EMILY STOPER has a Ph.D. from Harvard and is Professor of Political Science and Co-Director of the Women's Studies Program at California State University, Hayward, where she has taught courses on both state and local government and public policy on the family. She has published a number of articles about women, politics, and public policy, most recently focusing on the institution of motherhood—an interest stimulated by her experiences in raising her two children.

SUSAN WELCH is currently Carl A. Happold Professor of Political Science at the University of Nebraska—Lincoln. She has published previous articles on women and politics in a variety of journals. She is currently examining the impact of political structures on urban city councils.

ANNE WURR worked as Community Educator with Mid-Peninsula Support Network for Battered Women from 1980 to 1983. While a graduate student in Women's Studies at San Jose State University, she worked on the founding convention of the National Women's Studies Association, and, as an intern at Mexican American Community Services Agency, organized opposition to county jail construction. She founded and played viola in the Support Network String Quartet. She is presently traveling overland through Africa.